CASE STUDIES IN LEGAL RESEARCH METHODOLOGIES
Reflections on Theory and Practice

CASE STUDIES IN LEGAL RESEARCH METHODOLOGIES
Reflections on Theory and Practice

Edited by

LAURA CAHILLANE
JENNIFER SCHWEPPE

CLARUS
PRESS

Published by
Clarus Press Ltd,
Griffith Campus,
South Circular Road,
Dublin 8.

Typeset by
Deanta Global Publishing Services Limited

Printed by
SprintPrint
Dublin

ISBN
978-1-911611-11-0

Preface

This collection is a follow-on to *Legal Research Methods: Principles and Practicalities*. Given the success of the first volume, we decided to produce a second collection which would look at some further methods not included in the first book and would take a different approach in order to help PhD and early career researchers to better understand various different legal research methods. In this book we have used a case study approach so that readers can gain an insight into how the methods worked in practice using specific project examples. We hope that readers will benefit from the honest and insightful accounts given by authors describing their own experiences and challenges with research methods.

We would like to thank all the authors to this collection for their thoughtful, engaging, and reflective contributions.

We would also like to thank the School of Law at the University of Limerick, and particularly the Head of School, Professor Shane Kilcommins for all his support of this project.

This is the second time we have both been pregnant whilst editing a collection with Clarus Press, and we would like to thank our families and friends, but most particularly David McCartney of Clarus Press for his patience with us in finalising the copy of this text.

Laura Cahillane and Jennifer Schweppe
8 May 2019

Short Table of Contents

Detailed Table of Contents

Author Biographies

Una Woods is a senior lecturer in the School of Law, University of Limerick. She graduated with a BCL from University College Cork in 1995 and was awarded an LLM in Human Rights and Discrimination Law by Queens University Belfast in 1996. She qualified as a solicitor in 1999 and was awarded the Findlater Scholarship by the Law Society of Ireland. She joined the School of Law, University of Limerick in September 1999. In November 2006 she was appointed by the Minister for Justice as a member of the Property Registration Authority and, in November 2010, she was re-appointed for another 4 year term. In 2014, she completed her doctorate with Queens University Belfast on "The Irish Law on Adverse Possession - The Case for a Qualified Veto System". She has acted as a consultant to the Irish Law Reform Commission on the law in relation to cohabitants and adverse possession. Her publications focus mainly on land law and conveyancing law. Una's research interests lie primarily in the area of land law, the law of trusts, conveyancing law, succession law and matrimonial property law.

Conor O'Mahony is a senior lecturer at the School of Law at University College Cork, where he has lectured in constitutional law since 2005. His research interests lie broadly in the areas of constitutional law and child law, with a particular focus on constitutional interpretation, family and children's rights, educational rights and special educational needs. Examples of his comparative work include the rights of children with special educational needs (*Public Law*, 2008); human dignity as a source of constitutional rights (*International Journal of Constitutional Law*, 2012); models of reform on marriage equality (*Illinois Law Review*, 2016); and the constitutional protection of children's rights (*Human Rights Law Review*, 2019).

Laura Cahillane is a lecturer in the School of Law, University of Limerick. Laura undertook a Post Doctoral Fellowship in UCC and held lectureships in UCC and DCU before joining the School of Law at UL. Her research interests lie in the areas of Constitutional Law, Legal History, Judicial Politics and Comparative Law and she has published nationally and internationally in these areas. Her monograph on the 1922 Constitution was published by Manchester University Press in 2016. She is a frequent contributor to the media on legal and constitutional issues and has advised the Oireachtas on law reform on a number of occasions. She is editor of the Irish Judicial Studies Journal.

Clíodhna Murphy is a Lecturer in Law at Maynooth University. She has also held positions as a lecturer in Dublin City University and as a post-doctoral fellow at University College in Cork. She completed her thesis on legal aspects of migrant integration at Trinity College Dublin. Clíodhna lectures and researches in the areas of migration law, human rights, international law and company law. She has published widely in these fields, including in journals such as International & Comparative Law Quarterly; Human Rights Quarterly; Industrial Law Journal; and British Journal of Criminology. Her first book, *Immigration, Integration and the Law: The Intersection of Domestic, EU and International Regimes*, was published by Ashgate in 2013 and republished by Routledge in 2016. She is a member of the Ethical, Political, Legal and Philosophical Studies Committee of the Royal Irish Academy.

Mary Gilmartin is a Professor of Geography at Maynooth University. She completed her PhD at the University of Kentucky and worked at Nottingham Trent University and University College Dublin before joining Maynooth University in 2008. The main focus of her research is contemporary Irish migration and mobility. Her book on Ireland and migration in the twenty-first century was published by Manchester University Press in 2015, and she was Managing Editor of Social & Cultural Geography, a leading international geography journal, from 2014–2018.

Leanne Caulfield is a researcher in the Law Reform Commission. She is a graduate of University College Dublin (BCL 2014, LLM 2015). She has worked as a research assistant on a number of projects at the UCD Sutherland School of Law (2014, 2015 and 2017). Leanne was a research assistant at the Immigrant Council of Ireland in 2016 and at Maynooth University in 2017. In 2017, she also authored an information resource with the Immigrant Council of Ireland. She joined the Law Reform Commission as a researcher in January 2018.

Máiréad Enright is a Senior Lecturer in Birmingham Law School, which she joined in 2016. Her research is in feminist legal studies and law and religion. She is especially interested in how patriarchal legal and religious structures can be resisted and changed. Her research in this respect looks beyond traditional methods of law reform to consider illegality, protest, private litigation, and experimental legal drafting. She is Co-Director of the Northern/Irish Feminist Judgments Project and often consults with and advises groups campaigning around reproductive rights and historical gender-based violence in Ireland.

Aoife O'Donoghue is Professor of International Law and Global Governance in Durham Law School. Her research focuses on public international law and constitutionalism with a particular interest in global governance and legal theory. Aoife's work examines constitutionalism, tyranny, utopias and feminism, legal theory and international legal history. Currently Aoife is heavily engaged with research and policy debates on Brexit with a particular focus on Northern Ireland including the ESRC funded project Performing Identities: Post-Brexit Northern Ireland and the reshaping of 21st-Century Governance. Aoife is currently working on a monograph on tyranny and global governance to be published by CUP entitled 'Tyranny and the Global Legal Order'.

Ivana Bacik is the Reid Professor of Criminal Law, Criminology and Penology. She has a Law degree from Trinity College Dublin and an LL.M. from the London School of Economics. She is a barrister, and teaches courses in Criminal law; Criminology; and Feminist Criminology at Trinity. She is also a Senator for Dublin University. Her research interests include criminal law and criminology, constitutional law, feminist theories and law, human rights and equality issues in law.

Mary Rogan is an Associate Professor at the School of Law, Trinity College Dublin. She researches in the area of human rights and oversight in the penal system, access to justice, prison law, and prison policymaking. With Ivana Bacik, she is the co-editor of *Legal Cases that Changed Ireland* (Clarus, 2016). She is the PI on a project funded by the European Research Council entitled 'Prisons: the rule of law, accountability and rights' (PRILA), which examines the legal frameworks, lived experiences, and effects of prison oversight mechanisms. She was appointed by Minister for Justice and Equality to chair an Implementation and Oversight Group on reforms to penal policy in February 2015 and to the inaugural Department of Justice and Equality Research Advisory Group in 2019. Mary is also a representative of Ireland on the International Penal and Penitentiary Foundation.

Amanda Haynes is a senior lecturer in sociology at the University of Limerick. Amanda's research interests centre on the analysis of discursive, classificatory and physical violence, particularly those which are motivated by prejudice. She is a co-director of both the Hate and Hostility Research Group and the Power, Discourse and Society Research Group at the University of Limerick. Amanda's research has been funded by the European Union, the Irish Research Council and the Irish Council for Civil Liberties. Her research in the areas of hate crime, migration studies and stigma has been published in high ranking journals such as the Journal of Housing and the Built

Environment, Journalism: Theory, Practice & Criticism and New Media and Society and she is editor of collections with Rowman Littlefield International and Palgrave Macmillan. Following her service on the executive committee of the Sociological Association of Ireland, she was elected President of the Association for the 2008 term.

Jennifer Schweppe is a senior lecturer in the School of Law at the University of Limerick. She was President of the Irish Association of Law Teachers for 2009–2010. She completed a graduate diploma in Academic Practice at UL and won the Small Group Teaching Award at UL in 2010. She was awarded a National Award for Excellence in Teaching by the National Academy for the Integration of Research, Teaching and Learning in 2011 and was a finalist for the European Award for Excellence in Teaching in the Humanities and Social Sciences in 2012. She recently completed her PhD entitled: Legislating Against Hate Crime: Considering International Frameworks for an Irish Context. Her research interests lie in the areas of hate crime and reproductive justice, and she has published widely on these topics. She is co-editor of two major collections in the area of hate crime with Oxford University Press and Palgrave Macmillan, and has published in the Journal of Hate Studies, the Oxford Handbook Online in Criminology and Criminal Justice, the Northern Ireland Legal Quarterly and the Irish Jurist. She is co-director of the International Network for Hate Studies. She is also founder and co-director of the UL-based Hate and Hostility Research Group, the only academic research group in Ireland dedicated to exploring and understanding hate crime in an Irish context. Her work in the area of hate crime with Dr Amanda Haynes has been funded by the Irish Research Council, the EU DG Justice programme, and the Irish Council for Civil Liberties.

Niamh Dillon is a PhD candidate in the Department of Sociology at the University of Limerick. Her research focuses on asylum policy in Ireland, specifically the system of Direct Provision and its evolution. Niamh has recently published a paper on the barriers to integration for asylum seekers in Ireland. Her research interests include; Inequality & Social Exclusion, Migration, Gender & Sexuality, Racism and Hate Crime.

Claire Hamilton is a Professor of Criminology at Maynooth University Department of Law. She practised as a barrister in criminal law until 2004 when she became a full time academic. Prior to joining Maynooth University she worked for several years as a lecturer in criminology in Dublin Institute of Technology and Queen's University Belfast. She has published widely in various national and international legal and criminological journals including the *British Journal of Criminology, Theoretical Criminology* and the

European Journal of Criminology. She is the author/co-editor of five books, the most recent of which is *Counter-terrorism, Criminology and Contagion: Justice in the Shadow of Terror* published by Palgrave Macmillan.

Johnny Connolly is an Irish Research Council/Irish Council for Civil Liberties research fellow in the Centre for Criminal Justice and Victim Studies at the University of Limerick. His current research project is *Developing a comprehensive human rights based response to drug and gang-related crime and community violence*. He is also managing a research project titled Building community resilience – responding to criminal networks in Dublin South Central. Another project in which he is currently engaged as part of the National Drugs Strategy involves the development of a community crime impact assessment. Prior to joining UL, he spent 10 years as a research officer with the Health Research Board. He was Ireland's national correspondent to the European reference group on illicit drug markets and drug-related crime and the National Legal database on drug law and policy based at the European Monitoring Centre on Drugs and Drug Addiction in Lisbon. From 2005–2007 he was vice chairman of the criminal justice platform of the Pompidou Group of the Council of Europe. He was a member of the advisory group of the Drug Treatment Court for five years. In 2017, he was appointed by the Minister for Justice as a member of the Commission on the Future of Policing in Ireland.

Jonathan Ilan is a Senior Lecturer in Criminology in the Department of Sociology at City, University of London. He completed an LLB at Trinity College Dublin (2002) and a PhD in Social Sciences and Legal Studies at the Dublin Institute of Technology (2007). He was a project post-doctoral researcher at the School of Law, University College Dublin (2008–9) before moving across the Irish Sea to join the University of Kent first as a Lecturer (2009–15) then Senior Lecturer (2015–16) in Criminology. He publishes on a range of issues connected to crime, culture, control and marginalisation and is author of the book: 'Understanding Street Culture: Poverty, crime, youth and cool'; published by Macmillan Education UK in 2015. He is a member of the editorial board of the British Journal of Criminology.

Conor Hanly is a lecturer in law in NUI Galway. He graduated from NUI Galway with a B.A. in History and Legal Science in 1988, and with an LL.B. in 1990. In 1994, he completed an LL.M. by research at University College Dublin entitled "Pricing: A Behavioural Approach to Abuses of Market

Power", for which he was awarded First Class Honours. From 2003 to 2004, Conor was a Graduate Fellow at the Yale Law School, where he was conferred with a Master of Laws degree, and was awarded the Joseph M. Parker Prize in Legal History and Roman Law for his paper, "The Decline of the Civil Jury in Nineteenth Century England." He was also an editor on the Yale Law and Policy Review. In 2012 he completed his doctorate (JSD) on the criminal jury in Victorian England. Conor spent five years in a civil litigation environment in the Claims Department of Eagle Star Insurance Company. From 1995 to 2000, he was Lecturer in Law at Waterford Institute of Technology, and was an adviser to the Doras project, an outreach programme for those involved in juvenile prostitution in Waterford City. He joined the faculty at NUI Galway in 2000. He is a regular contributor to local, regional and national print and electronic media on matters of criminal law, especially those relating to sexual offences.

Mary Tumelty is a lecturer in law in University College Cork. She is a graduate of the University of Limerick (LL.B (Law and Irish); PhD) and has research interests in the area of Medical Law, Law of Torts, ADR, and Art Law. She is also interested in empirical legal research projects. In 2017 she completed her PhD entitled 'The spiralling costs, delays, and emotional burdens of medical negligence litigation: A socio-legal analysis of the current dynamic in Ireland', for which she was awarded a Research Scholarship by the Cluster for Understanding Emotions in Society, University of Limerick. Before taking up a Lectureship at the School of Law in UCC, Mary held the position of Postdoctoral Research Fellow with the Graduate Entry Medical School, University of Limerick. During this time, Dr Tumelty collaborated with colleagues in the Royal College of Surgeons, Ireland and conducted a nationwide survey to investigate the existence and extent of defensive medical practices among surgeons. Mary has presented her research at national and international conferences, and her work has been published or is forthcoming in the Journal of Patient Safety, the BMJ, the Medico-Legal Journal of Ireland, the Irish Jurist, the Irish Journal of Criminal Law, and the Commercial Law Practitioner.

Ciarán Burke is Director of Research at the Law Reform Commission. He holds a professorship in law at the Friedrich Schiller University of Jena in Germany. He was awarded his doctorate in 2011 by the European University Institute in Florence, and is an alumnus of the Vrije Universiteit (Amsterdam), Université Robert Schuman (Strasbourg), Université Toulouse-I and University College Dublin. His first book, *An Equitable Framework for Humanitarian Intervention*, was published in 2013. His second book, *Intelegere Drepturile Migrantilor - Un Manual pentru Republica Moldova,* was published in 2015. He has published in a wide array of renowned journals and in several languages. He has previously worked as a lecturer at the Universities of Passau, Dresden, and Kent, and has run projects for the European Commission, as well as government agencies in several states. He is the former Managing Editor of the European Journal of Legal Studies.

Raymond Byrne is a full-time Commissioner in the Law Reform Commission, appointed by the Government in April 2016 (following a TLAC/PAS public competition). Prior to his appointment, he was Director of Research in the Commission. He qualified as a barrister in 1982, and between 1982 and 2007 he was a lecturer in law in the School of Law and Government, Dublin City University. He is the author of a number of texts on safety and health law, including *Safety and Health Legislation: Annotated and Consolidated* (Round Hall Thomson Reuters, 2013). He is also co-author of *Byrne and McCutcheon on the Irish Legal System* 6th edition (Bloomsbury Professional, 2014) and of the *Annual Review of Irish Law* series (Round Hall Thomson Reuters). He was a contributor to Macleod and Hodges (eds), *Redress Schemes for Personal Injuries* (Hart Publishing, 2017) and Percival and Sayers (eds), *Changing the Law: A Practical Guide to Law Reform* (Commonwealth Association of Law Reform Agencies, 2017). Raymond chaired a Working Group whose work led to a Council of Europe 2009 Recommendation on Missing Persons and Presumption of Death. He is currently a member of the Research Ethics Committee of the Royal College of Physicians in Ireland. He was previously Chair of the Irish Council for Civil Liberties and President of the Irish Association of Law Teachers.

INTRODUCTION

Researching Law and Legal Research: Introducing the Case Studies Approach

Laura CAHILLANE *and Jennifer* SCHWEPPE

In our previous edited collection, *Legal Research Methods: Principles and Practicalities*,[1] we set out with the aim of introducing readers to the frameworks utilised in diverse legal methods and methodologies, as well as the 'how to' in each case, with the contributors also discussing the perceived advantages and disadvantages to the particular approach under discussion. However, whilst the authors described how the approach could be used in theory, we felt that there remained an outstanding question: how to use different approaches in practice. Thus, we approached a new set of contributors from a variety of legal disciplines to engage with this 'case studies' approach to understanding legal research.

The reason we drew together this collection was to highlight the processes that experienced researchers have engaged in when researching different and complex legal questions. There is no 'right' or 'wrong' way to conduct research, and as is highlighted throughout this collection, researchers consider a number of issues when determining which methodological approach to take to their research, and which methods to use in exploring their question. Indeed, some of these considerations may be outside the control of the researcher, either because of a mandated approach required by a funding body, or because a lack of funding required the researcher to seek cost-effective ways to answer their question.

In approaching each chapter, we asked the authors to consider using five key headings:

- What was the research question?
- What was the methodological approach and what were the methods used?

[1] L Cahillane and J Schweppe, *Legal Research Methods: Principles and Practicalities* (Clarus Press 2016).

- What were the challenges encountered?
- What ethical considerations were taken into account?
- What reflections do you have on the research?

In answering these questions, contributors each took different approaches, placing more or less emphasis on different sections. However, what we were particularly struck by in our review of the chapters was the deeply reflective approach the contributors took to their individual contributions. The authors highlighted the problems they encountered in conducting the research, highlighting what we think is a key point of learning from this text: there is no definitively right or wrong way to answer a research question. What is definitive, however, is the importance of a robust and clear methodology.

We observed in our previous text that it is only recently that legal researchers have begun to articulate a methodology in their work, and that law schools have been slow to engage in formal instruction in the subject matter. This, again, is a theme which emerges from this text – a number of contributors are either self-taught in research methods, either learning 'on the job' or upskilling for the purposes of a particular project. This, we believe, is no longer a sustainable position. We believe that every law student should have at least a rudimentary understanding of research methods at an undergraduate level, and that law schools – either individually or collectively – should provide comprehensive and extant training for their graduate students.

Until then, we hope that this collection will provide a useful resource to researchers seeking to engage in legal research.

In Chapter 1, Una Woods describes how she used primarily a doctrinal approach but supplemented this with a socio-legal approach and some comparative analysis in order to investigate reform of the Irish law on adverse possession. While much of the research was carried out in the traditional doctrinal sense, it was necessary to adopt a socio-legal approach when illustrating the impact of the current law of adverse possession in practice and also a comparative analysis of discrete aspects of the law in a number of other common law jurisdictions, namely England and Wales, Canada, Australia and the United States in order to recommend the most appropriate reform for Ireland.

Conor O'Mahony writes about comparative research in Chapter 2 in relation to his research which focused on the issue of marriage equality but also served as a case study for a project that was primarily an exercise in constitutional theory and comparative constitutional law. He examined the marriage equality issue, not by the arguments around what to decide but by the arguments around who gets to decide: the legislature, the courts, or the people in a referendum. Until 2015, no country had yet voted in favour of marriage equality in a national referendum but the issue had been the subject of a referendum in thirty states in the US. Ireland could have chosen any of these three ways. Comparative research thus offered a way to better understand how we might best address the issue here in Ireland, as well as to use marriage equality as a case study to explore constitutional theory questions about the relationship between formal constitutional amendment mechanisms and the posture of constitutional courts.

Laura Cahillane describes the approach she used in combining law and history in order to examine the drafting of the Irish Free State Constitution in Chapter 3. The historical approach was necessary for a project of this type which aimed to elucidate the original features of the Irish Free State Constitution but despite assumptions, the historical approach does not necessarily come naturally to lawyers. There are a number of factors which must be borne in mind and pitfalls to be avoided. Furthermore, combining a historical approach with a legal doctrinal approach requires careful consideration in order to obtain the best results from each discipline. Despite the challenges involved however, she also emphasises that using a mixed methods approach can be a very rewarding experience.

In Chapter 4 Clíodhna Murphy, Mary Gilmartin, and Leanne Caulfield explain how they used International Law in an Interdisciplinary Human Rights research project. The aim of the project was to conduct a comprehensive audit and critical human rights and equality review of migrant integration policy across public bodies in Ireland and through writing about their experience with this project, they point out that for the legal researcher, adopting elements of an international law approach can allow for the exploration of 'new' material and an original slant on aspects of the law which are already the subject of much scholarly analysis. Additionally, they note that an international law analysis can enrich and help to justify the recommendations for reform which form part of many doctoral theses and perhaps less obviously, the work of international organisations can also constitute an important source of legal information.

Máiréad Enright and Aoife O'Donoghue describe the feminist methodology they used in their The Northern/Irish Feminist Judgments Project in Chapter 5. The aim of the project was to rewrite 26 already decided judgments from several feminist perspectives, contextualised with accompanying commentaries and critical introductory chapters. Judgment writers were paired with commentators and each rewritten judgment was workshopped while still in draft. The primary goal was to address the marginalisation of feminist analysis within Northern/Irish legal traditions, and to demonstrate its value to judicial studies on the island. The authors were heavily influenced by the first such project in England and in this chapter they describe how they went about this unusual project.

The process involved in the 'Changing Ireland, Changing Law Research Project' is outlined by Ivana Bacik and Mary Rogan in Chapter 6. This project arose out of a desire to hear more of the stories behind some of the cases which have changed Ireland. The authors wanted to examine the personal impact that taking such litigation can have on individuals, as well as analysing the most effective ways in which to support both the litigants and the civil society organisations which work with them in using the law to secure change. The methods they used involved a form of narrative inquiry, where litigants spoke about their experiences alongside responses from academics and lawyers placing the case into a wider context. This approach provided a way for the lived experience of public interest litigation to be seen more clearly than is possible in legal analyses of such cases.

In Chapter 7, Amanda Haynes, Jennifer Schweppe and Niamh Dillon discuss the methodological approach utilised in an Irish Research Council funded piece of research. They sought to understand the experiences and perceptions of the Irish trans community of and with An Garda Síochána, and in doing so utilised a mixed methods approach. In this chapter, they particularly problematise the use of non-probability sampling methods in accessing a hard to reach population.

In Chapter 8, Claire Hamilton describes how she used social research and a mixed-methods approach in her project examining the concept of the 'new punitiveness' in three small jurisdictions; Ireland, Scotland and New Zealand from 1976 to 2006. A multi-method or triangulated approach including both qualitative and quantitative methodologies was adopted in order to attempt to more accurately grasp the punitiveness of each of the three countries. She discusses the challenges that she faced in identifying, collecting, and particularly interpreting and analysing, the quantitative data, as, like many lawyers, she had not been professionally trained in statistics or, indeed, the fundamental principles of social research. The message of this chapter is that collection of quantitative data acts as a powerful complement to both qualitative and doctrinal research and, as such, is certainly not something which legal researchers should dismiss out of hand.

Johnny Connolly also used methodological triangulation in his project examining illicit drug markets in Ireland and he explains how this worked in Chapter 9. The purpose of the study was to examine in particular how drug markets in four specific locations interacted with and impacted upon their local host communities. It sought to understand the thinking behind drug law enforcement and to describe the activities engaged in by An Garda Siochána drug units as they attempt to counteract local drug markets and to assess the activities from the perspectives of all sides. The study adopted a socio-legal approach but also combined ethnographic, qualitative, economic, quantitative, survey-based and criminological and law enforcement evaluation approaches. The author explains how methodological triangulation enables the obtaining of information on the same phenomena using two or more different methods, by using the strengths of one method to overcome the deficiencies of another, which achieves a higher degree of validity and reliability.

Jonathan Ilan outlines how he learned a new approach to research using ethnographic fieldwork during his project on young offenders in Chapter 10. The research involved looking at a particular group of young offenders and their interaction with wider society in order to try to understand their persistent involvement with the criminal justice system. The chapter provides a personal, reflexive account and explanation of ethnographic methods (research through immersion in a culture) and the qualities that make it distinctive.

In Chapter 11, Conor Hanly describes the methodology employed by Irish researchers from *Safe Ireland* and NUI Galway to document the response of the criminal justice system to incidents of domestic violence. This research was part of a wider pan-European study known as the INASC project – an acronym for *Improving Needs Assessment and Victims' Support in Domestic Violence-related Criminal Proceedings* and involved a quantitative analysis of a number of recent and completed official prosecutorial domestic violence files as well as surveys and face-to-face interviews with research participants.

Mary-Elizabeth Tumelty also explores the challenges and rewards involved in mixed methods approaches, this time in the context of medical negligence litigation in Chapter 12 with regard to her research project which explored the existence and causes of delay in medical negligence litigation in Ireland. The research involved the use of both quantitative and qualitative methods alongside the traditional doctrinal approach. She observes that the employment of multiple research methods allowed her to capture the nuances of delay as it pertains to medical negligence claims.

Finally, Ciarán Burke and Ray Byrne write about the unique nature of research at the Law Reform Commission and how it differs from both academic and practitioner research. They note that research for law reform is neither an abstract exercise, nor an examination of the minutiae of an individual case, but rather is a 'happy medium' between the two. Thus, they note, law reform research lends itself to a distinct methodological approach. They describe the methodological approaches taken in a number of pieces of work undertaken by the Commission, highlighting the nimble approach the Commission takes to its research.

Chapter 1

The Case for a Qualified Veto System of Adverse Possession in Ireland: A Doctrinal Approach with 'Bells and Whistles'

*Una Woods**

1 – Introduction

This chapter discusses the methodology and methods adopted to write my PhD thesis.[1] The thesis argued for the reform of the Irish law on adverse possession by the introduction of a qualified veto system of adverse possession, which would confer additional protection on the owner and prevent 'undeserving' adverse possessors from relying on the doctrine. Although a number of reform options were considered,[2] the reform ultimately proposed achieves the vital objective of ensuring 'the baby is not thrown out with the bathwater'. The number and variety of functions performed by the doctrine of adverse possession present a challenge for those interested in instigating its reform. However, conferring a qualified veto on an owner notified of an adverse possession application would refine and hone the operation of the doctrine, ensuring that it continues to perform certain valuable tasks, but in a manner that achieves a fairer result. Part 1 (chapters 1–5) of the thesis made the case for the introduction of the proposed reform. It explained why the doctrine, in its current state, fails to confer adequate protection on the owner against the dangers of losing title to an adverse possessor and it illustrated how the law permits 'undeserving' adverse possessors to acquire title. The proposed reform would permit an owner who has not abandoned the land to veto an adverse possession application unless the applicant qualifies under one of the exceptions to the scheme. In Part 2 (chapters 6–9) of the thesis the qualifications to the veto were formulated. The qualifications were carefully designed to preserve the operation of the

* Dr Una Woods, Senior Lecturer in Law, University of Limerick.

[1] See U Woods, *The Irish Law on Adverse Possession: The Case for a Qualified Veto System* (PhD thesis, Queen's University Belfast, 2015).

[2] For example, the introduction of a mandatory court application or a compensation requirement, ibid, ch 5.

doctrine for certain 'deserving' adverse possessors. Accordingly, the owner's veto would be ineffective against an adverse possession application by an applicant who entered possession pursuant to an informal or a defective title or an adverse possessor of boundary land who believed the land to be their own. The formulation of these exceptions required an examination of the modern role played by adverse possession in resolving different types of land law disputes and the doctrine's suitability as a remedy. It was also necessary to address certain challenges presented by the design of the appropriate qualifications to the veto system.

II – Research Question

The various roles which have been ascribed to the 'strange and wonderful' doctrine of adverse possession[3] and the 'ideas of right and wrong'[4] which the doctrine raises make it a fascinating topic for land law students and provided ample, absorbing material for a doctoral thesis. My research engaged with both aspects of the doctrine: it examined the importance of adverse possession as a remedy in the resolution of a broad range of land law difficulties and it considered whether the doctrine should be reformed so that it operates in a manner that produces a fairer result.

The proposal for the thesis was formulated against a backdrop of increasing unease in relation to the fairness of the doctrine of adverse possession, which became evident in certain jurisdictions around the turn of the new millennium. In England and Wales, concerns relating to the fairness of the doctrine, coupled with a desire to align the doctrine with registration principles, prompted the reforms to the law on adverse possession introduced by the Land Registration Act 2002. The 2002 Act applied a qualified veto system of adverse possession to registered land in England and Wales. Certain states in the United States had also recently attempted to make the doctrine fairer by introducing reforms to the doctrine, which impose a good faith requirement on the adverse possessor.[5]

In Ireland, the Law Reform Commission published a Report on Reform and Modernisation of Land Law and Conveyancing Law in 2005 and an awareness of this discomfiture with the doctrine was very much in evidence. The Law

[3] See JE Stake 'The Uneasy Case for Adverse Possession' (2000–2001) 89 Georgetown Law Journal 2419, 2419.

[4] See R Auchmuty, 'Not just a good children's story: A tribute to adverse possession' [2004] Conveyancer and Property Lawyer 291, 307.

[5] For example, Oregon introduced a mandatory good faith requirement in 1989 while New York introduced a more limited good faith requirement in 2008, see Woods (n 1) ch 4, pt 1.

Reform Commission noted that the law on adverse possession had become the subject of increasing controversy.[6] It argued:

> it must be recognised that on occasion the doctrine may operate unfairly, especially where it appears to enable a person, who deliberately sets out to take advantage of it, to use it as a means of obtaining ownership of someone else's land without paying any compensation. The same applies where it appears to exact a very severe penalty on a landowner (the loss of the land) through a mere oversight or mistake.[7]

The Commission included a number of provisions in the draft Land and Conveyancing Law Reform Bill set out in its report which were clearly intended to provide added protection for the owner and to streamline the operation of the doctrine, so that it would continue to apply only where necessary to restore the marketability of abandoned land and in certain other limited circumstances. These proposals were jettisoned in response to critical submissions made to the government by the Law Society's Conveyancing Committee, mostly related to the workability of the proposed scheme.[8] Consequently, the Land and Conveyancing Law Reform Bill 2006 was published without the inclusion of any reforms dealing with the law on adverse possession.[9]

The widespread unease with the fairness of the doctrine also permeated judicial thinking in England and Wales. It was quite evident in the *Pye* litigation which involved an adverse possession claim governed by the old law (operating before the Land Registration Act 2002 came into effect). As this case wound its way through the domestic courts, a number of judges condemned the doctrine from the bench.[10]

In the House of Lords, Lord Hope observed:

> The unfairness in the old regime which this case has demonstrated lies not in the absence of compensation, although that is an important factor, but in the lack of safeguards against oversight or inadvertence on the part of the registered proprietor.[11]

---

[6] *Report on Reform and Modernisation of Land Law and Conveyancing Law* (LRC 74—2005).

[7] ibid para 2.06.

[8] These proposals are discussed in ch 5, Woods (n 1).

[9] The Land and Conveyancing Law Reform Act 2009 was enacted on 1 July 2009 and all of its provisions, with the exception of s 132, came into operation on 1 December 2009. s 132 came into force on 28 February 2010.

[10] See *JA Pye (Oxford) Ltd v Graham* [2000] Ch 676, 710 (Neuberger J).

[11] *JA Pye (Oxford) Ltd v Graham* [2002] UKHL 30; [2003] 1 AC 419, [73].

The *Pye* case originated in an action brought by JA Pye (Oxford) Ltd to recover possession of 25 hectares of land in Berkshire from the personal representatives of Michael Graham, who had been a neighbouring farmer and claimed to have established adverse possession of the land. When the House of Lords ruled in favour of the Grahams, Pye Ltd proceeded to bring an application against the UK government pursuant to Art 34 of the European Convention on Human Rights. The company alleged that the law on adverse possession, through which it had lost land with development potential, violated its right to property as guaranteed by the Convention. On 30 August 2007 the Grand Chamber of the European Court of Human Rights delivered its judgment in *JA Pye (Oxford) Ltd v United Kingdom.*[12] It held by ten votes to seven that the English law on adverse possession, as set out in the Land Registration Act 1925 and the Limitation Act 1980, did not violate Art 1 of the First Protocol to the European Convention on Human Rights, which protects property rights.[13] This application represented the high point of culminating concerns in relation to the fairness of the doctrine, and had implications for other contracting states (such as Ireland[14]). The Grand Chamber decision in *Pye* eliminated doubts over the acceptability of the law from a human rights perspective and crushed any possibility that the Convention would act as a catalyst for the reform of the Irish law on adverse possession. However, the controversy generated by this litigation, reforms to the doctrine introduced in other jurisdictions and the unremitting debate in academic literature concerning the doctrine's modern relevance[15] were all critical in the formulation of my research question. This question involved two components: (1) whether there was a case for reforming the Irish law on adverse possession in Ireland on the basis that it is unfair (i.e. inadequately protects the owner and facilitates claims by undeserving squatters) and (2) how could the law be reformed to produce

[12] (2008) 46 EHRR 45.

[13] The judgment reversed the Chamber decision delivered on 15 November 2005 which found by four votes to three that there was a violation of the property rights guarantee.

[14] The Irish government made a third-party submission to the European Court of Human Rights which emphasised the important functions performed by the doctrine, see *JA Pye (Oxford) Ltd v United Kingdom* (2008) 46 EHRR 45 [50]–[51].

[15] See, for example, M Dockray's article, 'Why do we need adverse possession?' [1985] Conveyancer and Property Lawyer 272; L Fox and N Cobb, 'Living outside the system? The (im)morality of urban squatting after the Land Registration Act 2002' (2007) 27(2) Legal Studies 236; JE Stake 'The Uneasy Case for Adverse Possession' (2000–2001) 89 Georgetown Law Journal 2419; LA Fennell, 'Efficient Trespass: The Case for "Bad Faith" Adverse Possession' (2006) 100 Northwestern University Law Review 1037; TW Merrill, 'Property Rules, Liability Rules and Adverse Possession' (1984–85) 79 Northwestern University Law Review 1122; WG Ackerman and ST Johnson, 'Outlaws of the past: A western perspective on prescription and adverse possession' (1996) 31 Land and Water Review 79; CN Brown and SM Williams, 'Rethinking Adverse Possession: An Essay on Ownership and Possession' (2009–2010) 60 Syracuse Law Review 583.

a fairer result but also preserve the valuable role that the doctrine currently plays in resolving certain property disputes?

III – Methodological Approach and Methods Used

The analysis of the law and the case for reform were conducted by relying primarily on a doctrinal methodology, although a socio-legal approach was also adopted when illustrating the impact of the current law of adverse possession in practice. While the thesis was devoted chiefly to an examination of the Irish law in this area, it also engaged in a comparative analysis of discrete aspects of the law in a number of other common law jurisdictions, namely England and Wales, Canada, Australia and the United States.

A doctrinal approach

In adopting a doctrinal approach, the thesis could be described as following a well-worn, traditional path popular with academics engaging with research questions involving a critique of the law and the need for reform. While an exclusively doctrinal approach may be appropriate and effective in making an original contribution to the literature on a subject, in my research the doctrinal approach acted as a lynchpin or framework for a project which also drew on other methodological approaches.

The analysis of certain aspects of the law on adverse possession conducted throughout the thesis relied heavily on primary and secondary sources of law to elucidate the development and current status of specific rules in the area. The law was explained by referring to legislation and case law in Ireland, the United Kingdom, the United States, Australia, and Canada, and also scholarly interpretations of the primary sources located in texts and journal articles. As is increasingly the case with this method of research, electronic resources were invaluable in gathering this material. In addition to databases (such as Lexis, Westlaw, Heinonline, and Justis), resources made available on governmental websites and the websites of the various law reform bodies proved extremely useful. On occasion, when older reports had not been uploaded to the websites of law reform commissions, the material was scanned and emailed by helpful employees.

One of the basic claims or assumptions of the black letter tradition is that legal doctrine possesses a 'logical coherence' or an 'underlying rationale'.[16]

[16] M Salton and J Mason, *Writing Law Dissertations: An Introduction and Guides to the Conduct of Legal Research* (Pearson Longman 2007) 68, 75. See also T Hutchinson, 'Doctrinal Research' in D Watkins and M Burton (eds) *Research Methods in Law* (Routledge 2013).

The aim of substantive sections of the thesis was, therefore, to identify the principles which help make sense of the unwieldy mass of case law decisions.[17] As Richard Posner observes, 'The messy work product of the judges and legislators requires a good deal of tidying up, of synthesis, analysis, restatement, and critique.'[18] Researchers adopting a doctrinal approach are also ideally placed 'to confront the conundrums and uncertainties which arise at the frontiers of the law.'[19] The approach is perhaps best illustrated by referring to an example of a doctrinal analysis of the law conducted in chapter 1 of the thesis.

In examining the case for the introduction of additional protection for the owner against the dangers of losing title through adverse possession, a necessary first step was an analysis of the extent to which the Irish law in the area currently protects the owner. During the human rights controversy sparked by the *Pye* litigation, it was argued in some quarters that the owner was better insulated against inadvertently losing title under the Irish law on adverse possession than the English law (before the reforms introduced by the Land Registration Act 2002).[20] The additional protection was alleged to be a by-product of the application of certain judicial techniques or glosses on the law which make it more difficult to prove that an owner has been dispossessed and would, it was implied, have prevented a positive outcome for the Grahams if the *Pye* litigation had occurred in Ireland. For example, in a relatively recent High Court case, *Feehan v Leamy*,[21] it was held that the owner could maintain possession of the land, thus preventing adverse possession, by simply looking over a hedge or gate onto the land. In contrast, in *Pye*, although a representative of the company visited the disputed land to inspect it on one occasion and viewed it from the road, it was not suggested

[17] Salton and Mason, ibid 68.

[18] R Posner, 'In Memoriam: Bernard D Meltzer (1914-2007)' (2007) 74 University of Chicago Law Review 409 435.

[19] In the words of T Hutchinson, 'Doctrinal Research' in D Watkins and M Burton (eds) *Research Methods in Law* (Routledge 2013) 14. See, for example, the discussion of whether adverse possession must be obvious in Woods (n 1) ch 3, pt 3, or when the limitation period begins to run in the context of an informal transaction in Woods (n 1) ch 6.

[20] See N Buckley, 'Adverse Possession at the Crossroads' (2006) 11 (3) Conveyancing and Property Law Journal 59, 60; The summary of the law contained in the Property Registration Authority Practice Direction, *Title by Adverse Possession to Registered Land*, para 2.1, lends support to such an argument. This Practice Direction is available at <www.prai.ie/adverse-possession-title-by-adverse-possession-to-registered-land> accessed 18 January 2018. Note that the website specifies that Practice Directions are published for guidance only and should not be regarded as legal interpretations. Although reasonable care is exercised in their compilation no representation is made as to their accuracy.

[21] [2001] IEHC 23.

that this was sufficient to constitute an act of possession by the owner. It has also been suggested, that the rule in *Leigh v Jack*[22] may still apply in Ireland,[23] which would make it more difficult to prove adverse possession where the owner had future plans for the property. Pye Ltd had purchased the disputed land with the intention of retaining it until planning permission could be obtained for its development. In *Pye*, the rule in *Leigh v Jack* was definitely rejected by the House of Lords when Lord Browne-Wilkinson described the notion that sufficiency of possession can depend on the intention of the true owner as 'heretical and wrong'.[24]

Therefore, the first substantive chapter of my thesis required a doctrinal analysis of the relevant Irish case law in an attempt to ascertain whether it can be comfortably asserted that the owner is less easily dispossessed under Irish law and to assess the accuracy of such an interpretation of the law.[25] This involved an examination of any case which focused on the owner's actions and future plans in relation to the land in determining whether he or she had been dispossessed by an adverse possessor. The aim was to place the decision in *Feehan v Leamy* in context and to clarify the current status of the rule in *Leigh v Jack*. It also involved an examination of the relevant legislative provisions and various interpretations of the law set out by academic writers in textbooks and journal articles. The forensic examination of judicial dicta carried out by a doctrinal lawyer should result in the piece-by-piece construction of a judicial jigsaw revealing the main principles which the judiciary has relied on to reach their decisions. The aim is to differentiate the good law from the bad law and identify instances where a judge may have gone astray in his or her application of the law. The conclusion reached following the analysis of the law in this particular context was that it cannot be confidently asserted that the Irish law confers more protection on the owner. More specifically, the analysis illustrated why the ruling in *Feehan v Leamy*, that looking over a hedge prevents dispossession must be regarded as questionable. It also revealed that although the Supreme Court has yet to rule on the issue, the High Court has, for the most part, leaned against the adoption of the rule in *Leigh v Jack*. The review of the case law demonstrated that

[22] (1879) 5 Ex D 264. While the rule held sway in England and Wales, it was applicable if the owner had a plan to use the land for some specific purpose in the future and, in the meantime, some other person took physical possession of it. The rule prevented adverse possession from taking place if the adverse possessor's current use was not inconsistent with the owner's future plan for the property.

[23] See N Buckley (n 25) 64; Property Registration Authority Practice Direction (n 25) para 2.5.

[24] *JA Pye (Oxford) Ltd v Graham* [2002] UKHL 30; [2003] 1 AC 419.

[25] Note that an early draft of this chapter formed the basis for a published article: U Woods, 'The Position of the Owner under the Irish Law on Adverse Possession' (2008) 30 Dublin University Law Journal 298.

although references to *Leigh v Jack* appear in many Irish adverse possession cases, many of these references cannot be taken as a direct endorsement of the rule itself as the case is frequently cited to support other arguments.

In recent times there has been much criticism of doctrinal legal research. Van Gestel and Micklitz note that doctrinalists are often perceived to be 'intellectually rigid, inflexible, formalistic and inward-looking.'[26] They continue:

> Other accusations include that doctrinalists show an unhealthy preoccupation with technicalities, often focus on unimportant topics, repeat existing knowledge, and fail to connect law to life by assessing the real world consequences of doctrinal frameworks.[27]

The doctrinal analysis adopted in my thesis was necessary to clarify specific aspects of the law which had become obfuscated by certain judicial rulings and academic commentary. Although many areas of land law, including the law on adverse possession, may be perceived as technical, its application by the courts has critical implications for the litigants involved who may acquire or lose valuable real estate depending on the outcome of a case. Twining states that the central weakness of the expository tradition:

> is that typically it takes as its starting point and its main focus of attention rules of law, without systematic or regular reference to the context of problems they are supposed to resolve, the purposes they are intended to serve or the effects they in fact have.[28]

However, Hutchinson points out that the first step in a legal research project is to understand the content of the law before being concerned about its derivation or effects on society;[29] understanding the law necessarily precedes empirical research. My doctrinal analysis was a necessary precursor to the substantive portions of my thesis which were devoted to a discussion of the problems that adverse possession is supposed to resolve and the practical effects of the doctrine's application. The thesis, therefore, also had a non-doctrinal or a socio-legal dimension.

---

[26] R Van Gestel and H Micklitz, *Revitisalizing Doctrinal Legal Research in Europe: What about Methodology*? (European Institute Working Papers Law 2011/05) 2, referring to D Vick, 'Interdisciplinarity and the Discipline of Law' (2004) 31(2) Journal of Law and Society 164.

[27] ibid, referring to R Cotterell, 'Subverting Orthodoxy, Making Law Central: A View of Sociolegal Studies' (2002) 29 Journal of Law and Society 633.

[28] W Twining, *Taylor Lectures 1975 Academic Law and Legal Development* (University of Lagos Faculty of Law, 1976) 20.

[29] Hutchinson, 'Doctrinal Research' in *Research Methods in Law* (n 19) 17.

The 'bells and whistles': a socio-legal approach

The thesis could be described as adopting a 'problem, policy and law reform' based approach.[30] It highlighted certain problems with how the law on adverse possession currently operates and proposed reforms to the doctrine designed to preserve its operation for specific policy objectives. The main difficulty identified was the increasing tendency of legal academics, members of the judiciary and the public to view the outcome in certain adverse possession scenarios as unfair. The policy objectives traditionally assigned to the doctrine were examined and it assessed how the law could be reformed to meet the objectives which continue to be relevant, while resolving the issue which has arisen over the fairness of the doctrine.

To many, a pure socio-legal approach will involve a substantive interdisciplinary focus, or comprise of a large-scale data collection and analysis exercise involving the compilation of statistics and/or carrying out surveys or interviews. The socio-legal dimension to my research was less pervasive as the empirical research was limited and relied primarily on secondary data. This aspect of the research was made up of two components, both of which had the common goal of analysing how the law on adverse possession is applied in practice. It involved an analysis of a sample of adverse possession applications made to the Property Registration Authority (known as 'section 49 applications')[31] and the reported Irish case law on adverse possession.[32] For a number of reasons, mainly pragmatic, the data analysed in connection with the adverse possession applications was secondary. Reliance was placed on an internal survey which the Authority recently carried out.[33] Although the organisation's aim coincided with my own (identifying how the doctrine is relied on in practice), as the Authority was the primary data collector, it decided on the survey's scope and other aspects of how the survey was to be conducted. While the sample of section 49 applications surveyed was small (one month's applications in 2008 in respect of two counties – 88 cases in total), the results accurately reflected the experience of examiners of title who dealt with such applications on a daily basis. The counties sampled were Waterford and Cork which contain a good mix of both urban and rural properties. An analysis of this survey and other data made available from the Authority highlighted the surprisingly

[30] I Dobinson and F Johns 'Qualitative Legal Research' in M Mc Conville and W Hong Chui (eds), *Research Methods for Law* (Edinburgh University Press 2007).

[31] Registration of Title Act 1964, s 49.

[32] 34 cases are listed in Woods (n 1), Appendix 1.

[33] For the results of the survey and additional data, see Woods (n 1) Appendix 2. I am grateful to the Property Registration Authority for sharing this information with me, particularly CEO, Liz Pope, who patiently discussed it with me.

high volume of successful adverse possession applications which are made to the Property Registration Authority on an annual basis[34] and illustrated the most common functions performed by the doctrine in a registered title context: namely, updating ownership of property forming part of unadministered estates; tidying up informal transactions; restoring abandoned land to the market and resolving boundary disputes.[35]

The analysis of the case law conducted using this method was completely different to the doctrinal analysis carried out in chapter 1 of my thesis which was designed to clarify the law. The goal of this analysis was to identify how the law is relied on in practice: namely, the circumstances of the adverse possessor and the owner. It involved distinguishing the successful claims from those which had failed and categorising the relationship between the owner and the adverse possessor (family/neighbours/contractual/strangers).[36] Finally, an attempt was also made to identify the prevalence of 'bad faith' adverse possession (i.e. where the adverse possessor is aware that they are not the owner) from the case law. The presence or absence of a belief in ownership (or good faith) is generally regarded as irrelevant when it comes to establishing the mental element required to prove adverse possession, namely *animus possidendi* (an intention to possess). However, a seminal article published in the United States in 1983[37] negates the conventional wisdom on this issue. In his article on 'Adverse Possession and Subjective Intent' Professor Helmholz reached an unexpected conclusion. Following a survey of 850 appellate decisions, Helmholz noted that a bad faith adverse possessor is less likely to succeed in court despite the absence of an explicit good faith requirement. He deduced that the courts prefer the claims of an honest person over those of a dishonest person and distinguish the claims through the application of the

[34] Over 1,000 adverse possession applications are made to the Property Registration Authority in relation to registered land on an annual basis and the majority of these applications are successful. This level of applications appears to be quite consistent: 1,378 section 49 applications were received in 2007 and 1,081 applications were received in 2011. Eight-hundred-and-eighty-four applications were completed in 2007. Seven-hundred-and-seventy-eight applications were completed in 2011. The rest were abandoned, withdrawn, refused or transferred.

[35] Fifty-six percent of the section 49 applications surveyed involved adverse possession between family members, typically in relation to property forming part of an unadministered estate. Twenty-five percent of the applications involved lost or informal transfers, while 12 percent of applications involved strangers to title (frequently in relation to abandoned land). Six percent of applications involved boundary issues.

[36] In 16 of these cases there was a family relationship between the parties; 14 cases involved neighbouring landowners; three cases involved a pre-existing contractual relationship between the parties; only one case involved strangers.

[37] RE Helmholz, 'Adverse Possession and Subjective Intent' (1983) 61 *Washington University Law Quarterly* 331.

more elastic elements of the doctrine. In essence, his research could be described as illustrating the gaps in understanding which a pure doctrinal analysis of the law may produce. It was impossible to replicate a Helmholz-style analysis of the relevant Irish case law, as most adverse possession claims are made by application to the Property Registration Authority and, consequently, there are not enough reported cases on the topic. Also, it was difficult to determine from the facts of some of the cases whether the adverse possessor believed he was the owner.[38] In the vast majority of the 34 cases reviewed, however, it seems likely that the adverse possessor did not possess 'in good faith'.[39] Despite the presence of bad faith, the adverse possessor was equally as likely to succeed. Counter-intuitively, good faith had the potential to create more difficulties in proving *animus possidendi*.[40] This analysis of the case law revealed that the Irish law on adverse possession facilitates claims by bad faith adverse possessors, frequently considered to be unworthy beneficiaries of the law. In light of this conclusion, it was then necessary to assess the case for the introduction of a more restrictive regime which would preclude claims by bad faith adverse possessors. This discussion involved a critique of certain academic literature which put forward a defence of bad faith adverse possession.[41] While the main arguments made by these writers were of limited relevance in the Irish context, the articles were useful in illustrating the dangers of relying solely on the criterion of good faith for the purposes of distinguishing a deserving adverse possession claim from an undeserving claim.

Teitelbaum recommends greater use of empirical research to advance our understanding of law. He notes as follows:

> If laws are intended to produce certain results, questions about whether they do produce the expected results, whether they produce other results and whether the identifiable results are as consistent with the reason for law as one might have anticipated, are all important to examine.[42]

---

[38] In some cases, it was possible to hazard a reasonable guess in relation to the presence of good faith or bad faith based on the circumstances presented. For example, it was assumed that the adverse possessor who went into possession following an intestate death on title was aware of the entitlements of the other next-of-kin. Therefore, these claimants were categorised as bad faith adverse possessors in the Appendix, see e.g. *Martin v Kearney* [1902] 36 ILTR 117; *Christie v Christie* (1917) 1 IR 17.

[39] It was only possible to identify two cases where the court seemed to accept that the adverse possessor believed he was the owner: *Murphy v Murphy* [1980] IR 183 and *Kelleher v Botany Weaving Mills Ltd* [2008] IEHC 417.

[40] See *Kelleher v Botany Weaving Mills Ltd* [2008] IEHC 417.

[41] LA Fennell, 'Efficient Trespass: The Case for "Bad Faith" Adverse Possession' (2006) 100 Northwestern University Law Review 1037 and L Fox and N Cobb, 'Living outside the system? The (im)morality of urban squatting after the Land Registration Act 2002' (2007) 27(2) Legal Studies 236.

[42] LE Teitelbaum, 'An Overview of Law and Social Research' (1985) 35 Journal of Legal Education 466.

The value of such an empirical analysis of the impact of the current law on adverse possession in practice is illustrated by certain academic commentary which followed the introduction of the reforms to the English law on adverse possession. Although the fundamental reforms introduced to the English law by the 2002 Act appear to have been ushered in with a minimum of fuss,[43] after the event, Fox and Cobb raised some profound questions about whether the reform was desirable.[44] They argued that the owner who lost title through the traditional adverse possession regime was a bad land steward and that many adverse possessors were resourceful individuals in need of housing. In analysing the Irish data, therefore, it was important to consider if the introduction of reform in Ireland was likely to promote bad stewardship practices and punish homeless urban squatters. In a nutshell, it was critical to examine whether the circumstances of the typical owner and squatter warranted the introduction of the proposed reform.[45]

The examination of the reported case law on adverse possession revealed no obvious surprises and confirmed the writer's suspicion that many litigated disputes involved family members or neighbouring land owners.[46] More astonishing was the high number of adverse possession applications involving family members, revealed by the Property Registration Authority's internal survey.[47] These results immediately raised concerns about the vulnerability of owners in this neighbourly or familial context. It is easy to imagine very little, if any, conversation taking place between the parties to form the basis of an express or implied licence which would prevent the limitation period from running against the owner. The owner may assume that formalising the occupation is unnecessary, or he or she may be embarrassed to raise the matter, or reluctant to do anything which might jeopardise or further damage an existing relationship with a neighbour or sibling. There was strong evidence in the Irish context to indicate that the typical owner could not

[43] See Woods (n 1) ch 2.

[44] L Fox and N Cobb, 'Living outside the system? The (im)morality of urban squatting after the Land Registration Act 2002' (2007) 27(2) Legal Studies 236.

[45] These questions are discussed in Woods (n 1) chs 3 and 4.

[46] See Woods (n 1) ch 3, pt 2 for an analysis of the case law.

[47] Fifty-six percent of applications involved adverse possession between family members, typically in relation to property forming part of an unadministered estate. It was confirmed that objections are made in relation to the majority of section 49 applications, and 70 percent of these objections were based on an entitlement to the land under the unadministered intestate or testate estate of the registered owner. Of course, once the limitation period has expired, such an objection has no legal basis and will not prevent registration in the absence of another valid ground for objection, for example, proof that the objector continued to engage in acts of possession or that the applicant was not in possession or was in possession pursuant to an express or an implied licence.

justifiably be labelled as a 'bad land steward' and the vulnerability of these owners renders the case for additional protection particularly strong.

The empirical analysis also revealed that in Ireland the doctrine is not frequently relied on by a resourceful urban squatter; the most frequent applicant to the Property Registration Authority relies on the doctrine to extinguish the intestate entitlements of siblings who are out of possession.[48] This raised an interesting question about whether the doctrine continues to be relied on within families to up-date the ownership of farms, a peculiarly Irish justification traditionally advanced for the doctrine.[49] It is arguable that the historical role played by the doctrine in this agricultural context was an expedient and practical response to the problems generated by a reticence on the part of small farmers to make a will, widespread emigration from rural Ireland and a reluctance to extract grants to administer the estates of small farmers. It is also important to envisage the social and cultural context of the inheritance of small family farms in the early to mid-twentieth century. Up until relatively recently, it was commonly expected that the eldest son would inherit the family farm[50] and many important financial decisions followed on from this expectation. For example, other children may have been provided with an education or had provision made for them on marriage. It is no longer the case that such assumptions will be made in relation to the inheritance of farms. Many daughters now show an interest in farming and it cannot be assumed that one child will benefit on the basis of their order of birth. In any event, the ownership of farms tends to be updated on death more assiduously in more recent times than in the past. As this particular problem with unadministered estates no longer exists, it was timely to assess whether the acquisition of title by adverse possession is an appropriate remedy to make available to one sibling who remains in possession of a property forming part of the estate of a deceased parent. Nowadays, the property in question could be land or a valuable urban dwelling and it was submitted that the doctrine of adverse possession is unnecessary to protect a child with a moral claim to the property (e.g. if they

[48] ibid.

[49] It is frequently asserted that the doctrine of adverse possession performs a valuable social function in Ireland by allowing the ownership of land forming part of an unadministered estate to be updated many years after the death of the owner. More specifically, it is argued that this role is particularly important in rural Ireland where historically will-making was uncommon, emigration was widespread and grants of representations were rarely extracted in relation to small farms. See A Lyall (with A Power), *Land Law in Ireland* (Dublin: Round Hall, 3rd edn, 2010) 990; JCW Wylie, *Irish Land Law* (5th edn, Bloomsbury Professional 2013) para 23.42; RA Pearce, 'Adverse possession by the next-of-kin of an intestate' (1987) 5 Irish Law Times 281; Law Reform Commission, *Report on Reform and Modernisation of Land Law and Conveyancing Law* (LRC 74-2005) 331–332.

[50] This approach may have been a hangover from the rules of primogeniture which favoured the eldest male heir.

sacrificed opportunities to care for a parent on the basis of an expectation of inheriting property created by that parent). The more appropriate legal response, in such circumstances, is to provide a remedy to the child under the doctrine of proprietary estoppel or s 117 of the Succession Act 1965.[51] Having established that many owners are in need of additional protection and that 'undeserving' possessors are relying on the doctrine, the dilemma became how to reform the law to address these issues in a manner which would allow the doctrine to continue to perform certain valuable functions. The qualified veto system of adverse possession provided an ideal solution.[52]

The 'bells and whistles': a comparative approach

Although the thesis discussed the Irish law on adverse possession and considered reform in an Irish context, it considered these issues in light of developments which had occurred elsewhere. The recent reforms in England and Wales to the doctrine featured most prominently in this comparative analysis, which makes sense given the broad similarities between the property law systems of both jurisdictions. However, certain other land law remedies from further afield such as the United States, Australia and Canada, which fulfil some functions typically performed by adverse possession, were also examined. The aim of this micro-comparison[53] was to assess how well such reforms and remedies would work in Ireland, bearing in mind possible differences in social context.

Those who attempt to incorporate comparative analysis into their research are engaging in a risky business. It is easy to be labelled a 'dabbler' by academics who devote much of their energy to examining the theory and method of comparative law.[54] Although the identification of the aims of comparative law is not free from controversy,[55] two benefits of this type of

[51] See Woods (n 1) ch 7; See also Woods, 'Adverse Possession and Unadministered Estates: An Unfair Solution to a Redundant Irish Problem' (2016) 67(2) Northern Ireland Legal Quarterly 137.

[52] Alternative reform options were considered in ch 5, Woods (n 1).

[53] This is the term Rheinstein adopts for the comparison of aspects or topics of two or more legal systems, in contrast with a macro-comparison which involves the comparison of two or more entire legal systems. See M Rheinstein, 'Teaching Tools in Comparative Law' (1952) 1 American Journal of Comparative Law 95.

[54] J Hendry, 'Legal comparison and the (im)possibility of legal translation' in S Glenart (ed) *Comparative Law – Engaging Translation* (Routledge, 2014) 95.

[55] See the discussion of the functions of comparative law in WJ Kamba 'Comparative Law: A Theoretical Framework' (1974) 23(3) International and Comparative Law Quarterly 485, 489–505. Hendry notes that those who engage in comparative legal studies are under considerable pressure to prove the legitimacy of this field of legal research. She continues, 'A sceptic could argue, of course, that the fact that such enquiries are so often repeated rather suggests that the answers have remained somewhat inadequate. But this claim does not withstand scrutiny.' See Hendry ibid 88.

research are difficult to dispute. First, looking at the problems faced by other legal systems and the solutions adopted to these problems greatly assists legal researchers, commentators and students conducting a critical assessment of the position within their own jurisdiction. As Kamba notes:

> When one is confined to the study of one's own law within one's own country and thus within one's own cultural environment, there is a strong tendency to accept without question the various aspects (norms, concepts, and institutions) of one's own legal system. One is inclined to think that the solutions of one's own legal order are the only possible ones. This leads to an idealisation of one's legal institutions and to treating them as inherent in the general nature of law.[56]

Second, comparative law provides a valuable resource for legislators engaged in making law and reforming the law. According to Maine, 'The chief function of comparative jurisprudence is to facilitate legislation and the practical improvement of the law.'[57] This aim appears to be the basis for the functionalist 'better solutions' approach to comparative legal research. The classic explanation of this approach is provided by Zweigert and Kotz who assert that 'the legal system of every society faces essentially the same problems' and argue that the object of comparison should be to identify a much richer range of model solutions to these problems.[58] Von Mehren agrees:

> ... insight into how other legal systems have dealt with particular problems not only stimulates the jurist's imagination but reveals the strengths and weaknesses of particular solutions. Comparative study thus assists legal reform as well as lawyers' efforts to find creative solutions for problems that arise in legal practice.[59]

Of course, for some, the notion that a solution from another jurisdiction can be successfully 'transplanted' into the host nation is seriously problematic. This difficulty relates principally to the emergence of a contextualist approach to the field of comparative legal studies.[60] For the more committed advocates of the contextualist approach 'the deep structures of law in a specific context

[56] Kamba, ibid 491.

[57] See Kamba, ibid, 496, referring to Maine, *Village Communities* (1871), 4.

[58] See K Zweigert and H Kotz, *Introduction to Comparative Law* (3rd edn, OUP 1998) 34.

[59] See CA Whytock 'Legal Origins, Functionalism and the Future of Comparative Law' Brigham Young University Law Review (2009) 1897, 1883, referring to AT Von Mehren, 'The Comparative Study of Law' (1991–92) 67 Tulane Civil Law Forum 43, 47.

[60] See Hendry (n 54) 98–99.

cannot be and will never be, fully understood by outsiders'.[61] However, even more moderate adherents, such as Gutteridge, acknowledge that 'laws must be examined in the light of their political, social or economic purpose, and regard must be paid to their dynamic rather than to their static or doctrinal aspects'.[62] Kamba sums it up as follows:

> the 'perfect' comparatist is one who is fully conversant with the socio-cultural totality of the legal systems he examines comparatively. Clearly the standard of scholarship demanded of comparative lawyers is extremely high – well-nigh impossible to attain. It is hard enough to gain mastery of the socio-economic environment of one's own legal system, much less that of two or more systems.[63]

If perfection is required, it could be argued that there is no point in engaging in comparative legal research. However, a cursory glance at the reports published by law reform bodies across the globe highlights that it is happening, and presumably on a less than perfect basis. Perhaps, it is simply more pragmatic to accept that a legal transplant in its purest form is impossible, but that borrowing certain elements of an approach from another jurisdiction facing a similar problem may sometimes make sense. Teubner points out that the transplant may act as a 'legal irritant' and the newly introduced law may develop in a different way, perhaps leading to unforeseen consequences.[64] However, Watson provides rich historical evidence showing that transferring legal institutions between societies has been an enormous historical success despite the fact that these societies display a bewildering diversity of socio-economic structures.[65] I am wholly convinced of the benefits of borrowing from other jurisdictions, when feasible and sensible, and consequently I adopted a 'functionalist' 'better solutions' approach to the comparative material when assessing the difficulties with the current Irish adverse possession regime and how they could be remedied. However, where significant differences in context were apparent, they were highlighted, and these differences, in certain circumstances, had a significant impact on

---

[61] See Hendry (n 54) 99.

[62] See Kamba, (n 55), 514 referring to HC Gutteridge, *Comparative Law* (2nd edn, Cambridge 1949) 12.

[63] Kamba (n 55) 514–515.

[64] G Teubner, 'Legal Irritants: Good Faith in British Law or How Unifying Law Ends up in New Divergences' (1998) 16(1) Modern Law Review 11.

[65] See Teubner, ibid, at 15, referring to A Watson, *The Evolution of Law* (Johns Hopkins University Press 1985); 'Evolution of Law: Continued' (1987) 5 Law and History Review 537–570; *Legal Transplants* (2nd edn, University of Georgia 1993) 'Aspects of Reception of Law' (1996) 44 American Journal of Comparative Law 335.

my conclusions in relation to the value of the lessons to be learnt from other jurisdictions.[66]

A philosophical approach?

Although, this research focused on whether the existing law is fair and discussed how it could be made fairer, it is important to state that the goal of this thesis was not to engage in a philosophical assessment of the morality of the doctrine of adverse possession.[67] However, a concerted effort was made to vigorously defend any arguments proposed on the basis of fairness. In addition, any classifications which were made on the basis of the merits or deserts of claimants were carefully considered in as objective a manner as possible. It is also important to stress that I did not seek to contribute to the debate between natural lawyers and legal positivists about the law's relationship to morality.[68] If pressed, I would subscribe to an inclusive rather than an exclusive positivist approach, which recognises the separability rather than the strict separation of law and morals.[69] Although law and morality do frequently intersect, it is equally the case that they occasionally do not. Where a disconnect emerges between the law and morality, this may sometimes prove problematic and it is submitted that the doctrine of adverse possession presents as such a problematic area. According to Merrill and Smith, 'the core of property law must rest on a simple foundation of everyday morality.'[70] If rules, such as those governing adverse possession, are perceived as unjust and the legislature fails to respond in a timely manner, the danger is that eventually the judiciary may be tempted to interpret the rules in a very restrictive or liberal manner. This thesis highlights a number of examples of such judicial activity.[71] While a review of the Irish case law reveals occasional judicial expressions of sympathy for the owner or the adverse possessor, the overriding impression is of a judiciary which has striven to apply the law in an objective fashion. However, the danger of a Supreme Court endorsement of the rule in *Leigh v Jack*[72] and the favourable treatment recently received by

[66] For example, see the conclusions reached in Woods (n 1) ch 9 on whether Ireland should adopt marketable title legislation, akin to that which operates in the United States.

[67] The failure to clarify the meaning of the term 'morality' appears to be a surprising deficiency in the literature concerning the relationship between law and morality. See LL Fuller, *The Morality of Law* (Revised edn, Yale University Press 1969) 3. Fuller attempts to address this deficiency in ch 1.

[68] See, for example, D Dyzenhaus and A Ripstein (eds), *Law and Morality – Readings in Legal Philosophy* (2nd edn, University of Toronto Press 2001).

[69] As described by MH Kamer in *Where Law and Morality Meet* (OUP 2004).

[70] TW Merrill and HE Smith, 'Law and Morality: Property Law: The Morality of Property' (2007) 48 William and Mary Law Review 1849, 1851.

[71] See, for example, the discussion of *Feehan v Leamy* [2000] IEHC 118 in Woods (n 1) ch 1 or the discussion of the development of the inconsistent user test in ch 5, pt 1.

[72] (1879) 5 Ex D 264.

the owner in *Feehan v Leamy*[73] demonstrate the dangers of complacency in this regard.

IV – Challenges

Certain challenges encountered in writing this thesis were inextricably linked to the particular methodology adopted. In conducting my doctrinal research, it was essential to confront and re-examine long-standing, ubiquitous theories and expositions of the rules. This required the courage and impudence to second-guess assumptions made by very intelligent practitioners, academics and even members of the judiciary. Misconceptions about the law will persist and may eventually become law unless doctrinal lawyers occasionally intervene and review the relevant primary sources of law with 'fresh eyes'. My empirical analysis of the case law was hampered, although to a limited degree, by the absence of certain information (e.g. it was not always apparent from a reported judgment whether the claimant believed they were the owner or not). Finally, while engaged in my comparative analysis of differing approaches to certain issues across jurisdictions it was vital to consider the matter holistically – to take into account important historical and sociological factors and fundamental differences in conveyancing practises and procedures. It was impossible to be completely confident that my knowledge was sufficient in this respect, although this is a challenge facing all researchers who rely on this methodology.

V – Reflections

In retrospect, the methods used to conduct the research necessary for this thesis still seem entirely appropriate. The ability to conduct doctrinal research is part of the DNA of a lawyer and can be done intuitively by any experienced legal researcher. It is a hugely intellectually stimulating experience but may also, on occasion, be very challenging. The close reading of judicial dicta required could be compared to the careful scratching and scraping involved in the examination of an archaeological site. The numerous references to academic commentaries in case law are also testament to the value of doctrinal research in shaping the development of the law. However, I must concede an occasional pang of regret for the missed opportunity to engage in my own survey of adverse possession applications made to the Property Registration Authority. This would have involved upskilling in how to conduct this particular method of empirical research and the submission of an ethics application. In addition, conducting the survey itself would have extended the lifespan of the project. I decided ultimately that it made sense to

[73] [2001] IEHC 23.

rely on the secondary data which was kindly made available to me and could reasonably be relied on as accurate. An overriding concern for those conducting research must be pragmatism in relation to the methods they use; time and energy must be jealously guarded and maintained. Methods should be selected on the basis of their suitability and not whether they are currently popular or 'on trend'. The fundamental consideration should be whether the methodological approach will enable the researcher to answer their research question or make their central argument cogently and efficiently. An important research project with a tight deadline is not the time to dabble in an experiment with an unfamiliar methodology if it is unnecessary. There will be more appropriate research projects in the future to allow for the mastery of new research methods.

A huge advantage of having to write a PhD thesis in more recent times is the increased emphasis which is placed on requiring the writer to explain and justify their methodology. Academic lawyers were traditionally excused from having to explain how they conducted their research and why they relied on certain methods. Alternatively, a perfunctory reference to the analysis of primary and secondary sources of law would be accepted as adequate. In recent times the proliferation of PhDs in law and an increasing reliance on less traditional methodologies have driven this focus on methodology and methods. It should be welcomed and embraced as the development can only contribute to the quality of the work of a legal researcher and the rigour of their arguments. It also makes legal research more accessible to readers from other disciplines who expect and value a methodological discussion.

CHAPTER 2

Who Gets to Decide on Marriage Equality? A Reflection on Comparative Research

*Conor O'Mahony**

I – INTRODUCTION

Legal scholars in a jurisdiction as small as Ireland have no choice but to compare. The label of the 'best little country in the world to do XYZ' has been well-worn in recent years, but often, we forget just how tiny we are. Ireland makes up only 0.6 percent of the world's population, and over 120 countries are bigger than us, many of them by large multiples. In global terms, our collective experience is extremely limited, and so we cannot afford to ignore the wider world and what we can learn from it. But that is not the only reason to compare: sometimes, even where we have experience of an issue, we can learn more about ourselves by holding our system up against a different one. And importantly, the learning process is not a one-way street. In a global legal conversation, we should never fall into the trap of thinking that we have nothing to contribute just because we are small.

In Irish legal scholarship, the necessity to compare is fuelled further by the recent emphasis in third level institutions on publishing for an international audience. It is a lot harder to do this successfully if writing about an issue of narrow national concern. As a result, all of us are likely to engage in at least some comparative work at various times. But comparative work is hard, and good comparative work is exceedingly difficult. It requires a scholar to gain a deep appreciation not just of a specific point of law from another jurisdiction, but of the surrounding legal context, as well as political and social factors that shape how the law works in practice. All of this takes a considerable amount of time; and in a jurisdiction where we have to compare so much, we don't always have the time to compare to this level of rigour.

Scholars differ on how to define comparative law. According to Kamba, 'comparative law is the systematic application of comparison to law. Casual

* Dr Conor O'Mahony, Senior Lecturer, School of Law, University College Cork.

reference to, say, German law in a course on the English law of contract is not comparative law.'[1] As against this, Palmer has argued that the costs involved in undertaking comparative work on such a scale are such that 'realism demands that even simple methods, which it has long been fashionable to disdain, such as purely textual comparisons, or questionnaires devised to gather foreign-law data, or simple juxtapositions of materials without elaboration or comment ... could [all] have legitimacy and value in practical forms of legal research.'[2] Certainly, I have often engaged in the latter; many of my publications have incorporated comparative material at a level which has not delved deep beneath the surface of the law itself, but which nevertheless has added value to the analysis. However, I have also undertaken two projects that have involved the sustained investment of time and effort that is associated with what Kamba would consider to be a truly comparative approach. This chapter will reflect on one of those.

II – Research Question

This chapter is based on a comparative study which I began while on sabbatical leave from January to June 2012, and on which I continued to work sporadically until 2016. The work focused on the issue of marriage equality, but this really served as a case study for a project that was primarily an exercise in constitutional theory and comparative constitutional law. I was drawn to write about marriage equality not so much by the arguments around *what* to decide (I was always clear on who had the better side of that debate), but by the arguments around *who gets* to decide: the legislature, the courts, or the people in a referendum. Marriage equality had the dual appeal of being one of the signature controversies in constitutional law in a number of jurisdictions in recent years, and of being one that offered particular insights into the interplay between different branches of government and decision-making processes.

Some jurisdictions, such as England and Wales, New Zealand, the Netherlands and several other European countries, had introduced marriage equality by way of ordinary legislation; in others, including South Africa and Canada, the courts had played a key role by issuing decisions that acted as a catalyst for legislation. And while, until 2015, no country had yet voted in favour of marriage equality in a national referendum, the issue had been the subject of a referendum in 30 states in the US. In Ireland, potential existed for us to deal

[1] WJ Kamba, 'Comparative Law: A Theoretical Framework' (1974) 23 International and Comparative Law Quarterly 489.

[2] VV Palmer, 'From Lerotholi to Lando: Some Examples of Comparative Law Methodology' (2004) 4(2) Global Justice Frontiers 1, 3–4.

with the issue in any of these three ways. Comparative research thus offered a way to better understand how we might best address the issue here in Ireland, as well as to use marriage equality as a case study to explore constitutional theory questions about the relationship between formal constitutional amendment mechanisms and the posture of constitutional courts.

The latter point became the particular focus of my research. A huge volume of constitutional theory literature approaches the question of the appropriate posture of constitutional courts through the lens of the US Constitution, where it is exceedingly difficult to amend the Constitution in response to an unpopular court decision, and where accordingly there is a particularly strong case for a deferential posture. Far less attention has been paid to how these arguments might be modified in a jurisdiction where the constitution is comparatively easier to amend.

The experience of California—where two separate referendums prohibiting marriage equality were overturned by courts as unconstitutional—was of particular interest to me. I wanted to explore in depth an argument briefly raised by Gerry Whyte some years ago: that the counter-majoritarian objections raised to judicial review by commentators in the US should be less of a concern here in Ireland, where a court decision can be comparatively easily overturned by a referendum on a constitutional amendment.[3] The Californian marriage equality case law, as it wound its way through state and Federal courts, offered an opportunity to test this claim against both a system where the Constitution is easier to amend than in Ireland (i.e. the California state Constitution) and one where it is harder to amend (i.e. the US Federal Constitution). This would shed light on the Irish situation from both directions, and provide the opportunity to examine the relationship between depth of entrenchment and judicial posture along a spectrum of deep, moderate and shallow entrenchment.

III – Methodological Approach

The project was inherently comparative in nature and there was really no other way of addressing my research questions. Funding had no impact on my research design, in that I didn't have any: I was unsuccessful in a Fulbright

[3] G Whyte, 'The Role of the Supreme Court in our Democracy: A Response to Mr. Justice Hardiman' (2006) 28 Dublin University Law Journal 1, 12–13. Whyte makes the same point elsewhere; see 'Discerning the Philosophical Premises of the Report of the Constitution Review Group: An Analysis of the Recommendations on Fundamental Rights' in *Contemporary Issues in Irish Law and Politics (No 2)* (Round Hall, Sweet and Maxwell 1998) 232–233 and Social Inclusion and the Legal System: Public Interest Law in Ireland (2nd edn, Institute of Public Administration 2015) 65–67. See also WJ Parker, 'Must Constitutional Rights be Specified? Reflections on the Proposal to Amend Article 40.3.1°' (1997) 32 Irish Jurist 102, 117.

application. I did manage to spend two months on a research trip in the US, which was made possible by a creative combination of small grants, personal resources and frugality.[4]

Although there are various approaches to the process of comparison, a well-established common denominator is that properly executed comparative research needs to look beyond the narrow legal source material to place the law in its surrounding context.[5] Law does not exist or operate in a vacuum, and a fulsome understanding of the law necessitates an examination of the political, social and historical factors that have shaped its enactment, evolution and day-to-day operation. Moreover, recommendations for reform in one jurisdiction that are based on laws from another jurisdiction need to be particularly aware of such factors. Just because a particular law or legal doctrine flourished in one environment does not mean that it will do so when transplanted to another.

To an extent, it may be possible to gain an appreciation of political, social and historical factors through desk-based research drawing on literature from those disciplines. However, there is a natural limit to this. Much of how a legal system operates is attributable to how legal professionals work and think rather than merely what the law says on paper. A statute, a judgment or even a textbook or article only tells part of the story. Razi has observed that a legal system 'is not made of rules alone but is also characterised by its institutions, practices, standards, methods of research and even the mental habit of lawyers, judges, legislators and administrators.'[6] This is true of any area of law, but is perhaps particularly true of constitutional law, where the legal framework is relatively sparse and the line between law and politics is especially thin.[7] Many of the rules are unwritten, and exist by of way of judicial and political practice built up over time. For this reason, detailed comparative research really needs to incorporate a visit to the comparator jurisdiction, since the only way to come to terms with this aspect of

---

[4] Between January and March 2012, I visited Emory Law School in Atlanta, Temple Law School in Philadelphia and Brooklyn Law School in New York. I was able to access a small travel fund at University College Cork, and I identified a conference in Florida at the beginning of my trip that offered bursaries for international speakers; this paid for my flight into the US and onwards to Atlanta. In Atlanta and Philadelphia, I managed on an accommodation budget of US$50 per night by settling for basic but well-located hotels. I was fortunate to be given the use of a vacant apartment in New York by relatives.

[5] See, e.g., EJ Eberle, 'The Method and Role of Comparative Law' (2009) 8(3) Washington University Global Studies Law Review 451, 457–460.

[6] GM Razi, 'Around the World's Legal Systems' (1959) 5 Howard Law Journal 1 at 11.

[7] Brest, 'Interpretation and Interest' (1982) 34 Stanford Law Review 765, 773 states that 'the line separating law from politics is not all that distinct and ... its very location is a question of politics'.

comparative work is to spend time discussing your work with people from the jurisdiction in question, and—ideally—by presenting it in front of an informed audience. For the purposes of my project, the well-established tradition of the Faculty Colloquium at US Law Schools provided the ideal opportunity to do so, and the level of attention and rigour that is brought to these events is truly impressive.

In my research on constitutional law and marriage equality in the US, there were all sorts of things that were difficult to fully grasp by sitting in a library. Books and articles have been written about how politicised the US courts have become,[8] and so it was of course essential that I read this material to gain an appreciation of the general tendency and how it differs to Ireland.[9] But how was this likely to play out on the issue of marriage equality? The debate was too new for there to be any quality scholarship available addressing the point; however, scholars had plenty to say about it in conversation, and this pointed me in the right direction. Equally, the strategic litigation approach that had been adopted by the American Civil Liberties Union (ACLU), and the timing of the *Perry* litigation out of California,[10] was another issue that was difficult to fully understand without discussing it in an American environment. What to me looked like a straightforward and inevitable legal challenge in federal court against a state law turned out to be a much more complicated story involving celebrity lawyers (who had argued on opposite sides of *Bush v Gore*)[11] teaming up to pursue marriage equality in the face of resistance from LGBT advocacy groups who feared that the timing was wrong and that the case might do more harm than good.[12] The question of timing is one that I will return to below; it became central to my analysis, and I would never have fully appreciated some of the nuances of the litigation I was studying without having had the opportunity to discuss the surrounding context with American scholars who knew the things that the literary sources were not telling me (at least not at that time). For these and other reasons,

8 See, e.g., EJ Segall, *Supreme Myths: Why the Supreme Court Is Not a Court and Its Justices are not Judges* (2012) and M Marcus, 'Is the Supreme Court a Political Institution?' (2004) 72 George Washington Law Review 95.

9 See J Carroll, 'You Be the Judge: A Study of the Backgrounds of Superior Court Judges in Ireland in 2004 Part I' (2005) 10 *Bar Review* 153, 167 (citing empirical evidence that Irish superior court judges are reluctant to self-identify as holding a political ideology, and that they believe ideology has no place in the judiciary).

10 *Perry v Schwarzenegger*, 704 F Supp. 2d 921 (ND Cal 2010); *Perry v Brown*, 671 F 3d 1052 (9th Cir 2012); *Hollingsworth v Perry*, 133 S Ct 2652 (2013).

11 531 US 98 (2000).

12 J Capehart, 'The Road to Marriage Equality: Boies and Olson's Wedding March', *The American Prospect*, 17 June 2014, available at <http://prospect.org/article/road-marriage-equality-boies-and-olson%E2%80%99s-wedding-march> (Accessed 12 March 2019).

I could not properly address my research questions without spending a lengthy period based in my comparator jurisdiction. I am inclined to think that this holds true for every proper piece of comparative work.

Limited funding meant limited time, and so this meant I had to be very focused in what I wanted to get out of this trip. I decided that the whole purpose of travelling to the US was to interact with scholars who would be interested in my work and in a position to put me right when I missed out on nuances of the US system. There was no point in sitting in libraries, well stocked as they might be. For a comparative study on the US, everything you need is accessible nowadays through online databases and online bookstores (Amazon Marketplace is a particularly effective way of accessing US law texts second-hand for very little money). I could sit in a library when I got home. My time in the US was devoted to meeting people, sitting in on classes, teaching a few classes myself, and presenting my work at Faculty colloquia. The academic culture in the US is extraordinarily welcoming and the benefits I derived from this trip cannot be overstated. It shaped my thinking and allowed me to build a network of contacts that proved invaluable after my return home as a means of seeking out feedback and advice.

In some ways, constitutional structures in the US and Ireland are very different. The US is a huge federation consisting of 50 states, with significant powers of government existing at both state and federal levels. Ireland is a small unitary republic (slightly smaller in both size and population than South Carolina) with highly centralised government. The US model of the separation of powers, with completely separate executives and legislatures at both state and federal level and features such as executive veto, differs from Ireland's Westminster-style integrated parliament and executive. The combined effect of these differences is that the normal, everyday politics of the two countries have relatively few similarities.

However, there are far fewer differences when it comes to major national disputes that affect religious-moral questions with implications for constitutional rights. A number of the fundamental features of the constitutional structures of the US and Ireland are very similar. Both are liberal democracies; both systems operate under entrenched written constitutions that are the supreme source of law; and both have full-blown judicial review, under which judges may strike down legislation by reference to vague language in constitutional rights provisions (or, indeed, by reference to unenumerated rights not even specified in the text of the constitution itself). Each country has a history of significant matters of religious-moral controversy resulting in landmark Supreme Court decisions, with numerous such decisions (for example on sodomy laws,[13] contraception[14] and assisted suicide[15]) containing distinctly similar reasoning.

In pursuing the comparative analysis, I began with the well-recognised functional approach – i.e. to identify and compare the legal provisions in each jurisdiction that performed the same function.[16] This turned out to be relatively straightforward, and certainly more straightforward than my last major comparative study – namely, my PhD thesis comparing the right to education for children with special educational needs in Ireland and in England and Wales. On that occasion, it was necessary to compare a framework based largely on vague provisions in a written constitution (as interpreted in lengthy judgments in which judges had the power to enforce constitutional rights against the other branches of government) with a system lacking entrenched constitutional rights, but based instead on detailed legislation and judgments which were mostly short and fact-heavy.[17] By contrast, on this occasion, the relevant functions were the laws regulating who may marry; the laws regulating rights relevant to same-sex marriage, such as the right to marry and constitutional guarantees of equality and non-discrimination; and the laws governing constitutional amendment. The provisions in question look very similar to each other in each of Ireland,[18] California[19] and the US federal jurisdiction[20] – a statutory provision governing capacity to marry and a discrete number of constitutional provisions and associated case law, drawing on very similar principles.

Since the provisions looked so similar on their face, the issue was more about identifying the differences that might not seem so obvious from the legal text. From a methodological perspective, this highlighted the limits of a narrow

[13] Compare *Bowers v Hardwick* 478 US 186 (1986) with *Norris v Attorney General* [1984] IR 36.

[14] Compare *Griswold v Connecticut* 381 US 479 (1965) with *McGee v Attorney General* [1974] IR 284.

[15] Compare *Washington v Glucksberg* 521 US 702 (1997) with *Fleming v Ireland* [2013] 2 IR 417.

[16] K Zweigert and H Kötz, *Introduction to Comparative Law* (3rd edn, Clarendon Press 1998) at 34: '… in law the only things which are comparable are those which fulfil the same function.' See further R Michaels, 'The Functional Method of Comparative Law' in M Reimann and R Zimmermann, *The Oxford Handbook of Comparative Law* (OUP 2006) at 349–382. For a critique of excessive focus on the functional approach, see Palmer, 'From Lerotholi to Lando: Some Examples of Comparative Law Methodology' (2004) 4(2) Global Justice Frontiers 1, 23–24.

[17] For an example of this work, see, e.g., *C O'Mahony,* 'Constitutionalism and Legislation in Special Educational Needs Law: An Anglo-Irish Perspective' [2008] *Public Law* 125–151.

[18] Civil Registration Act 2004, s 2; Irish Constitution, Arts 40.1, 40.3 and 46; *Ryan v Attorney General* [1965] IR 294.

[19] California Family Code §§ 300, 308.5 (Deering 2013); California Constitution, Art I, § 7 and Art XVIII, §§ 3 and 4; *Re Carrafa*, 77 Cal App 3d 788 (1978).

[20] US Constitution, Art V and the Fourteenth Amendment; *Meyer v Nebraska*, 262 US 390, 399 (1923); *Loving v Virginia*, 388 US 1, 11–12 (1967).

functional approach that focuses on the functionally equivalent laws and the necessity to look beyond those laws to see how they operate in context. For example, looking at the formal rules governing how a constitution is amended tells only part of the story. It is immediately clear that the US Constitution (for which proposed amendments must be approved by a two-thirds majority of both houses of Congress and subsequently ratified by the legislatures of three-quarters of the 50 states[21]) is more difficult to amend than the California Constitution, where amendments can be passed by a simple majority of voters in an initiative process without any legislative involvement.[22] However, further research is needed to identify the fact that the political dynamics in each jurisdiction have exacerbated these tendencies, making the US Constitution all but unamendable,[23] while the California Constitution has been described as suffering from 'hyper-amendability'.[24] Similarly, in Ireland, it is necessary to engage with the political science literature to understand how the politics surrounding referendums in Ireland, particularly on religious-moral issues, has historically acted as something of a conservative brake on reform, notwithstanding the relative ease with which the Constitution may be amended.[25]

Moreover, any analysis of the compatibility of laws prohibiting same-sex marriage with constitutional guarantees related to equality and the right to marry would be incomplete without having regard to theoretical debates around judicial posture and the trends in American and Irish courts in litigation of this nature. A successful case would have to convince a court not just that the constitution precluded such laws, but that it was legitimate for the court to force legal change on a sensitive issue that is the subject of moral dispute. Recent trends in the Irish Supreme Court, whose output has been characterised by restraint and deference since the turn of the millennium,[26] seemed to suggest that our courts were always going to be unlikely to rule in favour of marriage equality, whereas it seemed likely that the time would come sooner rather than later when the US

[21] US Constitution, Art V.

[22] California Constitution, Art XVIII, §§ 3 and 4.

[23] See, e.g., B Ackerman, *The Living Constitution* (2007) 120 Harvard Law Review 1737, 1741–1742.

[24] See, e.g., BE Cain and RG Noll, *Malleable Constitutions: Reflections on State Constitutional Reform*, (2009) 87 *Texas Law Review* 1517, 1521–25; B Cain et al, *Constitutional Change: Is It Too Easy to Amend Our State Constitution?* in BE Cain and RG Noll (eds), *Constitutional Reform in California: Making State Government More Effective and Responsive* (Institute of Governmental Studies Press 1995) at 265–90.

[25] See, e.g., M Gallagher, 'Ireland: The referendum as a conservative device?' in M Gallagher and P Uleri (eds) *The Referendum Experience in Europe* (Hampshire: Macmillan Press, 1996) 101–102 and C O'Mahony, 'Falling Short of Expectations: The 2012 Children Amendment, From Drafting to Referendum' (2016) 31(2) *Irish Political Studies* 252, 253–254.

[26] See, e.g., *Sinnott v Minister for Education* [2001] 2 IR 545; *TD v Minister for Education* [2001] 4 IR 259; *MD (A Minor) v Ireland* [2012] 1 IR 697; *Fleming v Ireland* [2013] 2 IR 417; and *MR v An tArd Chláratheoir* [2014] IESC 60.

Supreme Court would be fertile ground for such an argument.[27] Again, gaining an appreciation of these points this required engagement with a broader body of case law and literature in each jurisdiction, so that the specific issue before the courts could be placed in its surrounding politico-legal context

IV – Challenges

There are a number of common challenges in comparative research, which apply to a greater or lesser degree, depending on the specific project involved. For this project, since I chose to compare English-speaking, common law legal systems, I did not have to grapple with the significant challenges involved in comparing across (e.g.) common law and civil law jurisdictions, where the legal sources look very different and command of more than one language is often a necessity. I also did not have to overcome any difficulties in accessing materials. For the US, it is extremely easy to access literature – journal articles in particular, which are almost invariably accessible through HeinOnline, but also books, which can be sourced inexpensively. Judgments and official publications are widely available online. A project involving a different jurisdiction might pose significantly greater challenges.

While the degree of difficulty involved in accessing and interpreting materials will vary from project to project, probably every comparative project involves the challenge of simply demanding too much from the researcher. I have already considered the range of political, social and historical factors that a comparative researcher needs to factor in. In this regard, Kamba has made the following compelling observation:

> ...the good if not the 'perfect' comparatist is one who is fully conversant with the socio-cultural totality of the legal systems he examines comparatively. Clearly the standard of scholarship demanded of comparative lawyers is extremely high – well-nigh impossible to attain. It is hard enough to gain mastery of the socio-economic environment of one's own legal system, much less that of two or more systems.[28]

There is no escaping our human limitations, and to a degree, it is inevitable that comparative work will fail to grasp all of the local nuances. I know I have read work by highly-regarded international scholars who have made

---

27 Writing in 2012, M Klarman accurately predicted that in the short term, the Supreme Court would possibly refuse to grant review in a marriage equality case, but that once public opinion had shifted and a clear emerging consensus could be identified, it was 'almost certain' to rule in favour of marriage equality. Both of his predictions came to pass within just three years. Klarman, *From the Closet to the Altar* (OUP 2013) at 207.

28 WJ Kamba, 'Comparative Law: A Theoretical Framework' (1974) 23 International and Comparative Law Quarterly 489, 514–515.

reference to Ireland in ways that I would take issue with. Perfection is probably unattainable; all we can do is be cognisant of this, and of the reasons why, and strive to get as close as possible to perfection. If the headline issues are accurately represented and misunderstandings limited to discrete or peripheral points that do not affect the overall argument, then the comparatist is doing quite well. In my case, I have little doubt that some American scholars would pick up on points that I could have addressed more clearly or accurately; but having presented the work to American audiences on a number of occasions, and published it in well-regarded US law reviews, I feel re-assured that any significant errors or omissions have been ironed out by now.

Aside from the usual challenge inherent to large-scale comparative work, the other main challenge I encountered in this project was that there is simply no end to the volume of literature that could potentially inform a piece of work like this. When I completed an LLM by Research on an Irish law topic (with no comparative component) in 2001–2002, I could confidently claim by the end of it to have read and engaged with every relevant secondary source available. That would be harder to do today; but in a small jurisdiction like Ireland, it may still be achievable, depending on the topic. By contrast, scholars in the US have been churning out vast quantities of constitutional theory literature for decades, much of it very high-quality, and the trend is ever-upwards. You have to accept from an early point that you could never read everything, and be ever mindful of the danger of not being able to see the wood for the trees. The balance between rigour and overload is a precarious one; you have to say 'stop' at some point, but inevitably, readers will be able to point to relevant sources you have missed.

V – Ethical Considerations

The project was blissfully free of ethical considerations. There was no empirical component and thus no concerns related to informed consent, confidentiality, or data storage. Once I observed normal academic conventions, I was free to approach the project however I wished.

VI – Reflections

The project produced four main outputs. A paper considering whether Irish judges can afford to be less restrained in light of the relative ease with which the Irish Constitution can be amended was presented at a conference marking the 75th Anniversary of the Irish Constitution in 2012 and subsequently featured as a chapter in the edited collection arising from that event.[29] An

[29] *C O'Mahony,* 'Constitutional Amendment and Judicial Restraint: How Restrained should an Irish Court be?' in E Carolan (ed), *The Constitution of Ireland: Perspectives and Prospects* (Bloomsbury 2012) at 161–178.

article looking specifically at marriage equality in Ireland, and considering the respective roles of the courts and the legislature in addressing the issue, was published in the 2012 Dublin University Law Journal.[30] The main output from the 2012 sabbatical leave – a 20,000 word article – was published in the 2014 Harvard Human Rights Journal.[31] All of this work formed the basis of a later comparative paper reflecting on the advent of marriage equality by way of referendum in Ireland and by way of Supreme Court decision in the US, which I presented at a conference on comparative constitutional history in Chicago in 2016, and which was published in the Illinois Law Review in 2017.[32]

This has probably been the most enjoyable project I have undertaken in my career to date, but in other ways the most challenging, particularly in terms of securing recognition for the work produced. It has involved working in a very crowded space: this raises the level of competition, making it harder to secure publication opportunities and for outputs to be cited once they are published. As such, perhaps the obvious thing that I could have done differently would have been to focus entirely on my constitutional law research rather than dividing my time between the marriage equality project and other unrelated projects on children's rights law. This would have allowed me to engage with the issues in more depth and keep up with the level of research evident in the work of scholars who are solely focused on this field. This is an ongoing identity crisis of mine. I have always enjoyed working in both constitutional law and children's rights law, and my research and teaching span both areas; however, it is challenging to be research active in both to the standard that I would like.

The benefits which I derived from the comparative aspect have transformed both my research and my teaching. After some uncertainty early in my career, the exposure to a significant quantity of US literature has allowed me to identify a position in the great constitutional theory debate between activism and restraint that I feel I will be comfortable with for the foreseeable future. The more time I spent working on the issue and tracking its progress in both Ireland and the US, the more persuaded I became by Alexander Bickel's theory of the passive virtues, as advanced in *The Least Dangerous Branch*[33]

[30] C O'Mahony, 'Principled Expediency: How the Irish Courts can Compromise on Same-Sex Marriage' (2012) 34 Dublin University Law Journal 199–228.

[31] C O'Mahony, 'If a Constitution is Easy to Amend, Can Judges be Less Restrained? Rights, Social Change, and Proposition 8' (2014) 27 Harvard Human Rights Journal 191–242.

[32] C O'Mahony, 'Marriage Equality in the United States and Ireland: How History Shaped the Future' (2017) University of Illinois Law Review 681–711.

[33] A Bickel, *The Least Dangerous Branch: The Supreme Court at the Bar of Politics* (2nd edn, Yale University Press 1986).

and subsequently elaborated on by Cass Sunstein.[34] I found Bickel's work to be both descriptively accurate and normatively persuasive when applied to marriage equality (as well as to other comparable moral issues which provoke particularly strong feelings that may ultimately be channelled into backlash against court decisions). From an Irish perspective, Bickel's central concern about decisions needing to be able to gain acceptance in the foreseeable future was of particular relevance, given the fact that our method of amendment can be used relatively easily to overturn an unpopular Supreme Court decision (and indeed has been on several occasions).[35]

But since Bickel's work was rooted in the US Constitution and the case law of the US courts, it would not be possible to make sense of how he intended it to operate, or how it might need to be adapted when applied in a different jurisdiction, without undertaking detailed comparative research within the US system first. The devices which Bickel called the 'passive virtues', such as the rules governing standing and *certiorari*, operate in a very particular way in the US. In the case of *certiorari*, we did not have any equivalent method of docket control in the Irish Supreme Court at that time, and our rules of standing are applied rather flexibly. However, through detailed examination of Bickel's theory, the surrounding literature, its application in case law, and conversations with US scholars, it was possible to identify ways in which an Irish court might 'decide not to decide' (as advocated by Bickel) even in a different doctrinal and procedural context.

Most of all, the juxtaposition of the Irish and American systems allowed me to gain a different and (I hope) better understanding of both. This became particularly clear to me in the aftermath of the 2015 marriage referendum. Having worked on the issue academically, it was always my intention to write a piece reflecting on the referendum once it was over. That same summer, I had just completed a similar piece on the 2012 children referendum.[36] However, unlike the children referendum (on which I knew exactly what I wanted to say as soon as it was over), I spent the weeks immediately after the marriage referendum struggling to make sense of the events of the previous months and of what my contribution to the academic debate would be. Most likely, this was

[34] C Sunstein, 'If People Would be Outraged by their Rulings, Should Judges Care?' (2007) 60 Stanford Law Review 155.

[35] I elaborate on these points in 'Principled Expediency: How the Irish Courts can Compromise on Same-Sex Marriage' (2012) 34 Dublin University Law Journal 199 at 217–226.

[36] C O'Mahony, 'Falling Short of Expectations: The 2012 Children Amendment, From Drafting to Referendum' (2016) 31 Irish Political Studies 252–281.

attributable to having been active in the campaign; I was still too close to the issue to have any scholarly perspective.

It was only when, five weeks later, the US Supreme Court ruled in favour of marriage equality in *Obergefell v Hodges*[37] that I was able to see where the Irish referendum fit into the work I had completed up to this point. In particular, I was struck by Justice Scalia's protestations in his dissenting judgment in *Obergefell*, in which he described the judgment as a 'judicial putsch' and claimed that if such major questions could be decided by a majority of five out of nine unelected judges, the United States 'does not deserve to be called a democracy.'[38] I was reminded of Michael Klarman's recent and accurate prediction that the US Supreme Court would—having perhaps declined to hear the issue at first—rule in favour of marriage equality once public opinion shifted and a clear emerging consensus could be identified. Klarman's rationale was that '[t]hat is simply how constitutional law works in the United States'.[39]

As I found myself thinking that Justice Scalia was protesting too loudly, given that he knows well that this is simply how things are done in his country, my mind was drawn to a significant volume of commentary both in the lead up to and aftermath of the Irish referendum which argued that marriage equality, as a minority rights issue, should not have been the subject of a referendum in Ireland.[40] While sympathetic in principle to this argument, it occurred to me that the response to Justice Scalia's protestations in the US had resonance in Ireland also. If criticisms of *Obergefell* as undemocratic are overstated because they fail to take account of deeply embedded practice in the US, then by the same token, criticisms of the Irish referendum as unduly majoritarian are overstated because they fail to take account of a deeply

---

[37] 135 S Ct 2584 (2015).

[38] ibid at 2627, 2629.

[39] M Klarman, *From the Closet to the Altar: Courts, Backlash and the Struggle for Same-Sex Marriage* (New York: OUP, 2013) 207.

[40] See, e.g., C Browne, 'In the Face of Political Inaction, It Is up to Us to Back the Rights of Minority Groups', *Irish Independent*, 12 May 2015, <http://www.independent.ie/irish-news/referendum/inthe-face-of-political-inaction-it-is-up-to-us-to-back-the-rights-of-minority-groups-31214250.html> (Accessed 12 March 2019); S Kamali Dehghan, 'A Referendum is not the Way to go When it Comes to Gay Rights or Minority Issues', *The Guardian*, 22 May 2015, <https://www.theguardian.com/world/commentisfree/2015/may/22/a-referendum-is-not-the-way-to-go-when-it-comes-to-gay-rights-or-minority-issues> (Accessed 12 March 2019); OG Encarnación, 'Ireland's Referendum, However Inspiring, is not a Step Forward for Gay Rights', *The Irish Times*, 26 May 2015, <http://www.irishtimes.com/opinion/ireland-sreferendum-however-inspiring-is-not-a-step-forward-for-gay-rights-1.2225587> (Accessed 12 March 2019); L Weeks, 'Rule by Referendum is not the Best Way to Make Decisions', *The Irish Times*, 2 June 2015, <http://www.irishtimes.com/opinion/rule-by-referendum-is-not-the-best-way-to-make-decisions-1.2233896> (Accessed 12 March 2019).

embedded practice of referendums on issues of deep religious-moral controversy. It is particularly striking that the same means has been used to determine the legal position on marriage equality and abortion in each country: Supreme Court decisions in the US and referendums in Ireland.

There are reasons for this – reasons which are peculiar to the legal and political systems and cultures of both countries. Thus, my reflection on the advent of marriage equality in the US and Ireland in the summer of 2015 was to argue that the criticisms of the *Obergefell* decision as too undemocratic and of the Irish referendum as too majoritarian failed to take account of these political-constitutional dynamics and deeply embedded practices. I doubt that my conclusion would have looked like this had I not immersed myself in a comparative study of the US debate over the previous four years: by holding my own country up against the experiences of another, I gained an element of distance and perspective that led me to what I now feel is a more nuanced and defensible analysis. Moreover, the comparative dimension made this analysis relevant to an international audience and adaptable to the circumstances in other countries. I was able to draw on it when writing on a subsequent controversy in Australia as to whether marriage equality should be the subject of a plebiscite or simply legislated for by Parliament, when I argued that Australia had no tradition of plebiscites on social issues and that accordingly a plebiscite on marriage equality would, in that country, rightly be criticised as too majoritarian.[41]

VII – Conclusion

Comparative work is an uncomfortable experience, in that it has the tendency to expand your sense of the 'known unknowns': the more of it you do, the more you realise just how much you have yet to learn. But that is also why it is so rewarding, and why it repays the effort involved. In recent years, I have gained experience of qualitative methodology, which is a very different approach and which has many merits. But I can genuinely say that nothing else I have undertaken has challenged my preconceptions and informed my view of the law to the same extent as large-scale comparative work. By its nature, you may fall flat on your face a few times in the early stages of a project. But if you embrace the uncertainty and work hard to fill the gaps, making the best use of both documentary and human resources, the end result is a richer piece of scholarship and an awareness of a far wider range of possibilities for publication and for future projects.

[41] C O'Mahony, 'Ireland's vote on marriage equality holds many lessons – but are any relevant to Australia?', *The Conversation*, 27 September 2016, <http://theconversation.com/irelands-vote-on-marriage-equality-holds-many-lessons-but-are-any-relevant-to-australia-65872> (Accessed 12 March 2019).

Chapter 3

Researching the Irish Free State Constitution: Law and History

*Laura Cahillane**

I – Introduction and Research Question

Professor Jim Phillips has written that 'legal developments cannot be separated from other historical trends' and that 'a sense of history is vital to understanding the law, even if (or perhaps because), it tends to highlight the limitations of law.'[1] While the study of legal history or the use of history in legal research has never been fashionable in law schools in Ireland, and indeed some might struggle to see its importance, internationally it is recognised that the use of history in legal research serves to enrich legal analysis and can offer new insights and a deeper understanding of legal issues and developments. As more young researchers begin to carry out research on aspects of law and history which are directly relevant to Irish law and the Irish State, the benefit of such research becomes more apparent. As Phillips further elaborated:

> [I]t is always better to understand not just the shape that some aspect of our present world takes, but also how it got that way. Moreover, our history is more than an explanation of past developments, it is an essential form of understanding of the world around us, because it is invariably still with us, aspects of it remain embedded in every part of our society.[2]

Because it is a practice which is very much under-developed in Ireland, one of the aims of this chapter is to demonstrate that inter-disciplinary research in general, but research in law and history in particular, is not something to be fearful of and in fact can be very worthwhile and rewarding.

In this context, the project I have chosen to write about is my PhD which was entitled 'The Genesis, Drafting, and Legacy of the Irish Free State

---

* Dr Laura Cahillane, Lecturer in Law, University of Limerick.

[1] See J Phillips, 'Why Legal History Matters' (2010) 41 (3) Victoria University of Wellington Law Review 293.

[2] ibid.

Constitution'. I was interested in challenging some of the myths which abound concerning Independent Ireland's first Constitution. As an undergraduate law student, I had heard very little about this document and the impression gained was often negative. Thus, the aim of the thesis was to examine the manner in which the Irish Free State Constitution was drafted and to discover what was originally intended by that Constitution, as well as the reasons why it did not function as anticipated. The question of how the Constitution was drafted was important because by looking at who was involved and what sources were used, it shed light on the other research questions related to the purpose and aim of many of the provisions. Trying to discover the original intent of various provisions was tricky but this was where the mix of research methods became useful in analysing both the historical sources and the legal text and cases. The final question on why the Constitution did not function as anticipated was more analytical and based on answers garnered to the second question. I decided to take a thematic approach to the examination and after first outlining and analysing the drafting stages using a chronological approach I then turned to consider the central themes underlying the document. This was possible because of the methodological approach chosen.

II – Methodological approach and Methods used

Due to the nature of the topic and the research questions, the approach I took was a combination of the traditional doctrinal approach along with a historical approach. I described the overall methodological framework in the thesis as one which sought to gain a holistic view of the Irish Free State Constitution and one which was informed both from a historical and a legal perspective because each of these has a distinctive and important role to play in allowing us to properly and fully understand the document.

Early on into my work on the thesis I discovered that the doctrinal approach would not be sufficient in order to answer my research questions and that the historical method was essential since any research of this type involves interpreting documents from the past. For the most part, the historical method focuses on sources. The secondary sources which were used in the project included biographies of members of the Constitution Committee and many text books and articles written about the Constitution. The primary sources were more diverse and included the following: the Irish Free State Constitution; the three original Drafts;[3] all of the existing Irish documentation on the drafting in the National Archives of Ireland;[4] various Irish Provisional

[3] National Archives of Ireland (NAI) Department of the Taoiseach S8953.

[4] NAI 3/493/5 and files from the Department of the Taoiseach including: S8952, S8953, S8955.

Government Cabinet Minutes and Dáil Éireann papers;[5] the debates in the Constituent Assembly on the Constitution;[6] the British Record of Negotiations on the Irish Conference from the British National Archives;[7] the papers of EM Stephens[8] (Secretary to the Constitution Committee) which include his record of the Committee meetings; the papers of Hugh Kennedy;[9] the papers of Alfred O'Rahilly[10] as well as the papers of various other figures[11] and the writings of members of the Constitution Committee.[12]

The historical approach also aims to elucidate the political climate of the day and establish the context in which events took place. This is an important consideration and one which legal scholars sometimes neglect. It is said that lawyers fail to take context into account, but instead look to use material from a completely different time period, in order to interpret legal provisions.[13] By concentrating on the historical method, it was possible to avoid this practice of 'presentism' and instead focus on trying to view events through the eyes of the people of 1922 and to take into account the social, political and economic climate and conditions of the time. Of course there are also difficulties and certain limitations involved in using historical documentation and at all times during the project, regard was had to the possibility of bias or the existence of gaps in the documentation and a critical textual analysis was carried out on all of the sources used in order to minimise the possibility of an erroneous interpretation.

For example, when reading the British and Irish accounts of the negotiations on the Constitution in London, I had to bear in mind the potential slants both sides would put on their reports and to identify common elements in both in order to establish an accurate account. Similarly, when reading the personal

---

5 These include: (NAI) PG 1/2, PG 2, PG 5 and DE1, DE 2/341, 2/279, 2/467.

6 Dáil Deb, 18 September–25 October 1922, vol 1.

7 British National Archives, CAB 43/7.

8 EM Stephens Papers, Trinity College Dublin Archives, 4234–41.

9 H Kennedy Papers, University College Dublin Archives, P4.

10 A O'Rahilly Papers, University College Dublin Archives, P178 and Special Collections, University College Cork.

11 These include the papers of George Gavan Duffy (University College Dublin Archives, P152); Eamon de Valera (University College Dublin Archives, P150); John A Costello (University College Dublin Archives, P190); Desmond Fitzgerald (University College Dublin Archives, P80); JM Kelly (University College Dublin Archives, P147) and Michael Rynne (in the possession of Etienne Rynne, Galway).

12 M Collins, *The Path to Freedom* (Welsh Academic Press Wales 1996) (First published by Talbot Press in 1922); D Figgis, *The Irish Constitution; explained by Darrell Figgis* (Mellifont Press 1922), A O'Rahilly, *Articles* (Special Collections, University College Cork).

13 For example, see JP Reid, 'Law and History' (1993) 27 Loyola Law Review 193.

papers of the various figures involved, I had to be cognisant always of potential personal bias on different issues. With all sources it was necessary to note potential gaps, exaggerations, understatements, etc. and to keep a record of these to cross-check with other sources. Eventually by comparing these it is possible to build a picture of the most likely scenarios.

While the historical approach was crucial in order to engage in any real depth with the historical material, the project was still a legal analysis of the Constitution and so the doctrinal approach was also important. The doctrinal method was an essential element of the parts of the thesis which analysed the draft documents and which examined various constitutional provisions in detail and the case-law surrounding them. The legal perspective was crucial to the thesis as a whole because it represented a different point of view to that of historians or political scientists, who had previously dominated the literature on the Constitution and that period in Irish history. FW Maitland has written that lawyers and historians operate on completely different wavelengths, in that historians are interested in the 'logic of evidence', while lawyers look for the 'logic of authority'.[14] This is a criticism of lawyers and it points to the 'propensity of lawyers to misread and misuse history'.[15] However, Wilfrid Prest has pointed out that: 'whether or not lawyers are prone to distort or oversimplify historical evidence, historians, for their part, frequently misinterpret legal sources.'[16] Lawyers are necessarily more aware of the fact that a constitution is a living document and thus an attempt was made throughout the thesis to examine the Irish Free State Constitution as a dynamic entity by relying on both historical and doctrinal methods.

The fact that both the historical and legal methods were used means that a more complete picture was attained from the research. This was one of the unique aspects to the thesis. The methodological framework allowed for a multi-perspective analysis of the Irish Free State Constitution and a detailed analysis of the meaning and impact of the Constitution both as a legal and a historical document.

[14] FW Maitland, 'Why the History of English Law is Not Written' in HAL Fisher (ed) *The Collected Papers of F W Maitland* (Cambridge University Press 1911), 490–491. See also See L Cahillane, 'The Use of History in Law – Avoiding the Pitfalls' in L Cahillane and J Schweppe, *Legal Research Methods: Principles and Practicalities* (Clarus Press 2016) 57.

[15] W Prest, 'Law for Historians: William Blackstone on Wives, Colonies and Slaves' (2007) 11 Legal History 105 at 105.

[16] ibid at 106.

Dipping into other areas

In certain places throughout the thesis, it was necessary to step outside of the boundary of the doctrinal or historical methods. Because the early part of the thesis dealt with the 'genesis' of the Constitution, it explored the context into which the Constitution was born and also many of the ideas and philosophies behind the document. The analysis necessarily involved some sociological and anthropological considerations in order to properly explain how the document developed as it did. I also decided to consider the personalities behind the document as part of the investigation into the reasons behind certain provisions. In order to fully comprehend the Constitution as originally drafted it was important to gain an insight into those involved in the drafting process and thus in this section, the research method involved examining the biographies and personal papers of the members of the Committee. However, this was sometimes a difficult task, as apart from Michael Collins, biographies have been written about only two of the Committee members in book form.[17] Also, as with personal papers, in reading biographies the researcher must always be alert to the possibility of bias and so a similar exercise in cross-checking information was necessary. In addition, a further chapter explored the idea of anti-party politics in the Constitution and this required a political science-type analysis and sources used included articles from political science periodicals[18] as well as political science monographs.[19] These additional methods were necessary to explore very specific parts of the thesis and they complemented the doctrinal and historical approaches used throughout the thesis.

III – Challenges

There certainly are many challenges involved in both historical and doctrinal research. One of the biggest challenges with historical research, I found, was time. It was necessary to spend vast amounts of time visiting archives

[17] JA Gaughan, ed, *Memoirs of Senator James G. Douglas (1887–1954), concerned citizen* (University College Dublin Press 1998). JA Gaughan, *Alfred O'Rahilly* (Kingdom Books 1986). The short biographies which have also recently been produced online by the Dictionary of Irish Biography for certain Committee members were also considered. William Murphy wrote a biography of Darrell Figgis; Ronan Keane wrote one on Hugh Kennedy and James Murnaghan; Michael Kennedy wrote one on James McNeill; Gerard Hogan wrote one on John O'Byrne and Marie Coleman wrote one on Kevin O'Shiel. These are published by Cambridge University Press and available at <http://dib.cambridge.org/>.

[18] AE Malone, 'Party Government in the Irish Free State' (1929) 44(3) Political Science Quarterly 363.

[19] For example, W Moss *Political parties in the Irish Free State* (Columbia University Press 1933); M Gallaghar, *Political parties in the Republic of Ireland* (Gill and Macmillan 1985); D O'Sullivan *The Irish Free State and its Senate: a study in contemporary politics* (Faber and Faber 1940); in M MacCarthaigh and M Manning *Houses of the Oireachtas* (IPA 2010); C O'Leary *Irish Elections 1918–1977: Parties, Voters and Proportional Representation* (Gill and Macmillan 1979).

collections, in particular in University College Dublin, Trinity College Dublin and the National Archives. While it is important to prepare well in advance and be familiar with descriptive lists (which contain skeletal information on what the archives contain), you will never know what you will find until you start looking. The process requires careful methodical processing of all of the information. Also, it is necessary to be familiar with the rules and regulations of the different institutions which house the archives. Some places will not permit photography or photocopying and so in many cases, I sat for hours typing contents of documents into my laptop and in one case writing pages and pages of notes in pencil. It is so important to label everything so you know where it came from and what it relates to. Often the significance of a document will only become apparent later as the research progresses and sometimes multiple trips to return to various documents are necessary. All of this is very time consuming and depending on where you are based, it involves some expense too.

A related challenge is that of distraction. Combing through archives can be fascinating! I spent many an hour reading unrelated newspaper reports of irrelevant but intriguing material, as well as interesting letters and memos. Someone once pointed out to me that the old newspaper ads are often the most interesting material in the archives. An hour can easily pass with such an activity and if your time is limited this is certainly something to watch out for. On the other hand, if you have plenty of time – enjoy this foray into times gone by!

A more unwelcome challenge presented itself when I discovered that many of the files on the descriptive list of the National Archives are missing. I tried in vain to contact various people about this but never received a response apart from a guess from a staff member that things may have been mislabelled in the move to Bishop Street in 1991.[20] This is a concern particularly with historical research that is focused on earlier periods but can arise even for modern history.

There are also some traps which those unfamiliar with historical research would be wise to avoid.[21] For example, the practice of 'presentism' or 'Whig history' is a potential danger for lawyers using history in their research. A crude explanation of this approach is that the researcher assumes that

[20] See T Mohr, 'Legal Material and Historical Research' in L Cahillane and J Schweppe, *Legal Research Methods: Principles and Practicalities* (Clarus Press 2016) 71.

[21] See L Cahillane, 'The Use of History in Law – Avoiding the Pitfalls' in L Cahillane and J Schweppe, *Legal Research Methods: Principles and Practicalities* (Clarus Press 2016) 57.

because society is constantly evolving, then what has happened in the past is in some way primitive and that modern day developments are necessarily better. This approach also fails to consider elements of the past in their proper context, instead measuring them against modern values and conditions. While it can be difficult to look at things with the eye of someone from that period, that is essentially what the researcher must attempt to do in order to avoid distorting historical elements.

Another trap which is related to the idea of presentism, and which is particularly relevant to this type of research project, is sometimes referred to as the danger of 'history as authority'. Lawyers and judges are sometimes guilty of looking to the past in order to pluck some legal principle from its context and use it to justify some modern argument. However, it is possible to avoid this by using historical elements as evidence not simply authority and to properly weigh them up and analyse them in their proper context. As mentioned earlier, lawyers are often criticised for using history simply to justify a conclusion already reached or prove a point rather than looking to understand. The danger here is that the lawyer will rely on the aspect of history without seeing the bigger picture and truly appreciating it in its context; this can then lead to misinterpretations. These potential dangers were not something I was aware of when I began the project but they became apparent as I did more reading about the historical approach and this knowledge certainly made me more careful in my approach when assessing various elements of the Constitution.

Also, an activity I found very useful was to talk to historians, political scientists, children of contemporaries, etc. These were not qualitative interviews for research purposes but informal chats which often revealed new avenues, opinions, approaches or sources I had not come into contact with previously. Of course such conversations did not form part of the research output as such but together with the archival material and doctrinal analysis, it often helped to build up an overall picture and was sometimes a helpful nod in the right direction.

The doctrinal part of the research may have seemed straight forward at times but there are also challenges here. The principal one being that doctrinal research may not offer a complete picture and may not answer all of your questions, particularly the 'why' questions. This is where the historical research came in to build on the doctrinal work and to provide answers where the doctrinal approach could provide none.

IV – Reflections

A key issue for me in this project was locating my work within the existing scholarship. There was already a wealth of material on that period in history. So, I needed to demonstrate that there was indeed a (glaring) gap and to show how my research filled that gap. Luckily, very few legal scholars had focused on the Irish Free State Constitution. In fact, there has been very little academic writing in general on this subject. A very comprehensive work was published by a German lawyer in 1932: Leo Kohn's *The Constitution of the Irish Free State*.[22] Originally a doctoral thesis, the book provides a clear and penetrating commentary on the provisions of the Irish Free State Constitution. A particularly useful feature is the foreword by Hugh Kennedy, whose comments are particularly significant since he was a member of the 1922 Constitution Committee.

While this was certainly the most judicious treatment of the subject, it was somewhat out of date. At the date of publication of Kohn's book, the Irish Free State Constitution was undergoing a massive transformation and the fate of the document remained to be seen.[23] Furthermore, while Kohn may have had discussions with Kennedy and other members of government and administration, he did not have access to any of the documentation or original drafts. As a result, Kohn could only hazard a guess as to the reasons for inclusion of certain provisions and the drafting stages are not covered in the book. Thus, while the coverage of the constitutional provisions is very insightful, the lack of knowledge in relation to the drafting stages constituted a gap in the analysis.

Some 40 years after Kohn's book, some of the drafting documentation was made available and a number of the gaps were filled in by two series of articles by Farrell[24] and Akenson and Fallin.[25] Naturally, because of the nature of a series of articles, the treatment was still rather limited and there was little analysis of the original draft documents. There have been some excellent accounts of the Irish Free State Constitution produced in the fields

---

[22] L Kohn, *The Constitution of the Irish Free State* (George Allen and Unwin Ltd 1932).

[23] Furthermore, the Statute of Westminster had been passed in 1931 but Kohn seems to have failed to recognise the significance of this as there is no discussion of it in the book.

[24] B Farrell, 'The Drafting of the Irish Free State Constitution I and II' (1970) Irish Jurist 115 and 343; 'The Drafting of the Irish Free State Constitution III and IV' (1971) Irish Jurist 111 and 345.

[25] DH Akenson and FP Fallin, 'The Irish civil war and the drafting of the Irish constitution' (1970) Vol V (1) Éire-Ireland 10, Vol V (2) Éire-Ireland 42, Vol V (4) Éire-Ireland 28. These articles provide a good summary and give a good picture of the context of the time but because the focus is historical, there is little discussion on the actual draft constitutional provisions.

of history, political science and government.[26] However, these books do not examine the Constitution from a legal perspective. Thomas Mohr, an Irish legal historian had also examined the Constitution in his PhD thesis but the project was focused on external relations rather than an analysis of the document itself.[27] By analysing the existing literature and identifying the gaps in each piece, it was possible to demonstrate how my project would both build on the research which had already been carried out but also would go further by addressing issues and examining areas which had heretofore not been considered. In any thesis which looks at history, this is a crucial exercise as inevitably the subject will have been examined in some form already.

Another issue in this project was the interdisciplinary nature of the research. When I began this project with a mixed methods approach, I assumed both methods would work in harmony with each other and was not prepared for the fact that sometimes when dealing with two different disciplines you may find contradictions. The thing about doing research into how something was supposed to function or what original intentions were, is that it is often hard to come to concrete conclusions and inevitably, everything is subject to interpretation. I also met with competing advice from the disciplines of law and history on this as in law, we are usually trained to be measured in our conclusions whereas the advice given to me from historians was that I should form concrete opinions. Of course, as a lawyer this was sometimes difficult to do in the absence of authority for these opinions. Therefore it was necessary to find the balance between these positions, something which was not always easy.

It is always difficult to carry out research which straddles two disciplines, especially when you will invariably be an expert in just one of those disciplines. It can open you up to criticism from the secondary discipline, as the methods involved may differ and it may not always be possible to harmonise the approaches. The only advice I can offer is to immerse yourself as much as possible in your secondary discipline. I found it very useful to

[26] See for example, J M Curran, *The Birth of the Irish Free State 1921–1923* (University of Alabama Press 1980). N Mansergh, *The Irish Free State: its government and politics* (Allen and Unwin 1934). AJ Ward, *The Irish Constitutional Tradition: responsible government and modern Ireland, 1782-1992* (Irish Academic Press 1994). B O'Briain, *The Irish Constitution* (Talbot 1929). An Irish lawyer wrote this last book but it seems that this work was aimed at the average Irish citizen and does not therefore contain the same level of insight as works such as Kohn's. See E Wambaugh, 'Review of *The Irish Constitution* by Barra O'Briain' (1930) 43 (8) Harvard Law Review 1316.

[27] See T Mohr, *The Irish Free State and the Legal Implications of Dominion Status* (UCD Thesis 2007).

have meetings, information sessions, and conversations with many different historians and political scientists who were good enough to give of their time and offer their insights.

However, the difficulty involved in carrying out inter-disciplinary work was not always apparent to me at the time. It was mostly as I approached the end of the project and was faced with justifying my approaches that I became more aware of the difficulties and also afterwards when working on the text in order to publish it as a book. While members of the Department of History in UCC, where I carried out my research, were always very willing to answer my queries, in retrospect it would have been very useful to have had a co-supervisor from History or at least a person appointed who I could meet with on a regular basis to discuss the historical aspects of the thesis. In an ideal world, some sort of formal training in the other discipline would be the best option when considering a mixed methods approach.

However, it is important to note that there are also many advantages in using mixed methods – as Claire Hamilton points out in her chapter in this book, 'the weakness of one method can be offset by the strength of another.' Researchers should not be afraid of straying from what might be considered more 'comfortable' methods – if the project calls for a mixed methods approach then this should be embraced, both for the good of the project and for the enlightenment of the researcher. Furthermore, it can be very enjoyable to immerse yourself in a new discipline and learn new techniques and it is something that will contribute to and improve your future research when you can bring new insights from your secondary discipline.

Chapter 4

Using International Law in Interdisciplinary Human Rights Research

*Clíodhna Murphy, Mary Gilmartin, and Leanne Caulfield**

I – Introduction

Even outside of pure international law scholarship, there are both scholarly and instrumental benefits to incorporating an international law dimension into one's research. Some reference to international law is often necessary to engage in the most basic doctrinal analysis: for example, where international instruments are fully incorporated into domestic law (e.g. the European Convention on Human Rights in Ireland), or have strongly influenced an area of law (as is the case in Irish refugee law), one needs to examine the instrument itself in order to fully understand and explain the black-letter position in national law. From a normative perspective, international instruments can act as an external benchmark for domestic laws and help to bolster rights-based arguments in contested fields (the legal literature on abortion law in Ireland provides some good examples of this).[1] Indeed, in the case of legal research adopting a human rights approach or making normative rights arguments, there would be a glaring hole in your work if you ignored international human rights law completely.

For the legal researcher, adopting elements of an international law approach can allow for the exploration of new material and an original slant on aspects of the law which are already the subject of much scholarly analysis (e.g. examining the work of the International Labour Organisation on the labour rights of migrant domestic workers).[2] An international law analysis can enrich and help to justify the recommendations for reform which form part of

* Dr Clíodhna Murphy, Lecturer in Law, Maynooth University, Professor Mary Gilmartin, Professor of Geography, Maynooth University, and Leanne Caulfield, Legal Researcher, Law Reform Commission.

[1] See, for example, F de Londras, 'Fatal Foetal Abnormality, Irish Constitutional Law, and *Mellet v Ireland*' (2016) 24(4) Medical Law Review 591–607.

[2] C Murphy, 'The Enduring Vulnerability of Migrant Domestic Workers in Europe' (2013) 62(3) ICLQ 599.

many doctoral theses.[3] Perhaps less obviously, the work of international organisations can also constitute an important source of legal information. Soft law outputs of international bodies can provide the researcher with valuable, and credible, information in English on the legal framework and factual context in different countries, as well as rights gaps.[4] Similarly, global or regional reports on specific issues can identify common themes across borders and provide a form of ready-made conceptual framework for comparative analysis.[5]

From an instrumental point of view, it must be acknowledged that publishing in international peer-reviewed journals and obtaining funding is a key priority for many PhD students and early career researchers. Reference to international standards provides a means to generalise the appeal of research rooted mainly in domestic law (particularly important in a small country like Ireland). An international dimension can enhance the attractiveness of the work to international peer-reviewed journals, book publishers, and conference organisers. For these reasons, funders often like to see some sort of international element to grant applications.

This chapter describes and reflects on an interdisciplinary project conducted by the authors (two lawyers and a geographer) at Maynooth University, and funded by the Irish Human Rights and Equality Commission (IHREC). Its main focus is the international human rights law dimensions of the project methodology, but it also discusses wider issues relating to research involving the public sector, as well as interviews. In this contribution, we don't want to get bogged down in debates about the nature of international law, or the theoretical bases of international law methodology. Rather, the aim is to introduce and illustrate some of the possible benefits of adopting an international law approach; and give some practical guidance as to how to do this in a creative and rigorous manner, while avoiding potential pitfalls.

---

3 See, for example, V Mantouvalou, 'Am I Free Yet? Overseas Domestic Workers in Slavery' (2015) 42(3) Journal of Law and Society 329.

4 In the EU context, see for example EU Fundamental Rights Agency, *Severe labour exploitation: workers moving within or into the European Union States' obligations and victims' rights* (EUFRA 2015).

5 See for example International Labour Office, *Caught at Sea: Forced Labour and Trafficking in Fisheries* (ILO 2013).

Background to the project

The approach of public bodies towards migrant populations is often framed in terms of 'migrant integration'.[6] Ireland is now an immigrant-receiving society, with a long-established immigrant population. Census 2016 shows that 17.3 percent of the resident population of Ireland was born outside the country,[7] and it appears from both the census and the migration flow estimates that a considerable number of residents who were born in other EU countries have lived in Ireland for 10 years or longer. Our research project, entitled '"All the Children of the Nation": Integration Policy in Ireland Through the Lens of Human Rights and Equality', examined the development of migrant integration policy across the public sector in Ireland.

Research question

The aim of the project was to conduct a comprehensive audit and critical human rights and equality review of migrant integration policy across public bodies in Ireland. Our research question had three key dimensions. We wanted to:

1. Outline a best practice human rights-based model of integration;
2. Audit the extent to which public bodies in Ireland have developed integration policies or strategies; and
3. Assess the content of these policies against the human rights-based model.

The research topic was chosen for a combination of methodological and practical reasons. It builds on the existing expertise and research interests of the project team, and was designed to incorporate elements of both legal and social science methodologies. Both of the principal investigators had been working for some time in the field of migration and integration, and had previously engaged in critical analysis of Irish integration policy. This previous work had revealed a significant information gap relating to the extent and nature of integration policies of public sector bodies, and the process of developing such policies. Alongside this policy analysis work, one

[6] A Xanthaki, 'Against integration, for human rights' (2016) 20(6) International Journal of Human Rights 815; C Murphy, *Immigration, Integration and the Law: The Intersection of International, EU and Domestic Regimes* (Routledge 2013).

[7] Census 2016 Summary Results – Part 1 (Table EY020). Available online at <http://www.cso.ie/en/csolatestnews/presspages/2017/census2016summaryresults-part1/> accessed 20 October 2017.

of the principal investigators had already completed work on the potential usefulness of international human rights law in the development of a rights-based concept of migrant integration.[8] When the IHREC issued a call for its human rights and equality grant scheme in June 2016,[9] it was an ideal fit for the type of research which we wanted to conduct.

II – Methodological approach

The project was primarily desk-based, involving four main components. The first step was a review of the concept of integration in the academic literature and in international human rights law, and the development of a series of human rights indicators that would be used to benchmark integration policies. Secondly, we conducted an audit of the integration policies of public bodies. This involved developing a database of public bodies, requesting policy documents, and collating those documents when received. The third stage was assessing the policies received against the indicators identified. Finally, where the audit and review identified examples of good practice, as measured by the indicators, we carried out interviews with the official(s) in the relevant public body with responsibility for the policy.

For the purposes of this chapter, we focus on the following questions, which are useful to consider when deciding whether to use international human rights law as part of the overall methodological approach:

- What does international human rights law add to the proposed analysis?
- Are there other methods which could produce equally interesting or informative results? If so, why are they not being used?
- How exactly will international human rights law be incorporated into the methodology? Which legally binding instruments will be used as a touchstone; and/or what soft law outputs of international bodies might add to the analysis?

[8] C Murphy, 'Towards a Human Rights-Based Paradigm of Integration? The Contribution of International Law' (2013) 2 European Human Rights Law Review 166.

[9] The call is available at: <https://www.ihrec.ie/download/pdf/human_rights_and_equality_grant_scheme_2016_guidance_manual.pdf> accessed 8 January 2018.

- How does international human rights law fit into the overall methodological design of the project?

Why use international human rights law as the basis for developing human rights indicators?

Clearly, a superficial or tokenistic use of international human rights law is to be avoided: the first step must be to interrogate how international human rights law methodology addresses the research question. In the case of our project, the cornerstone of the research was the conceptualisation of 'integration' as a long-term process which aims to ensure the full protection of the human rights of migrants and their inclusion as equal members of society. This working definition of integration led us to propose the use of a human rights-based model of integration for the development and analysis of public sector integration policies. We decided to use international human rights law as the conceptual basis for this model. There are legal, theoretical and practical justifications for this use of international human rights law.

From the legal perspective, international human rights law, with its core content of rights applicable to all persons regardless of their legal status or any other pre-requisite, constitutes an important aspect of the overall legal framework within which integration policy must operate in Ireland. The international human rights treaties provide the basis for an equality-based paradigm of integration, by generally requiring state parties (including Ireland) to provide the rights enshrined therein to all persons on their territory without discrimination on the basis of nationality, race, religion or immigration status.[10] This links in to a more abstract point: international human rights law involves a reshaping of the relationship between the state and persons within its jurisdiction. By accepting human rights duties which transcend the state, the state loses a degree of control over the treatment of immigrants and non-citizens, such that it is no longer permitted to treat immigrants within its jurisdiction in ways which are contrary to its obligations under international human rights law. Through the engagement of supranational norms, the importance of the distinction between the individual as citizen and as foreigner, which is so central to the notion of state sovereignty as well as to national integration policies, begins to be broken down.[11]

[10] C Murphy, op cit n 6, at 244.

[11] E Guild, 'Cultural and Social Identity: Immigrants and the Legal Expression of National Identity', in E Guild and J Van Selm (eds), *International Migration and Security: Opportunities and Challenges* (Routledge 2005) 108.

Integration paradigms which are based on narrow conceptions of national identity and a strict dichotomy between the citizen and others are thus put under significant pressure by international human rights norms.

Aside from the state's international legal obligations and the universal nature of international human rights law, there are also more tangible ways in which an international human rights law approach 'added value' to our analysis. Previous research had shown that the UN human rights treaty monitoring bodies are, in their concluding observations on state reports, developing a nascent conception of integration which centres on a two-way, non-coercive process of the progressive realisation of equality for migrants.[12] We decided that this fledgling integration model emerging from the work of the UN treaty monitoring bodies would provide a useful, 'ready-made' framework for thinking about integration – and one which is firmly rooted in human rights.

Why were other methods not used?

It is also important to think through other possible methods. An alternative approach would have been to assess Irish integration policy against existing indicators and measurements of integration, rather than to develop our own human rights indicators. For example, the 'Zaragoza' indicators developed in the EU setting measure migrant integration outcomes in terms of employment, education, social inclusion and active citizenship;[13] and the Migrant Integration Policy Index (MIPEX) assesses integration policy using a variety of policy indicators.[14] Having reviewed these indicators and measurements of integration in the first stage of our research, we argue that current measurements of integration, which focus primarily on outcomes, are insufficient for the purposes of understanding how to develop effective and participatory integration policies. They do not track progress towards these outcomes, and they do not adequately identify the objectives which should inform state policy on integration. As a consequence, they miss opportunities for intervention directed at 'full participation and integration of migrants'.[15] In addition, the EU policy framework for integration has been criticised for an increasing tendency to focus on migrants' obligations to display 'respect for diversity

[12] See Murphy, op cit.

[13] T Huddleston, J Niessen and D Tjaden, *Using EU Indicators of Immigrant Integration* (Final Report for DG of Home Affairs 2013).

[14] Migrant Integration Policy Index 2015. *How countries are promoting integration of immigrants.* Available online at http://www.mipex.eu/ accessed 1 October 2017.

[15] CERD 2015. Concluding observations on the combined nineteenth to twenty-first periodic reports of the Netherlands. UN Doc CERD/C/NLD/19-21, 28 August.

and the EU's basic values', rather than on Member State obligations to take proactive steps to ensure equality of opportunity.[16] We argue instead for an explicitly human rights-based approach.

Description of the methods used

As already mentioned, our human rights model builds on previous work on the development of the concept of integration by the treaty bodies established under the International Covenant on Civil and Political Rights (ICCPR), the International Covenant on Economic, Social and Cultural Rights (ICESCR) and the International Convention for the Elimination of all forms of Racial Discrimination (ICERD).[17] Why did we select these particular instruments for guidance on best practice on integration? The primary rationale was one of universality of application – the ICCPR and the ICESCR apply to all persons in state parties and thus apply to all migrants in those states. In addition, ICERD applies to all victims of racial discrimination, as very widely defined in Art 5 as 'any distinction, exclusion, restriction or preference based on race, colour, descent, or national or ethnic origin', and so applies to all non-citizen migrants. The relevance of these treaties to integration policy is reflected in the development of a budding integration paradigm in the work of the corresponding treaty supervision bodies: the Human Rights Committee (UNHRC), the Committee on Economic, Social and Cultural Rights (CESCR) and the Committee on the Elimination of all Forms of Racial Discrimination (CERD). This paradigm is based on non-discrimination and the progressive realisation of equality for migrants.

The examination of the development of the concept of integration in the work of these UN treaty monitoring bodies was conducted primarily through an analysis of their concluding observations on state reports up to December 2017. Why focus on concluding observations? Reflecting state and civil society preoccupations with migrant integration, these concluding observations often expressly mention integration-related issues and the concept of integration. While concluding observations are generally not understood as having legally binding effect, nevertheless, as outputs of a treaty body, they have a 'notable authority, albeit unspecified', in particular where they purport to interpret treaty provisions.[18] While the Human Rights Committee (CCPR Committee) and the Committee on the Elimination of

[16] S Carrera, *In Search of the Perfect Citizen? The Intersection between Integration, Immigration and Nationality in the EU* (Martinus Nijhoff 2012).

[17] Murphy, op cit.

[18] M O'Flaherty, The Concluding Observations of the United Nations Human Rights Treaty Monitoring Bodies (2006) 6(1) Human Rights Law Review 27.

Racial Discrimination (CERD Committee) have the competence to consider individual complaints, the views of the CCPR Committee have not to date specifically referred to the concept of integration and the ICERD individual complaints procedure is rarely used. The general comments or recommendations of each of the three bodies have some useful information on the rights of non-citizens and the principle of non-discrimination,[19] but again there is little in the general comments which directly addresses integration policy. In contrast, integration-related issues as well as the concept of integration itself are often expressly referred to by the Committees in their concluding observations. For these reasons, our indicators are primarily drawn from the concluding observations of the Committees. We looked at the most recent set of concluding observations for all states, up to December 2017. The funding received from IHREC allowed us to employ a researcher to assist with the task of gathering and analysing the concluding observations of the relevant human rights bodies since 2013.

Devising a model of best practice

From our review of the literature as well as international human rights law, we concluded that a human rights and equality perspective in integration policies could be assessed with reference to structural issues, process and outcomes. We identified the following human rights and equality indicators of good practice.

Structural
The policy expressly identifies measures aimed at eliminating discrimination
The policy expressly addresses human rights
The policy identifies practical measures that promote equal access to these human rights
The policy expressly refers to respect for cultural, linguistic or other forms of diversity

[19] See, for example, HRC General Comment No 15, 'The position of aliens under the Covenant' (11 April 1986); HRC General Comment No 18, 'Non-Discrimination' (10 November 1989); HRC General Comment No 23, 'The rights of minorities (Art.27)' (8 April 1994); CESCR General Comment No 20, 'Non-discrimination in Economic, Social and Cultural Rights (art.2, para. 2)' (10 June 2009); CESCR General Comment No 21, The Right of Everyone to Take Part in Cultural Life (21 December 2009); CERD Committee General Recommendation No 30, 'Discrimination Against Non Citizens' (1 October 2004).

Process
The policy is being implemented, with specific budget/staff allocations
The policy provides for sufficient coverage of target populations
The policy is being mainstreamed
Outcomes
It is clear how, and by whom, the effectiveness of the policy is being measured
The success of the policy is addressed in the annual report
The annual report provides for follow-up

Audit of integration policies of public bodies

Having devised a model of best practice and developed indicators accordingly, the next step was to gather integration policies from public sector bodies. Our first task was to define and identify 'public bodies' including those classified as public bodies for the purposes of the Regulation of Lobbying Act 2015. Our starting point was the Irish State Administration database, which provides a comprehensive overview of a wide range of public bodies. We checked the current status of public bodies listed on the database, and updated the database where necessary. We also sought, where possible, to identify the person/s within each public body with responsibility for integration and/or diversity policy, and we compiled a revised list of public bodies and relevant contact details.

When we had identified public bodies, we then wrote to all 432 of these bodies requesting a copy of their integration and/or diversity policy or strategy documents. We provided a deadline and, if this was not met, followed up with further letters, emails and phonecalls. In total, we contacted 432 public bodies, and we received responses from 223 bodies by 30 September 2017. Almost 50 percent of these 223 bodies which responded stated that they had no relevant policies. A small number of bodies provided documents which were subsequently found to have no provisions relevant to integration or interculturalism. Thirty-four percent of the bodies which responded provided us with a relevant document.

Review of integration policies of public bodies

We developed a template for the review of integration policies based on the indicators. We used this template to review each of the policy documents that we received following our written request(s). When the individual reviews were completed by the project researcher, we then analysed the reviews as a whole in order to identify broad trends and patterns in the integration policies of public bodies in Ireland, which included identifying the extent to which integration policies are, or are not, informed by human rights and equality perspectives.

Interviews

In the process of reviewing integration policies, we identified a small number of public bodies that, based on the criteria shown in the table above, had policies that we considered to be good practice. The bodies identified each had strong policies on equality, integration and/or interculturalism. One body's policy was particularly strong on the human rights dimension (Irish Prison Service). We wanted to interview a selection of different types of public body based in different parts of the country; so we included a state company (Dublin Bus); a local authority (Limerick City and County Council); a cultural institution (Chester Beatty Library); a regulatory body (Central Bank of Ireland); and a university (Trinity College Dublin). In advance of making further contact with these public bodies, we received ethical approval from Maynooth University Social Research Committee to conduct interviews. In total, we conducted 6 interviews with 11 representatives.

The purpose of the interviews was to gain an understanding of the process of developing effective integration policies; and the extent to which the policies of these organisations (which seemed to represent good practice) were rooted in human rights considerations. For these reasons, we asked about, for example, the impetus for the development of the policy within the particular organisation; whether the national Migrant Integration Strategy was considered; and whether and how the idea of 'human rights' motivated the development of the policy in any way.

We presented the findings from the interviews as mini 'case studies' in the report, which we felt would assist public bodies in seeing what a 'good practice' policy would look like in practice; how this policy was developed on the ground; and what resources were used in the elaboration of the policy.

Synthesis report

We drafted a report synthesising our findings and launched this report at the Irish Human Rights and Equality Commission. The report included practical guidelines for public bodies to assist in the development and analysis of integration policy.[20]

III – Challenges

It was important to us that our project report would include practical recommendations to public bodies on how to translate the human rights objectives of integration policies into tangible results. One challenge which arose in this context was that although the UN treaty monitoring bodies require the effective implementation of integration policy, and set out the basic structural objectives of such policies, they provide little specific guidance on how to achieve effective practical implementation. We realised that we would need to draw on additional material for the 'process' domain. We went 'back to the drawing board' and further researched the work of international human rights bodies in this field and identified that the Office of the UN High Commissioner for Human Rights (OHCHR) has provided a guide to measurement and implementation of human rights norms in policymaking generally.[21] Of particular interest to us were the 'process indicators' designed by the OHCHR, which help in assessing a state's efforts to transform its human rights commitments into the desired results. We used this OHCHR guide to assist in our development of process indicators for integration policy in Ireland.

IV – Ethical considerations

As the material being analysed was voluntarily provided outputs of public bodies, the desk-based research did not raise ethical considerations. However, as mentioned, the later stages of the project involved interviews with public officials with specific responsibility for integration policies or strategies. The interviews focussed on the process of developing the policy in order to provide practical guidelines for other public officials and bodies. The material was thus of a non-sensitive nature and ethical considerations did not impact on the chosen methodology. However, we understood that it was possible that participants might make personal statements that, on reflection, they did not wish to be publicly associated with. We went through the process of gaining ethical approval for the interviews well in advance of the planned interviews to ensure that it was in place in plenty of time. Participants were

[20] The full text of the report is available here: <https://www.maynoothuniversity.ie/social-sciences-institute/news/developing-integration-policy-public-sector-human-rights-approach> accessed 27 November 2017.

[21] OHCHR [UN Office of the High Commissioner for Human Rights] 2012. Human Rights Indicators: A Guide to Measurement and Implementation, HR/PUB/12/5.

provided with an information sheet and a detailed consent form. They were asked, as part of the consent process, whether or not they wish to be publicly identified in any presentations, publications or other outputs from the project.

V – Reflections

We were satisfied that our research objectives were clear and that each stage of the project was carefully designed at the outset. This meant that the project ran reasonably smoothly, which was important given the limited project duration and budget. One issue which arose with the audit highlights the importance of being as specific as possible with requests for information. Some of the public bodies seemed uncertain as to what we meant by 'integration' policies. We had tried to address this definitional issue in the letter by being very broad in what we requested. We explained that we were collating 'policies and/or strategy documents of public bodies … which relate to migrant integration, diversity or interculturalism'. However, on reviewing the responses, we felt that some bodies might have had relevant policies that they did not think would be of interest to the project. Other bodies passed on everything in which they thought we might be broadly interested, and which were indeed relevant to our analysis: for example, the Irish Prison Service supplied us with their policy on access to psychology services for foreign national prisoners. One thing which we might have done differently to prevent this slight imbalance would have been to give a list of concrete examples of policies which might fall within the category of 'integration policies'.

One piece of advice which we could offer to those engaging in research with public sector bodies is to 'budget' plenty of time for bodies to respond. We were still receiving policies until very close to the launch of our report, which left us with a tight timeframe for the analysis and synthesis of our findings for the project report. Remember that a request to a public body will likely result in internal consultation and work to collate the relevant information, meaning that it may take some time for the body to provide what is requested.

As already mentioned in the section on 'challenges', we learned the importance of maintaining flexibility in the methodological approach. Our main source for a human rights-based model of integration was the concluding observations of the three UN treaty monitoring bodies selected. However, when this did not bring enough substance to the 'process' domain of indicators, we went back to first principles and found a very useful alternative source in the work of the Office of the UN Commissioner for Human Rights.

VI – Conclusion

The human rights-based model of integration developed in our project illustrates just one of the ways in which international law could be used in human rights research. There is a sliding scale of methods for incorporating international law into doctoral research – from mentioning international law standards applicable in a particular area; to (for example) a chapter on international human rights obligations in a particular area; to a comprehensive international human rights law methodology. Above all, in all cases the methodology needs to go beyond superficial references to international human rights law. In particular, the researcher needs to understand and factor in the limits of 'soft law' as a binding source of law; and acknowledge widespread non-compliance by states. It is also necessary to maintain a critical perspective: the contestation of international human rights law framework is important and includes feminist and 'third world' critiques, for instance. Research based on international human rights law needs to have considered all of these points at the preliminary stages, otherwise cracks will appear in the methodology and findings.

CHAPTER 5

The Northern/Irish Feminist Judgments Project: Experiments in Feminist Legal Research

Máiréad ENRIGHT *and Aoife* O'DONOGHUE*

I – INTRODUCTION AND RESEARCH QUESTIONS

Feminist judgments projects (FJPs) are a form of experimental legal writing. Participants rewrite already decided judgments as if they were a sitting feminist judge. *Northern/Irish Feminist Judgments: Judges' Troubles and the Gendered Politics of Identity* consists of 26 judgments rewritten from several feminist perspectives, contextualised with accompanying commentaries and critical introductory chapters. Judgment writers were paired with commentators and each rewritten judgment was workshopped while still in draft. Our main aim was to address the marginalisation of feminist analysis within Northern/Irish legal traditions, and to demonstrate its value to judicial studies on the island. Although some work has been undertaken on gender and judicial diversity in both jurisdictions,[1] there has been less analysis of Northern/Irish judicial craft. Shawn Wilson has written that research reveals not only unanswered questions, but unquestioned answers.[2] In this vein, feminist judging disturbs pre-conceptions of judgment writing by putting feminist critique into

* Máiréad Enright, Senior Lecturer, Birmingham Law School, University of Birmingham and Aoife O'Donoghue, Professor of International Law and Global Governance, Durham Law School.

[1] Bacik and E Drew 'Struggling with juggling: Gender and work/life balance in the legal professions' (2006) 29(2) Women's Studies International Forum 136–46; I Bacik, C Costello, E Drew, *Gender InJustice: Feminising the Legal Professions?* (Trinity College Dublin 2003); D Feenan, 'Women judges: Gendering judging, justifying diversity' (2008) 35(4) Journal of Law and Society 490–519; M Fox and J Morison, 'Lawyers in a Divided Society: Legal Culture and Legal Services in Northern Ireland' (1992) 19(1) Journal of Law and Society 124–45.

[2] S Wilson, *Research is Ceremony* (Fernwood, 2015) 6.

practice.[3] We did not invent feminist judging[4]: we were heavily influenced by the scholars who produced the first feminist judgments project in England, and included them as consultants on our project. We borrowed their method because it allowed us to openly question the assumption that judges are master-practitioners of impartiality and neutrality.[5] Feminist judging insists that judicial fairness and independence are not compromised by acknowledging that judges bring their own political commitments and lived experiences to their decisions.[6] Regarding law as indeterminate, as capable of responding to outside influences including feminist insight, FJPs are about reform-via-deconstruction. They show that judicial decisions are not inevitable: that important cases could be decided differently if patriarchal habits of reasoning are overcome. Even where a feminist rewrite does not change the outcome of a given case, it can alter how that judgment participates in the construction of gendered legal discourses of identity, justice and belonging which resonate through wider society. FJPs ask whether it is possible, from this perspective, to transform judicial method.

An FJP may seem an unusual case study for an edited collection of this nature, for many reasons. First, it is a multi-authored project comprising a range of diverse pieces, and so our approach in this chapter is necessarily selective. Second, in many respects, because the project requires outputs to take the form of a recognisable appellate judgment, the methods of data collection and analysis involved are very close to traditional doctrinal legal research. Although some individual judgment-writers drew on their own empirical, historical and socio-legal research to inform their writing, the project did not require this. Third, research subjects were not directly involved in the collaborative inquiry, or in co-construction of the project; an issue we discuss later on. Although the project was participatory in a sense, there was no real distinction between researcher and stakeholder. For this reason, the project did not pose any classic dilemmas in research ethics. Nevertheless, the project raises a number of important methodological questions. FJPs connect with broader conversations about the delegitimation of the objective and neutral 'gaze' in legal research methods. Feminist work has uncovered

---

3 R Hunter 'Can Feminist Judges Make a Difference' (2008) 15 International Journal of the Legal Profession 7 K FitzGibbon and J Maree Maher 'Feminist Challenges to the Constraints of Law: Donning UnComfortable Robes' (2015) Feminist Legal Studies 253, A Lorde, *Sister Outsider: Essay and Speeches* (Crossing Press 1984) 110–114.

4 Special Issue: *ReWriting Equality* (2006) 18 Canadian Journal of Women and the Law 1; R Hunter, C McGlynn and E Rackley *Feminist Judgments: From Theory to Practice* (Hart 2010); R Hunter, 'The power of feminist judgments?' (2012) 20 Feminist Legal Studies 135.

5 R Hunter, C McGlynn and E Rackley, *Feminist Judgments: From Theory to Practice* (Hart 2010).

6 R Hunter, C McGlynn and E Rackley, *Feminist Judgments: From Theory to Practice* (Hart 2010) 31.

how particular gendered methods of representing 'research findings' have been encoded as authoritative, in the process marginalising other readings of social reality. In this chapter, we reflect on the legal writing practices employed in our FJP, drawing on illustrative quotations from presentations given at four drafting workshops held early in the life of the project.[7]

II – Methodological approach

New conversations on feminist research methodologies emphasise the transformative potential of re-shaping textual forms which are rarely used in academic writing.[8] Livholts writes that academic writing can sometimes appear 'unfeeling' and dislocated from the contexts it seeks to analyse, so that academics may need to resort to alternative forms to put 'flesh on the bones' of theory.[9] Feminist judging is work in this mould, because it engages scholars in practical judicial writing: a form of *praxis* which realises and enacts a vision of law as well as analysing or critiquing it. It is, in many ways, akin to what the ethnographer Norman Denzin has called 'performance writing'; writing which 'shows rather than tells'.[10] So how does feminist judgment writing show what feminist law would look like?

First, feminist judgments pay detailed attention to female experiences and voices often marginalised in legal discourse,[11] not merely for the sake of appearing to 'hear all sides', but so that those voices and experiences can directly influence the judge's reasoning. Feminist judgments should also avoid the use of stereotypes and assumptions which mute minority experience. Louise Kennefick explained her approach to re-writing a rape sentencing judgment in these terms:

> Our judgment does not assume the reaction of a victim ... the original judgment is very quick to tell a victim of rape how they should feel and how it affected their life, with the implication that if they do not feel this way, their reaction is in some way invalid ... Finlay CJ is presenting a stereotypical image of women that obscures, distorts, and even replaces

7 Full transcripts are on file with the authors. Our thanks to Sandra Duffy for her transcription and coding work.

8 See e.g. R Edmondson, 'Writing Between Worlds' in Anne Byrne and Ronit Lentin (eds), *(Re) searching Women* (IPA 2000) 188.

9 M Livholts, *Emergent Writing Methodologies in Feminist Studies* (Routledge 2012). See similarly R Lynn Doty, 'Maladies of our souls: Identity and voice in the writing of academic international relations', Cambridge Review of International Affairs 17, no 2 (2004): 377–378 on the 'calcified' language of the academy.

10 N Denzin, *Performance Ethnography: Critical Pedagogy and the Politics of Culture* (Sage 2003).

11 KT Bartlett 'Feminist Legal Method' (1990) 103 Harvard Law Review 829.

the descriptions which individual women themselves might otherwise present.

Second, judgments must 'ask the woman question'. This affects the selection of judgments for re-writing and the framing of the feminist judgment's argument, especially where the area of law at play is not only, or perhaps obviously, 'about women'. Aoife O'Donoghue explained:

> [The case I'm re-writing is] to do with treaty law, two men, and old Articles 2 and 3 of the Constitution but what intrigued me when I read it was the way it constructed community, citizenship, and how the value of their arguments was based on the McGimpseys' public life. [I asked] could a housewife from Northern Ireland or the Republic of Ireland be in a position to take this case?

Third, feminist judgments give credit to a range of forms of evidence.[12] Colin Murray, for example, emphasised a need to correct a judicial tendency to defer to police evidence,[13] noting 'if courts constantly take the line of the expert actor, in this case a hierarchy of police that is almost exclusively male, there is not going to be a space for any dissonance – no rupture, no point for change to occur.'

Fourth, feminist judgments reject abstract readings of core legal concepts, which tend to universalise legal frames of knowledge as uncontestable truths. This tactic can be framed in terms of Donna Haraway's 'situated knowledge'[14]; a rejection of the search for an external disembodied point of view in favour of one that pays close attention to the specific social environment in which the original judgment was handed down. Feminist judgments take account of the material implications of a judicial decision, and its capacity to reinforce exclusionary discourses around gender and national identity. Re-writing an abortion case, Ruth Fletcher was mindful that:

> I draw on sources to talk about pregnancy as a fragile, dependent – if wondrous – kind of thing, that women have engaged in voluntarily and sometimes at significant cost to themselves. If prenatal life is ever to get to the point where it is capable of sustaining itself, it requires the sustenance

[12] MJ Boxer 'Unruly Knowledge: Women's Studies and the Problem of Disciplinarity' (2000) 12 National Women's Studies Association Journal 119.

[13] M Fox, '*Barnes v. Belfast City Council*' in M Enright et al (eds) *Northern/Irish Feminist Judgments: Judges' Troubles and the Gendered Politics of Identity* (Bloombsury 2017) 612.

[14] D Haraway, 'Situated Knowledgers: The Science Question in Feminism and the Privilege of Partial Perspective' (1988) 14(3) Feminist Studies 575.

> of another person for nine months – so those material facts are relevant to deciding what the scope of the right to life is ...

Eoin Daly, in re-writing a judgment about the dismissal of a pregnant primary school teacher in a Catholic school, was conscious of its repercussions for gay teachers in contemporary Ireland:

> I have met a lot of gay teachers who, in the Republic of Ireland today, are in not that dissimilar a position to what women like Eileen would have been like in the 80s in the sense of precarity and apprehension of power that exists in denominationally managed institutions … Eileen Flynn was unusual in the openness of her transgression ... today the main harms from a similar position affect people who never experience dismissal or sanction because they self-censor in the first place ... the same issues are alive today in a very different legislative context.

This contextualising approach may influence whether a formalist or realist approach is taken to the interpretation of a statutory or constitutional provision or to the selection of analytic categories. Often a feminist goal can be achieved using traditional techniques; for example, citing useful precedents which were downplayed in the original judgment, expanding the reach of a precedent beyond its own narrow facts, insisting on closer scrutiny of the facts or more scrupulous application of procedure, or closely reading professional regulatory codes which the original judgment downplays. At other times, feminist interventions rest on novel and disruptive deployments of existing legal tools. For example, Marie Fox's judgment on the destruction of a pet dog seeks to confound the categories under which the dispute was originally analysed:

> I think what my feminist conclusion would be, is: given all the reasons we should not objectify dogs, we shouldn't treat them as property … what I try to do in my judgment is use the language of Lennox's name, because naming is so important, and try ... to situate him as a family member.

Fifth, as Irish courts are partial to long passages of historical or philosophical analysis, feminist judgments can replace these with alternative narratives.[15] Although many judgments drew on feminist theorists such as Judith Butler and Jennifer Nedelsky, judgment writers felt that judicial practice did not

[15] For an example of a feminist judgment that relies on an alternative history to that favoured by the original judge see M O'Rourke, '*O'Keeffe v. Hickey*' in M Enright et al (eds) *Northern/Irish Feminist Judgments: Judges' Troubles and the Gendered Politics of Identity* (Bloomsbury 2017) 325.

permit citation. So, Mary Donnelly observed, that a feminist judgments' text concealed much of the scholarly work needed to produce it; it was the 'tip of the ice-berg'. Judgments hide the collaborative character of law-making and interpretation; suggesting an intellectual isolation that is not reflected in practice; compressing a multitude of voices into one judicial voice. The commentaries giving context to the judgments were a significant element of the project in this respect because they could set out the methodological choices which the judgment writer made; the feminist concepts employed; the choices not made and why. Most participants agreed that it would not be possible to directly acknowledge relevant academic literature in the judgment text. Sara Ramshaw explained her role as Kathryn McNeilly's commentator as follows:

> In light of the fact that the structure and content of legal judgment has obvious limitations we wanted to tease out some things in the commentary that Kathryn was not able to talk about. She was very explicit about [the role of legal] indeterminacy [in her judgment], but there's only so far, a judge can go in saying that without destroying your own legitimacy! How do we approach that in legal judgment? ... Kathryn has also just finished a PhD on Judith Butler, so we wanted to talk about liveability and heteronormativity and biopower, all things that she hints to in her judgment but can't go into any details, so … we can use the commentary to tease that out more.

Finally, feminist judgments are accountable for the essentially political choices authors make in favouring one set of legal arguments over another. For example, Julie McCandless, rewriting a judgment about race and 'family resemblance' in assisted reproduction law, sought to draw attention to the political work done by the marginalisation of race in the original judgment, making race a central element of her own reasoning:

> I was quite annoyed by the judicial marking-off of racism or prejudice based on racial features as exceptional and ignoring that continuum of violent discrimination, prejudice … that weaves through the fabric of society … This case could have been really interesting … It could have been seen as a judicial opportunity to talk about multiculturalism in a much deeper way than it was in the case. What seems to happen in the case – the word 'race' is only used once... what the judges refer to instead is 'skin colour' – lighter, darker, skin colour. It's pitched almost like a physical variation, like height or hair colour or suntan.

Feminist method can be as much about how a text is produced as it is about the content of that text. We were interested in the collaborative feminist praxis underpinning FJPs, in particular, because the drafting workshops allowed us to engage in what Laurel Richardson calls 'writing as inquiry'.[16] In the process of writing together we were doing more than reporting the results of research already conducted. Rather, we learned collectively about judgment writing, and the challenges of developing feminist judicial method. We created a space where we could interrogate the ways in which we constructed knowledge about the law, the people affected by it, and ourselves as judges.

In the five-year life of the project we established an interdisciplinary network of 150 established academics, postgraduate students and early career researchers as well as activists, legal practitioners, artists and writers. Some were experienced in feminist research methods, and others adopted them for the first time. At the workshops, judgment writers and commentators presented together, having previously submitted a draft of their judgments and commentaries for the wider collective to read. Some judgments were also written in pairs. Project discussions allowed participants to draw inspiration from each other, to work their writing out of places where it had become 'stuck', and to confer on shared and recurring challenges in a supportive, constructive atmosphere. We also wanted to open the project up to interventions from outside academic legal communities. Each workshop incorporated critical interventions from academics in other relevant disciplines, activists with experience across multiple campaigns alongside artists, writers and poets.

We were also fortunate that several members of the judiciary were happy to come and discuss their experiences and the project. Activists, some of whom had been directly involved with the cases under discussion, analysed the political, social and economic contexts of these cases long-term impact on struggles for social change. Artists and writers allowed us to explore alternative modes of representing experience, law and context. The workshops were not passive events where an audience sat and listened with perfunctory questions at the end, but rather a fully engaged group debate. From the first

[16] L Richardson and E St Pierre, 'Writing: A Method of Inquiry', in NK Denzin and YS Lincoln (eds), *The Sage handbook of qualitative research* (Sage 2007) 959–978.

workshop at the University of Ulster the template for a spirit of co-operation, openness, support, debate, and even fun, was set.[17]

III – Challenges

A key challenge for the project was that of adapting to judicial writing. Feminist judging must find ways to negotiate masculinist modes of legal writing which have become authoritative under patriarchy, upsetting our ideas of what judicial writing ought to do and look like. Some FJPs allowed participants to abandon the strictures of traditional judgment writing and explore other forms. For example, Irene Watson, writing in the Australian project, rejected the judicial form altogether while the New Zealand project has incorporated Maori language and custom.[18] Our project largely operated within the confines of traditional judgment-writing as we understood them.[19] This was because our agreed aim, prescribed well in advance of beginning the project, was to construct feminist judgments that were plausible and recognisably 'legal', while taking account of feminist critique, imagination and insight. Plausibility is a concern for feminist methodology: some have suggested that feminist writing must reject established convention, pursuing nonconformist styles.[20] A tension arises here because, as Marjorie De Vault writes, we may need to adopt established writing formats to persuade audiences invested in tradition, of the legitimacy of a new endeavour.[21] One of our main goals for the FJP was that the rewritten judgments would be read and used by students, both as teaching tools and as models for their own writing, and indeed, today they are widely used in both Irish and Northern Irish law schools. For this reason, we wanted our 'outputs' to be familiar to students, judges, and practising lawyers. So, our participants agreed that the same law, doctrine, traditions

[17] R Fletcher 'FlaK: Mixing Feminism, Legality and Knowledge' (2015) Feminist Legal Studies 251; A Scales 'The Emergence of Feminist Jurisprudence: An Essay' (1986) 95 Yale Law Journal 1373; M Margaret Fonow and JA Cook (eds) *Beyond Methodology: Feminist Scholarship as Lived Research* (Indiana University Press 1991); EC DuBois, G Kelly, E Kennedy, C Korsmeyer, L Robinson (eds) *Feminist Scholarship: Kindling in the Groves of Academe* (University of Illinois Press 1987).

[18] I Watson, *Kartinyeri v The Commonwealth* [1998] HCA 22, First Nations Stories, Grandmother's Law: Too Many Stories to Tell' in H Douglas, F Bartlett, T Luker, R Hunter (eds) Australian Feminist Judgments: Righting and Rewriting Law (Hart 2015).

[19] R Hunter, C McGlynn and Erika Rackley, *Feminist Judgments: From Theory to Practice* (Hart 2010); M Davies, 'The Law Becomes Us: Rediscovering Judgment' (2012) 20 (2) Feminist Legal Studies 167; M Davies, 'Feminism and the Idea of Law' (2011) 1 *feminists@law* 1.

[20] As discussed in N Frost and F Elichaioff, 'Feminist Postmodernism, Poststructuralism and Critical Theory' in S Nagy Hesse-Biber (ed) *Feminist Research Practice: A Primer* (Sage 2014) 45.

[21] M DeVault, *Liberating Method: Feminism and Social Research* (Temple University Press 1999) 157.

of dynamic and conservative interpretation,[22] judicial conventions and evidence will bind them as bound the original decision-maker. This did not mean that all other perspectives were repressed within the project: this was, in part, why we included artists, activists and academics from other disciplines as participants. However, our concern for plausibility limited the inter-disciplinary possibilities of the project; so, for example, although we discussed aspects of judgments with poets and artists, opening the project to alternative writing methods might have enabled more creative direct collaboration with them which could have been embodied in the project publications.[23]

These constraints also generated discussion of the differences between an academic and a judicial orientation to law. For example, academic writing may give an author freedom to develop and invent new legal concepts, whereas a judge must work within established conceptual strictures. The feminist theorist of anti-oppressive research, Patti Lather, advocates for 'demastering' research; which would seek actively to undermine powerful discourses (like law) and strip them of their force and productivity.[24] It is not clear that feminist judging, at least as we applied it, could achieve this. Instead, the goal was to subvert or re-orientate concepts that could not be set aside. Sinéad Ring and Eilionóir Flynn in their shared judgment worked strategically with inherently patriarchal concepts of consent to sex which they reject in their own academic writing. Julie McCandless found herself wanting to resist fundamental concepts in medical and family law which grounded the decision she was re-writing:

> This is interesting for me, because I've spent most of my academic work critiquing that model of family law. So, am I bolstering it by saying that this is important and should get legal acknowledgment in a judgment? ... I'm thinking – am I doing the right thing, here? Is this good for feminist analysis? Because there are dangers associated with this. You're creating relationships between embryos and cells, and there are many contexts where we would want to resist that.

[22] See especially F de Londras, '*Zappone and Gilligan v Revenue Commrs*' in M Enright et al (eds) *Northern/Irish Feminist Judgments: Judges' Troubles and the Gendered Politics of Identity* (Bloomsbury 2017) 288.

[23] For an example of a feminist judgments project that goes further in this respect, see the Scottish Feminist Judgments Project <http://www.sfjp.law.ed.ac.uk/> last accessed 6 March 2019.

[24] P Leather, 'Against Proper Objects: Toward the Diversely Qualitative' <http://www.csri.mmu.ac.uk/siqr/keynotes15/lather15.php> last accessed 6 March 2019.

As Davina Cooper has noted,[25] 'imitative play'; pretending to be the judge, is a central aspect of FJPs. Participants were intrigued and challenged by the idea of finding a 'judicial voice'. Many of our discussions centred on the tension between the demands of plausible role-play and the inherent violence of certain authoritative, disinterested, modes of legal expression. The original judgments provoked strong emotions in some of our participants. Vicky Conway said of engaging with the Kerry Babies case, 'I found getting the right tone really hard because I, like anyone who's read any of this judgment, will want to curse and scream and do little else ...' At the same time, we debated the strategic value of dramatic judicial rhetoric. Could a phrase like this, discussed in our first workshop by Patrick Hanafin, survive the first draft? '[W]e as judges should not sit idly by in a case of such monumental cowardice and patriarchal posturing. It's our duty and responsibility in the name of equity to act to intervene in the name of individual choice.'

Several of our participants noted the difficulty of re-introducing feminist narrative techniques where the structure and language of original judgment was inherently inhospitable to them. Claire McCann observed: 'Actually the thing I've grappled with most is how to shoehorn the woman back into that narrative … sometimes I stuck references in and took them back out because it was just so incongruous'.

Participants also struggled with what is perhaps the essential distinction between the judicial and the academic role; the need to decide the conflict. Lorna Fox-O'Mahony described realising in re-writing her judgment in *Lynd*, a mortgages case, that 'you have to decide, you have to judge, and not avoid the hard issue … the [feminist judging] process ... forces you to be honest about the things you're critiquing and to find the evidence for it'.

Some participants made the difficulties of decision explicit within their texts. At the end of a complex discussion of the possibilities of different techniques of constitutional interpretation, Ruth Fletcher found herself unable to come to her desired decision, and wanted to signal her dissatisfaction to readers: 'I think there's a moment to carve out a voice of dissent, a judicial conscience articulating itself to say that I think this has to be the interpretation but I'm not happy about it'.

In many cases, therefore, a disjuncture emerged between the desire to produce a 'fractured' text, which would allow expression of authors' critique of the

[25] D Cooper, 'Retrieving the State for Radical Politics' (2016) 14(3) Journal of Social Policy 409.

law, and the need for a plausibly coherent judgment, understood as a monologue.[26] In many instances, the commentary on the judgment provided a parallel space,[27] where the affective and resistant dimensions of the feminist judgments could be presented. For example, in some commentaries, those directly involved or political engaged by the original dispute brought their own experience of anger, fear or joy to their commentaries. For example, Christine Bell's commentary on the Holy Cross conflict encompasses her vivid recollection of direct involvement in that dispute.

As discussed already, it was essential that our feminist methodology was set within wider feminist practices of collaborative and relational writing. We wanted collaboration to be generous and open,[28] ensuring that critique was engaged and constructive while avoiding the emergence of unnecessary hierarchies between participants. However, we encountered challenges in ensuring meaningful cross-disciplinary participation. All of our judgment writers, and most of those writing commentaries for the project were academic lawyers. The exclusionary legalism of the method is inescapable. It meant that we had to put some time into translating aspects of the project, its aims and utility for other audiences, ensuring that our workshops would be genuinely open to the interventions of the collaborators we had invited from outside 'the law school'. Nevertheless, two project participants—themselves experienced adoption rights activists and scholars—who had intended to re-write an adoption judgment found that their lack of legal training proved an insurmountable hurdle. This was disappointing because one of their aims in joining the project had been to de-mystify aspects of constitutional argument used to block activist work in this area. In practice, then, non-lawyers participated in our project as discussants and informants, and occasionally as commentators, rather than directly co-creating the written work. A further difficulty was the relative homogeneity of the Northern/Irish legal academy; by inviting participants who had worked on Northern/Irish legal issues before, we created an almost entirely White collective, even though many issues of race are considered within the

[26] Several judgments in the collection are co-authored, but the authors invented a 'hybrid' surname for the single judge identified as author of the feminist judgment.

[27] For more radical analogous techniques see A Mol, *The Body Multiple* (Duke, 2003), which contains two parallel texts in dialogue with each other; L Perriton's article in two columns, 'The Provocative and Evocative Gaze Upon Women in Management Developments' (1999) 11(3) Gender and Education 295 and P Lather and C Smithies, *Troubling the Angels* (Hachette 1997) which weaves several different formats and styles into a multi-layered narrative.

[28] On the experience of collaborative writing see M Gallant et al 'Retreating out of Ourselves: Sharing and Spilling the Lifeblood of Collaborative Writing' in Jane Speedy and Jonathan Wyatt eds *Collaborative Writing as Inquiry* (Cambridge Scholar Publishing 2014) 13.

project. This necessarily generated moments of difficulty around representation, which could never be entirely resolved. For instance, in rewriting *PM v Board of Management of St Vincent's Hospital*, we discussed how Mary Donnelly should engage with judicial norms of civility in addressing racial stereotyping in the judgment of the lower court. We agreed that a gentle rebuff would be more plausible, but an overt rebuke might be more disruptive of raced power relations within Irish law.[29]

Although we did not co-write with the surviving litigants who brought the cases being re-written, a feminist approach also required us to be mindful of them, not least because the members of the judiciary we consulted often said that they considered the parties to the case to be their first audience. Vicky Conway mobilised the symbolic weight of the judicial imaginary to offer an unprecedented apology, 'on behalf of the Irish judiciary' for the treatment of Joanne Hayes. More often, those re-writing judgments tried to honour the personal costs of participation for the original litigants. Lorna Fox O'Mahony explained:

> [On rewriting a mortgages case] She's the one fighting to keep a roof over their heads … it's the women in the family who are fighting the building societies and trying to the last hour to defend the property … I've tried signalling that it's her who's on the front line here.

Several judgment writers made contact with surviving litigants and their legal teams, and drew on interviews with them in their construction of the rewritten judgments. Others drew on published historical and archival sources. Participants re-writing judgments featuring very conservative litigants sometimes struggled to make contact. Describing an effort to get access to copies of legal submissions advanced by an anti-choice group in an abortion case, one participant noted; 'They did seem very positive … until I mentioned 'feminist!'. It was also important to be conscious of representation of litigants from minoritised groups, particularly where the original judgment was scant on the details of the litigant's own story. In that respect, our participants had to practice a certain reflexivity and consider their own investments in majority identities, and how these might intersect with the power dynamics of 'playing the judge'. As one of a handful of men writing for the project, Colin Murray noted:

[29] M Donnelly, '*PM v St. Vincent's Hospital*' in M Enright et al (eds) *Northern/Irish Feminist Judgments: Judges' Troubles and the Gendered Politics of Identity* (Bloomsbury 2017).

> … you come to [writing] the judgment knowing there's a real chance you're just adding another male voice to the law … you come to Northern Ireland in particular, where there is not a single female judge at High Court or Court of Appeal level, it does feel almost like you're taking the place of someone who could do this job better or more authentically, and certainly I've had that in the forefront of my mind.

Related issues arose around our representation of the judicial role. Judges are indirectly the 'subjects' of any FJP. There is very little judicial writing in either jurisdiction which discusses the process of judgment writing and no published empirical work, to our knowledge, on judicial decision-making practice. It is understandable that members of the judiciary whose cases are re-written may find the implicit criticism disagreeable.[30] We invited judges to enter into the project's spirit of collaboration by participating in drafting workshops. Of course, the ability to invite judges to participate is predicated on having academic capital to guarantee access and enable them to be sure of our credentials. We invited judges to participate in the project when most of our judgments were already drafted. This meant that our judgment-writers had begun to appreciate some of the difficulties inherent in assuming a judicial role. This enhanced our discussion with judges. That said, we might have benefitted from having these discussions before the project began in earnest: they might have freed us from some self-imposed constraints which judges, and especially novice judges, in practice do not necessarily share. Participants in drafting workshops speculated about the practical agency of judges which disclosed a prevailing frustration with, for instance, what were perceived as instances of poor judicial practice or wasted opportunities for judicial activism. Sometimes judgment writers articulated a detailed sense of their own imagined judicial role in constrained and technocratic terms. Claire McCann, for example, imagined herself as a High Court judge[31]:

> I think maybe if I take that idea and not think about myself as an actual High Court judge wanting to get a promotion to the Court of Appeal someday, it might be possible to be a bit more robust about it, because at the moment I'm feeling very constrained and held back ... I've taken out loads of things [that I feel didn't] belong in a High Court judgment, but

[30] Ms Justice A Donnelly 'Book Review: Northern/Irish Feminist Judgments Judges' Troubles and the Gendered Politics of Identity' (2017) Irish Judicial Studies Journal 90. Baroness Hale directly addressed this issue in the preface to the English book while in the Australian project a judge was given the opportunity to re-write one their own judgments.

[31] K FitzGibbon and J Maree Maher 'Feminist Challenges to the Constraints of Law: Donning UnComfortable Robes' (2015) Feminist Legal Studies 253.

> maybe I just need to be more out there. More outré. Get it overturned on appeal, who cares? Maybe I'll get a really positive Court of Appeal judge in the next instance …

Similarly, Fiona de Londras set limits to her drafting of a judgment on recognition of same sex marriage:

> [Something] that unconsciously restrained me ... was imagining that if I was a single judge, sitting on the High Court, first of all I would never have been assigned this case, because I am openly gay; secondly, if I had been assigned the case I would have been so cautious about my reasoning as a result of that that I would have engaged in quite conservative judicial interpretation.

Our ad hoc discussions with practising judges disrupted some of these assumptions. While the issue of plausibility was an on-going background concern in many ways, participants from the judiciary eased that anxiety by bringing their lived experience of judgment writing to the fore.

IV – Reflections

In the time since our FJP finished, its work has resonated with a revitalised feminist legal discourse in Ireland, driven by the movement to repeal the 8th Amendment, and by reflection during the Decade of Centenaries on the ways in which the newly independent state failed and mistreated women and children. The project has been important to artists[32] seeking to make space for survivor testimony of this legal experience. In our FJP, people who would not be appointed to the bench were able, however fleetingly, to occupy and subvert a judicial position. The FJP challenged and transformed our own sense of legal academics' relationship to judgment. As the project becomes embedded into the law school curriculum, it is doing the same for many students. However, it seems clear to us now that Irish feminist legal studies also requires a 'radical opening up' to dialogue with victims and survivors of legal violence. For example, we did not include litigants in our project even though, at present, feminist scholars are asking sustained questions about the Irish courts' poor treatment of survivors of sexual violence, people abused in religious institutions, pregnant women and

---

[32] S Browne, 'In the Shadow of the State' <http://www.sarahbrowne.info/work/in-the-shadow-of-the-state/> last accessed 6 March 2019. The artists were influenced by our FJP in developing their performances. A Roper, *No Country for Women* <https://www.rte.ie/player/gb/show/no-country-for-women-30005310/> last accessed 6 March 2019. The producer drew on our FJP in her preparatory research.

others. In this vein, Patti Lather argues that feminist researchers should tell research stories which situate researchers not as experts who 'say what things mean', but as witnesses who testify to the lives of others.[33] Despite the critical potential of feminist judging, we cannot say that it enabled us to escape the 'expert' position, merely to rethink it. The most important constraints imposed by FJPs in this respect are those of form and knowledge, which tend to empower participants who are already well versed in legal reasoning. It is doubtful whether the book of judgments the project produced is accessible, in itself, to women outside the academy.

Following on Lather's exhortion to build on 'failures',[34] our experience with the FJP has encouraged us to think about forming future inter-disciplinary research agendas which might be better equipped to overcome those limitations; allowing us to express legal ideas in a range of ways, and to avoid making participation conditional on narrow kinds of legal expertise. It may be that judgment itself is less hospitable to these efforts than, for example, a deliberative legislation project. It may be that a genuinely feminist judgments project will seek to reimagine, not only judicial texts, but the whole performance by which they are produced, re-staging tribunal hearings or even trials. Internationally, women's courts have created important opportunities for collaboration between lawyers, artists, activists and women with direct experience of legal processes. The Women's Court of Sarajevo,[35] for example, holds public hearings, and admits women's testimony in a range of artistic forms, bringing it into conservation with expert testimony and legal judgment. In this way it unsettles the univocality of legal texts, and lays open all stages of the remade legal process to the agency and critique of women affected by the law under analysis. Such modes of research might be less controlled, more halting, and more exhausting, but they may be able to reinvent the lessons of feminist judgments, to retrieve spaces for genuine co-production of new feminist legal knowledge.

---

[33] P Lather, *Getting Lost: Feminist Efforts Towards a Double(d) Science* (SUNY Press 2007) 41.

[34] P Lather, *(Post) Critical Methodologies: The Science Possible After the Critiques* (Taylor and Francis 2017) 115.

[35] <http://www.zenskisud.org/en/Metodologija.html>.

Chapter 6

'Changing Ireland, Changing Law': Access to Justice and Understanding the Lived Experience

*Ivana Bacik and Mary Rogan**

I – Introduction and Research Questions

Public interest litigation is notable for the long and arduous journeys behind the cases which are eventually discussed in legal books and articles. While the barriers to public interest litigation are well known, less is understood about the experiences and perceptions of those whose circumstances were behind those seminal decisions. This chapter provides reflections on a research project which sought to shed light on, understand and prioritise the voices of those who have taken cases in order to achieve progressive social change in Ireland. The 'Changing Ireland, Changing Law' project arose out of our desire, as lawyers and legal academics, to hear more of the stories behind some of the cases which have changed Ireland.[1] These cases do not just comprise a set of legal principles, as important as those principles are; they are also part of the personal history of an individual and a family. We wanted to examine the personal impact that taking such litigation can have on individuals, as well as analysing the most effective ways in which to support both the litigants and the civil society organisations which work with them in using the law to secure change. We also wanted to give prominence to the voices of the individuals with these experiences, as well as non-governmental organisations, using a form of co-production in our methods, whereby participants presented their experiences verbally at a series of seminars or workshops, and then wrote about them for an edited collection published subsequently. The methods we used involved a form of narrative inquiry, where litigants spoke about their experiences alongside responses from academics, civil society activists and lawyers placing the

* Ivana Bacik, Reid Professor of Criminal Law, Criminology and Penology, Trinity College Dublin and Mary Rogan, Associate Professor in Law, School of Law, Trinity College Dublin.

[1] The research ultimately culminated in the publication of Ivana Bacik and Mary Rogan, *Legal Cases that Changed Ireland* (Clarus Press 2016).

case into a wider context. This approach, in our experience, provided a way for the lived experience of public interest litigation to be seen more clearly than is possible in legal analyses of such cases. It also allowed for interactions between understandings of the broader social context or legal significance of the case and its day-to-day unfolding from the point of view of the person instigating it.

In order to allow for this interaction to unfold, our primary research method was to organise a series of seminars, open to the public, each based on a common theme, wherein litigants would speak about their experience of taking a particular, noteworthy case, accompanied by academic and legal experts on the area affected by the particular case. Relevant NGOs also participated, discussing the case and its implications, but also wider issues of strategy in trying to use the law to effect social change.

We recognised that the project was somewhat unusual, involving individuals and NGOs not as research participants in the traditional sense of the social sciences, and subject to traditional interviews, which are then coded and analysed, but rather as individuals speaking and writing directly and in public about their experiences. We wanted their voices to be made prominent and heard directly, rather than being mediated through our interpretations, reflecting a more general move towards participatory research in socio-legal studies. We also felt it to be a challenge to categorise the seminars or workshops in the ways that academia demands – did they constitute research, dissemination of research, or impact activities? In our experience, each seminar largely defied, or at least crossed, these traditional boundaries and provided the audience with a new insight into well-known legal cases, because they enabled the perspective of the litigant to be heard, as well as providing an opportunity to analyse the effect of each case and the broader social context. Each seminar generated a lively and dynamic engagement between litigants, lawyers and activists, and proved enriching and enlightening for all concerned. We wanted to capture the spirit of the seminars in the resulting edited collection. The result was that the workshops themselves were kinds of 'findings', allowing each participant, and the audience, to give their perspectives on the issues discussed. From those workshops, participants were then invited to review and revise their remarks in light of the discussion and provide a written account for publication in an edited collection.

While this method resulted in a traditional academic output, an edited collection, it is more difficult to characterise the other outcomes of the work. The workshops were ways of sharing information and for participants to discuss their views and opinions in public, but they were also encounters which shaped those ideas and formed the basis for the written pieces. Academic measurements need, in our view, to be modernised to take account of the particular nature of community-based research methods and activities such as those embarked upon in this project. More importantly, however, we encourage other academics to consider these kinds of methods, having found them to be amongst the most rewarding and inspiring professional activities we have ever undertaken.

II – Methodological Approach and Methods Used

The idea for the project grew out of conversations we had been having together about the way in which specific legal cases had brought about social change in Ireland. We agreed that it would be a worthwhile exercise to explore some of these cases in more detail and to uncover more about the human stories behind them, so in 2015 we applied to the Irish Research Council (IRC) seeking funding for a research project into public interest litigation, with a focus on how individual legal cases had brought about social change. Through the project, we sought to promote public discussion and reflection on how law and social change interact in Ireland. We called our project 'Changing Ireland, Changing Law' (CICL), and were delighted to be awarded funding for the project under the IRC's 'Engaging Civic Society' stream of its New Foundations scheme. The research was undertaken jointly between the Dublin Institute of Technology and Trinity College Dublin Law School (our then respective institutions), and additional funding was also secured from both the Trinity College Dublin Equality Fund, and the TCD Arts and Social Sciences Benefactions Fund.

The methodology that we envisaged for the project was unusual and, we hoped, innovative for a legal research project. We sought to gather but also disseminate material on public interest litigation through organising a series of four seminars, which took place between May and October 2015. In each of these seminars, we sought to explore the relationship between legal action and social change on a range of specific topics: women's rights, LGBT rights, immigration cases and public interest litigation generally.

We were conscious that very little literature exists in Ireland on public interest litigation or on the background to particular transformative cases.[2] We wished to build on the academic work of our colleague Gerry Whyte, and

[2] For the stories behind some leading cases taken before the Supreme Court, see R Mac Cormaic, *The Supreme Court* (Penguin Ireland 2016).

his insights were crucial to the project and the publication.[3] We also wanted to build on these approaches, which primarily engage in the examination of case law with legal and policy analysis of the implications of a particular judgment. Our approach sought to facilitate the telling of the stories behind the cases, to examine what drove the litigants to take these actions, and the consequences for them.

We chose four topics for the workshops. Though conscious that there are many other areas which we could have explored, and would ideally like to do so again, those four areas were: women's rights; LGBTQ+ rights; immigration; and, finally, the potential role for public interest litigation to influence social change generally. We selected the topics for the seminars on the basis that we both knew of key cases that had been instrumental in achieving change in those four areas; while being conscious that there were many other potential headings that a research project such as this could have examined: disability rights, children's rights, environmental rights, or the rights of Travellers, for example. The topics we chose gave an insight into the core aspects of our research question from a variety of angles. While the specific issues were different, all participants had gone through similar processes in which they had sought to vindicate their rights. This was the key interest of the project, the lived experience and reflections of those involved in the cases, placed into a wider context.

In each seminar, we sought to bring together former litigants, lawyers, NGOs, academics and those interested in the connections between law and social change. Research assistants (Lynsey Black and Colette Barry) worked with us to take a written note or summary of each contribution made at the seminars, having taken a decision that contributors, particularly individual litigants, would feel constrained in speaking freely about their experiences if the seminars were recorded by other means.

In keeping with the requirements of the IRC's 'Engaging Civic Society' funding stream, the project was run in partnership with four non-governmental organisations that have a history of using litigation to further their aims. These were: the Public Interest Law Alliance (PILA), the National Women's Council (NWCI), the Gay and Lesbian Equality Network (GLEN) and the Immigrant Council of Ireland (ICI). We had approached each of these organisations in advance of making our funding application, and our contacts within these non-governmental organisations (NGOs) all expressed great

[3] See G Whyte, *Social Inclusion and the Legal System: Public Interest Law in Ireland* (2nd edn, IPA 2015).

support for the concept behind the research, namely the desire to explore the context for particular cases, the story of the individual litigants involved, and the impact of litigation in bringing about social change. We also wanted the perspective of the NGOs to be part of the research, and to provide an opportunity for them to share their experiences of seeking social change through using law and other means, such as campaigning and advocacy. This collaborative approach with NGOs proved invaluable in supporting our tracing of individual litigants to tell their stories in each seminar.

At each seminar, we heard the perspectives of litigants, practitioners, academics and activists. The first seminar examined how cases on women's rights have changed law and changed Ireland.[4] The litigant's perspective was provided by Máirín de Búrca, one of the two plaintiffs in *de Búrca and Anderson v Attorney General*,[5] the case establishing the right of women to serve on juries; and also by Dr Micheline Sheehy-Skeffington, who in 2014 won a significant claim before the Equality Tribunal on the basis that her employer, NUI Galway, had discriminated against her for promotion on gender grounds.[6] An activist contribution was provided by Orla O'Connor, Director of the National Women's Council of Ireland (NWCI), who gave an overview of some of the key cases that have brought about positive change for women in Irish society.

Professor Yvonne Scannell of Trinity College Dublin spoke of her involvement as one of the initiators of the legal action taken to secure equal taxation rights for married women in the *Murphy v Attorney General* litigation.[7] Mary O'Toole SC provided a practitioner's perspective on the legal cases that have brought about change for women in the context of family law, and Professor Aileen McColgan of King's College London considered the merits of using litigation to bring about change for women's rights. All of the speakers emphasised the personal difficulties encountered in embarking on litigation, including the impact upon private and family life. But litigants and lawyers alike also recognised that change for women's rights has always been hard-fought; and that individual cases have played a vital role in bringing about progress towards gender equality.

[4] The first seminar, 'Women Changing Law, Changing Society', organised with the National Women's Council of Ireland (NWCI), took place on 8 May 2015.

[5] *De Búrca and Anderson v Attorney General* [1976]1 IR 38 (SC).

[6] Equality Tribunal, 13 November 2014, DEC-E2014-078.

[7] *Murphy v Attorney General* [1982] IR 241 (SC).

The theme explored in the second seminar was that of 'Sexual Identity, Law and Social Change'.[8] Senator David Norris spoke eloquently of his own personal experience as a litigant back in the 1980s in the key case leading to the decriminalisation of homosexuality in Ireland.[9] Dr Ann Louise Gilligan and her wife Dr Katherine Zappone (later to become Minister for Children), whose High Court litigation seeking recognition for the right to marry pre-dated the referendum establishing the right to marriage equality, also spoke powerfully about their personal experience of taking this ground-breaking case.[10] The seminar also included contributions from Brian Sheehan of the Gay and Lesbian Equality Network (GLEN), speaking of the extensive and very positive recent legal changes for the rights of LGBT persons in Ireland. Professor Mark Bell of Trinity College Dublin contributed an academic perspective, speaking about the impact that litigation has had for LGBT rights generally. The themes that emerged from these contributions and the engagement with the audience, as in the earlier seminar, included the personal impact of that taking litigation has upon the individual; frustration with court processes and delays was also a significant factor in the cases discussed. But again the desire of litigants and their legal teams to address injustice through the courts was emphasised as the driving force behind these cases. The opportunity to discuss these issues between litigants, academics, activists, lawyers and the audience meant that perspectives emerged which may not have done so through individual interviews. In a traditional interview setting, the interaction is between the participant and the researcher, often involving an interview guide. In this case, litigants were asked to speak about their experiences and memories of the process of taking the case, allowing them to shape and construct their contribution as they wished. The accompanying responses of the academic and legal experts, and the NGO participant prompted further reflection and dialogue, meaning that new perspectives and shared understandings of the subject were developed. The academic contribution, for example, discussed the consequences of the case for later policy or cases, which those involved in the immediate and specific details of the original case may not have been aware of. Similarly, those experts were able to hear about the processes by which certain arguments came to be

---

[8] The second seminar, jointly hosted with the Gay and Lesbian Equality Network (GLEN), took place on 10 July 2015.

[9] *Norris v Ireland* [1984] IR 36 (SC) and [1988] ECHR 22.

[10] *Zappone & Gilligan v Revenue Commissioners* [2006] IEHC 404, [2008] 2 IR 417 (HC).

made before the court or tribunal, and to see how legal strategy can play a key role in the development of jurisprudence The addition of a public audience, and the questions posed from its members, also added an additional, collaborative dimension which an interview setting with a single interviewer could not provide.

The third theme dealt with 'immigration, asylum and legal change'.[11] The seminar on that theme included contributions from Catherine Cosgrave of the Immigrant Council of Ireland (ICI), and from Ghandi Mallak, the individual litigant in a critical Supreme Court case on citizenship rights, *Mallak v Minister for Justice, Equality and Law Reform*.[12] The applicant, originally from Syria, had endured a Kafkaesque process in trying to get Irish citizenship as his applications were continuously refused, with no reasons given for refusal. His persistence in seeking an explanation—and his successful appeal to the Supreme Court against the State's refusals—established the important principle that Ministers and other public bodies must provide reasons for important decisions like denial of Irish citizenship. Dr Patricia Brazil from Trinity College Dublin, and Professor Cathryn Costello from Oxford University, made contributions from a practitioner and an academic perspective about the national and international legal issues involved in this area. The highly complex nature of immigration law was noted as a central theme, along with the State's resistance to recognise immigrant rights. Once again, frustration with long delays in court processes and the consequently detrimental impact upon family life, emerged as a key theme in this seminar.

In the fourth seminar, effectively a capstone session looking at more general themes in public interest litigation, we sought to explore the barriers faced by those seeking to take cases which have an important social dimension more directly, examining the crucial question: 'Public interest litigation; does it work?'.[13] Contributors included litigant Dr Lydia Foy, who challenged the State's failure to provide for transgender rights in *Foy v An t-Ard Chláraitheoir*.[14] Kevin Brophy, of Brophy Solicitors, provided a practitioner's view of his involvement in a series of different public interest cases; and Professor Gerry Whyte, of Trinity College Dublin, gave an academic

[11] The third seminar, 'Immigration, Asylum and Legal Change in Ireland', organised with the Immigrant Council of Ireland (ICI), took place on 18 September 2015.

[12] *Mallak v Minister for Justice, Equality and Law Reform* [2012] IESC 59, [2012] 3 IR 297 (SC).

[13] The fourth seminar, held in conjunction with the Public Interest Law Alliance (PILA), took place on 16 October 2015.

[14] *Foy v An t-Ard Chláraitheoir* [2007] IEHC 470, [2012] 2 IR 1 (HC) [137].

overview of public interest litigation and identified some key themes that have emerged from many such cases, including the themes of personal impact and frustrating delays, as discussed further below. This session acted to consolidate many of the themes which had emerged in previous seminars, and shaped our thinking on the recommendations we wished to make about public interest litigation and access to the courts.

While this project had always intended to conduct public workshops with the participants followed by, if they so wished, an opportunity to provide a paper for an edited collection, it is interesting to consider how the perspectives might have been different had we conducted interviews in private and with the contributors to the seminars individually. While such methods would also make for a most interesting study, allowing for common themes to be developed in particular, we feel our approach had particular merit in this context. It allowed litigants to speak directly about the case, and for recollections and perspectives to emerge from shared reflections and in response to the analysis of others. This was a key rationale behind choosing the workshop method. We wanted to ensure there was a dialogue between academics, lawyers, those working in NGOs and litigants so that they could reflect, collectively, on the processes involved in bringing a case with a strong social dimension, and the consequences of doing so, personally and more broadly. This interaction, along with the participation of the audience, allowed for the development of discussions with the involvement of a variety of experts which could not have taken place with a single interviewer.

Another approach to this topic would be to conduct interviews with public interest law litigants and draw themes from those interviews. Researchers could do so on an anonymous basis, or by identifying the litigant involved, with their consent. Both strategies would result in important insights into how public interest litigation is experienced in practice. Our experience was that our chosen method was a better way of achieving the objective of giving prominence to the voice of the litigant. First, the views and opinions of the litigant were given directly at the workshops and in the edited collection. Second, having an anonymous interview would have severely constrained our ability to refer to the features of the case which were of central interest to the research, as doing so would have made them identifiable. Thirdly, the litigant was able to respond directly to the contributions made by others, with a chance to give their own view and take on the interpretations and contextualisations that were made.

We also presented our findings from the research project at a public hearing before the Oireachtas Joint Committee on Justice on 25 November 2015.[15] At that hearing, we made presentations alongside the spokesperson for our lead NGO partner, Rachel Power from PILA. We spoke on a number of the key themes that had emerged from our research at that point; including the importance of NGOs in raising awareness of issues which require legal reform and social change; the problem of delay, identified as a critical difficulty for individual litigants in all the seminars; the personal impact of taking litigation; and problems around limited provision for civil legal aid and the very real prospect of being sued for costs. This part of the project fulfilled our aim of bringing the learning from the sharing of experiences to policymakers.

We had planned to make this presentation, following the conclusion of the seminar series, in order to inform lawmakers about the potential difficulties facing litigants, and about possible legal reforms to facilitate the practice of public interest litigation in Ireland. But we had not necessarily anticipated the production of any further research output from the project. This project had been essentially a tentative, even experimental, research endeavour. For us, a major objective—providing space and time for litigants, lawyers, activists, academics and policymakers to share their experiences in public—had been fulfilled.

However, as it transpired, the seminars were so well-attended, and provoked such a positive reaction from audience participants, both lawyers and non-lawyers, that we then decided to develop the material further. During 2016, we worked with the seminar contributors on working the proceedings into a publication, exploring how public interest litigation has contributed to social change in Ireland. Following the workshops, we received papers from our academic and legal experts and NGO representatives which were amended to take account of the discussion in the workshop. We also had notes of the contribution made by the litigants themselves, who also, in some cases, had their own prepared remarks to work from. We edited the contributions from the academic and legal experts in the usual way for an edited collection. As for the litigants, we sent them the notes made of their contribution at the workshop and brief guidelines about the expected length of a usual contribution. We offered support if this was desired. The litigants' contributions, which were at the heart of the project, were then very lightly

[15] See transcript of proceedings, headed 'Social Change in Ireland', at <http://oireachtasdebates.oireachtas.ie/debates%20authoring/debateswebpack.nsf/committeetakes/JUJ2015112500002?opendocument#AA00100> - accessed on 8 March 2019.

edited for conformance with the house style. The contributions were grouped by themes, in accordance with the themes for each workshop.

The book that arose from the seminar proceedings, *Legal Cases that Changed Ireland*, was published in November 2016 by Clarus Press. The book places the direct experiences of litigants alongside reflections from non-governmental organisations, practitioners and academics.

III – Challenges and Ethical Considerations

We encountered various practical challenges as we pursued this research project, at least partly because of the unusual methodology, specifically the fact that this was the first project in Ireland where litigants spoke directly on their own experiences of the process of taking public interest cases alongside NGOs and legal and academic experts. Unusually in this kind of academic research, however, funding was not a difficulty as we had secured sufficient resources to cover all the expenses associated with organising a series of seminars. However, we had difficulty initially in identifying and locating relevant individual speakers, particularly the litigants. We drew up a list of key cases that we had identified under each of the headings and then proceeded to seek to track down those individuals who had been most closely involved with those cases, as litigants, lawyers, activists or academics. We had particular difficulty in identifying individual litigants willing to come forward and speak publicly about cases associated with the assertion of rights of migrants to Ireland. However we sought and received vital support in identifying relevant individuals who were willing to speak through our NGO partners. As we sent out invitations and received responses, we had to modify our seminar plans accordingly. The date for the LGBT rights seminar, for instance, had to be changed due to the holding of the Marriage Equality referendum in May 2015, which obviously took over all the time commitments of our NGO partner, GLEN, during that period.

Once we had secured attendance of key contributors for each of the seminars, a further challenge arose in the decision about how to record the seminars. We took the decision that conducting audio or audio-visual recording would operate to constrain the contributions made by speakers; we wanted to ensure that all present, including those in the audience, felt free to contribute 'off-the-record'. Thus our only record of contributions made was the written summary or note taken at each seminar by our research assistants. This decision certainly meant that the seminars were lively and free-flowing, but we regretted subsequently that we did not have verbatim records of some of the powerful contributions made by the litigants, in particular, which would be very useful for all those interested in this area. A more accurate record would also have made the preparation of the book more straightforward. It is difficult to say with hindsight whether recording the proceedings would have resulted in a more restricted or guarded discussion. Our experience was that most of the litigants we worked with were highly adept public speakers and had previously discussed their stories in public. As such, we were probably overly cautious in our approach. However, future researchers dealing with more contemporary matters, or issues of particular sensitivity, may still wish to avoid contemporaneous recording to ensure a full and frank discussion can take place.

We also had to consider the ethical implications of the research, in particular for the individual litigants whom we were asking to speak personally about their experiences of taking legal cases. This was a priority in our work. We sought, and received, ethical approval for the work from the Dublin Institute of Technology Research Ethics Committee. We were aware that, although our participants had spoken about their experiences publicly before, there would be an emotional impact for them, both in giving the reasons for taking their cases in the first place, and in recounting their experiences of often arduous legal processes more generally. We, therefore, created an information sheet outlining the nature of the work and the fact that the seminars would be open to the public, and explaining that they would be named as the author of the resultant pieces in the edited collection. We created an informed consent form which we asked our litigant contributors to sign before taking part in the seminars. Participants were informed that they could choose not to participate in the seminars or the publication at any time, without giving a reason, with no consequences. We explained, further, that no direct benefits would accrue from participating, but that we hoped the work would inform policy and practice and might assist in formulating proposals for policy change and changes in practice. It was also very important to us that participants had the support of non-governmental organisations who could direct them to other supports if needed.

Other ethical considerations arose when asking practising lawyers to speak about cases in which they had been professionally involved. To address these considerations, we decided at the outset that we would only examine cases that had been concluded through the legal system, as this would make it easier for both litigants and lawyers to speak about their experiences. It would also mean that we could take a reflective approach in considering the impact of such cases on achieving social change in Ireland. We were also aware that lawyers are under professional obligations and subject to codes of practice which would determine what they could speak about.

IV – Findings and Reflections

Ultimately, we concluded that the legal cases examined in our research constituted tales of courage. The 'Changing Ireland, Changing Law' project highlighted the personal experiences of seven individual litigants, with six cases covered, spanning over 40 years. These litigants ranged from those wanting to highlight a particular issue to those who were truly in crisis, but all of whom felt they had been left with no option but to navigate the courts.

The stories they shared over the course of the project spoke to us of fear, desperation, and exhaustion. Those who have taken cases which have shaped Ireland have faced the daunting prospect of taking on the State and its powerful institutions. They have taken on the unfamiliar procedures and sheer inertia of the legal process, and have experienced the financial worries that embarking upon legal proceedings brings with it.

In all of this, they have had to endure the often immense personal pressure involved with participation in litigation, both for themselves and their families. In different ways, their cases have developed from very difficult circumstances – matters of deep personal importance, which chimed with emerging patterns of social change. Often, the courts have been the final port of call for litigants following an already long process, and often also following recourse to a succession of State bodies or institutions.

But the stories we shared during the project are also those of hope, humour, and a passion for fairness and justice. The support of family and friends, the enduring desire to be heard, to seek vindication, and the sheer indomitability of the individual litigants themselves, all shine through these accounts. The tenacity of the lawyers who fought on their behalf is also evident. The kinds of cases which impact on the public interest usually involve colossal effort, ingenuity, resilience and limited promise of reward. While those cases may eventually make ground-breaking precedent, the path to those judgments can be frustrating and exhausting. The lawyers involved in these cases are true defenders of the rule of law, giving those who might otherwise not be heard a path towards the vindication of their rights through litigation.

However, the range of obstacles involved in such litigation became increasingly apparent during the course of our research; in particular, obstacles related to time and money. Often already vulnerable as a result of the circumstances giving rise to the litigation, the legal process can be an additional heavy burden. The personal toll of legal action is often significant. At times, the adversarial nature of the legal process means that litigants can find that their own stories and experiences become lost. The long period of time involved, the possibility of intrusive publicity, and the complexity of the legal process all come at a substantial cost to those taking public interest cases.

We concluded that delay in securing access to justice, in fact, represents the most significant obstacle to justice experienced by litigants. Delay may be seen as an inevitable problem within the justice system, but some of the delay experienced in these cases was particularly severe. For example, it took 14 years for David Norris to see the decriminalisation of homosexuality take place; nearly 10 years for Ghandi Mallak to be granted Irish citizenship; over 10 years for Katherine Zappone and Ann Louise Gilligan to achieve their goal of marriage equality; and over 20 years for Lydia Foy to receive her new birth certificate.[16] True, Máirín de Búrca fared better in her 1970s case seeking equal rights for women to sit on juries. Indeed, the new Juries Act was passed in the same year as her successful Supreme Court decision, but this was still five years after her initial arrest.[17]

Thus, we found that public interest litigation represents a long and painful road for individuals, who often have to put their lives on hold while it is proceeding through the courts. But it does not have to be this way for public interest cases. We argued in the book resulting from the research project that fast track processes for litigation should be possible. Indeed, in Ireland, the Commercial Court has radically changed the litigation landscape to achieve speedy determination of high value commercial cases, and there is little dispute that it has done so efficiently and effectively. Commercial Court cases now tend to receive a trial date within five weeks of entry to the list. This is achieved through judge-managed litigation with strict application of short deadlines for exchange of legal documents, costs penalties for delays, and rules that have had a very significant impact on pre-litigation tactics. No other court list gets the judicial resources provided to the Commercial Court – and yet, while many of its decisions are clearly significant, the list

[16] *Norris v Attorney General* [1984] IR 36 (SC); *Norris v Ireland* [1988] ECHR 22; *Mallak v Minister for Justice, Equality and Law Reform* [2012] IESC 59, [2012] 3 IR 297 (SC); *Zappone and Gilligan v the Revenue Commissioners* [2008] 2 IR 417 (HC); *Foy v An t-Árd Chláraitheoir & Others* [2007] IEHC 470, [2012] 2 IR 1 (HC).

[17] *De Búrca and Anderson v Attorney General* [1976]1 IR 38 (SC).

has not made anywhere near the same contribution to jurisprudence in respect of public interest cases as other divisions of the High Court, or indeed the Supreme Court.

An inefficient courts system may be the predominant source of delay, but it has also arisen by virtue of the political process negating or impeding the effective implementation of judgments. In his 2007 High Court judgment in Lydia Foy's case, for example, McKechnie J expressed considerable frustration that the government had done nothing to legislate for the recognition of transgender persons in the previous five years, despite the fact that the European Court of Human Rights in Strasbourg had found against the United Kingdom in 2002 over the same issue.[18] Following that 2007 judgment, it took another eight years before legislation was finally passed to enable recognition of transgender persons. This delay seriously undermined, not only the rights of Dr Foy, and the rights of the transgender community in Ireland, but also the mechanisms of the ECHR Act itself and the perceptions around the prospect of enforcing rights under the Convention in this State.

We also found that the issue of money, and the fear that a losing party will end up facing a massive legal costs bill for their opponent's fees, remains a further significant barrier to public interest litigation. Because of the general 'costs follow the event' (i.e. that the losing party will pay the costs of the other side as well as his or her own costs) rule, the potential cost of fees for a litigant's own legal representatives tends not to be the main obstacle. Indeed, throughout the course of the 'Changing Ireland, Changing Law' seminars, lawyers were commended for their kindness and empathy in dealing with delicate cases, but they were also praised because money was rarely discussed with their clients. Lawyers taking on these cases tend to do so pro bono—or on a no foal, no fee basis—which means committing to extensive work without expectation of a fee. However, a game of financial roulette arises should the case lose and an adverse costs order be made against the plaintiff. That is the real reason why many people will be very afraid to take on such litigation.

Public interest litigation is unpredictable, inherently so, because the case is often being litigated in order to seek clarification of the law. There are very few cases where one can be certain of winning, and an adverse costs order on a sufficient scale could bankrupt an individual. Of course, in public interest litigation, the defendant is usually the government, and when the significant

[18] *Goodwin v United Kingdom* (2002) 35 EHRR 18.

resources of the State are weighted against those of the individual litigant, it is likely to 'chill' many individuals out of taking a case.

However, it is open to the Irish courts not to follow the usual costs rule where a case is considered of sufficient public interest, but this potential after-the-event approach provides plaintiffs with no certainty as to costs – although greater certainty could be provided for, through something employed in other jurisdictions, a Protective Costs Order. We argued in the conclusion to our book arising out of the research project that measures like Protective Costs Orders (PCOs) should be considered in public interest litigation. These are orders made at the outset of litigation, providing a plaintiff with certainty as to the costs outcome. This might provide that there will be no order as to costs, that the plaintiff's liability for costs will be capped at a certain amount, or that the defendant will pay costs, even if the plaintiff is unsuccessful. PCOs are already in existence in Ireland in relation to environmental cases under the Aarhus Convention, which provides that there should not be unduly prohibitive costs preventing the public from participating in environmental decision-making and procedures.[19]

A further point on the costs of litigation we found to be of critical importance: test cases and public interest litigation are specifically excluded from civil legal aid. In reality, the vast majority of public interest law cases are taken by small law firms, and some by independent law centres such as FLAC (Free Legal Advice Centres). But there are many cases with a point to be pursued, an anomaly or injustice a lawyer would like to challenge but simply cannot, because of the pressures of juggling cases and resources. A public interest case can be all-consuming, with no certainty as to getting paid. The pressures are no less real for independent law centres. When it may take eight years to implement a clear and unambiguous judgment, this becomes a huge undertaking for an organisation with limited resources – it means that equally pressing matters have to be put on hold indefinitely.

We concluded that civil legal aid needs much reform; to remove the ban on the Legal Aid Board taking or funding test cases would be a start. If this ban were removed, the Board could contract out work to the NGOs as the legal aid bodies have done in Britain – thus such cases would not necessarily represent a direct drain on the limited personal resources of the Board. This would be one creative approach to ensuring enhanced access to justice for public interest litigants.

[19] The United Nations Economic Commission for Europe, Convention on Access to Information, Public Participation in Decision-Making and Access to Justice in Environmental Matters (1998).

Finally, it became clear from our project that litigation alone should not be seen as a universal panacea for social problems. For various reasons, there are serious risks involved in launching any case; even apart from the practical implications for the individual litigant around time and money discussed above. Where litigation is used as a strategy in seeking to achieve change, it is best carried out alongside other strategies, including engagement with the political system and public awareness-raising. Embarking on any multi-faceted strategy like this will require a body of support around the individual litigant or litigants; in this respect, the experiences of litigants in public interest cases show the importance of effective non-governmental organisations.

Public interest litigation is not straightforward; even when a case is won, often that will represent only the start of a process, rather than the end. Experience shows that various strategies may typically have to be employed in order to translate a positive judgement into real social change on the ground, through public awareness or education campaigns. The critical importance of well-run and resourced non-governmental organisations for a healthy civic society is a key theme emerging from the research.

The findings from this project, we believe, were greatly enhanced by the methodological approach we took. Our research showed that the individual's voice was often lost in the legal process, which has its own language and constraints concerning the type of information which can be used in court. A reading of any of the judgments examined in our research can, inevitably, give but a glimpse of the personal story which led up to the decision. We wanted to emphasise those stories, and to hear directly from those who took the decision to litigate. Our methodology, where litigants spoke directly at workshops, responded to the interpretations of their particular case, and wrote personally about the legal process, allowed those voices to be centre-stage. This is perhaps the greatest strength of the methodology we employed.

The second characteristic which we consider contributed to the success of the project was our community-based approach. From the inception of the project we worked closely with NGOs in order to design the workshops and to ensure that the wider issues of strategy in using the law to effect change would also be discussed and examined in this research. As well as presenting findings concerning how public interest litigation works from an NGO's perspective, the seminars also acted as an opportunity for those NGOs to discuss litigation as a strategy with others.

The seminars that formed the core of this research project were, for us, among the most insightful and inspiring legal events we had ever attended. It is rare for lawyers or academics to hear from the truly courageous individuals who have given up years of their lives in many cases to pursue litigation, often thanklessly and against all the odds. Hearing the stories of individual litigants during each of the seminars provided us with an important reminder that the law is not abstract – it is about people, their lives, their stories and their experiences of a legal system that is simply not doing what it should to accommodate them.

On conclusion of the project, we reflected that the stories told in the seminars and the resulting book tell us much about Irish society, and how it has changed in the last four decades. They tell us about the tenacityof those who took landmark legal cases, and the indefatigability of the lawyers who represented them through the process. These individual litigants, and those who supported them, are champions of the rule of law in Ireland. A desire to bring their stories to greater public attention had initially prompted us to commence upon this project. We wanted to provide an opportunity to hear the personal accounts of the people behind some of the key cases which have changed Irish society.

We concluded, finally, that this research project had offered a rare opportunity to share experiences and stories as to how social change may best be effected through litigation. We had planned the research project on the basis that the substance of it was contained in the collaborative approach. In bringing together litigants, lawyers, activists, academics, policy makers and members of the public in attendance at these seminars, and in publishing papers arising from the seminars, we hope to have enabled the development of a mutual learning process. We believe this process will help to forge useful alliances between civil society activists and legal professionals, and to encourage reflection on how litigation may be used to advance progressive legal change in future.

CHAPTER 7

Researching with Hard to Access Communities: Understanding the Relationship between the Trans Community and An Garda Síochána in Ireland

Amanda HAYNES, *Jennifer* SCHWEPPE *and Niamh* DILLON*

I – INTRODUCTION

Ireland has the ignominious record of having the second highest prevalence of transphobic hate crime in Europe, and research conducted by the Hate and Hostility Research Group (HHRG) at the University of Limerick has shown the rates of police reporting for such crimes are extremely low. In this context, the HHRG in partnership with the Transgender Equality Network Ireland (TENI) sought funding from the Irish Research Council to explore the nature of the relationship between the trans[1] community and the police in an Irish context. The funding award was granted, and we undertook research with the purpose of providing an evidentiary base for inclusive policing for trans people in Ireland. This chapter will describe the context to the research, including a brief introduction to both the HHRG and TENI, outline the methodological approach, and then present our reflections on some of the challenges that we encountered in completing the research. We highlight the complexities of conducting research with a hard to access, vulnerable community, which extend beyond logistical to political and ethical dilemmas.

Transphobic hate crime in Ireland

In 2013 the European Union Agency for Fundamental Rights (FRA) carried out a survey on the experiences of transgender people living in the EU.

* Senior Lecturer in Sociology, University of Limerick; Senior Lecturer in Law, University of Limerick; PhD Candidate, Department of Sociology, University of Limerick.

[1] For the purpose of this report the term 'trans' is used as an umbrella term for gender-variant people. The sample is inclusive of trans, non-binary, gender fluid, genderqueer and androgynous people.

The survey *Being Trans in the European Union* highlighted the experiences of 6,579 transgender respondents.[2] The FRA survey included 139 respondents living in Ireland, who identified as transgender. There is no official enumeration of the trans community in Ireland,[3] however, by December 2017, 298 gender recognition certificates had been issued by the State.[4] While the number of trans people living in Ireland is undoubtedly multiples of this figure, the community is still relatively small.

The results of the 2013 FRA survey identified Ireland as having the second highest prevalence of hate-motivated violence against trans people among the EU Member States, with 13 per cent of respondents reporting that they had been physically attacked, sexually attacked or threatened with violence in the preceding 12 months, in contrast to the EU average of eight percent.[5] The Report also found Ireland to be among the five EU Member States in which trans people were most likely to have experienced hate-motivated harassment in the preceding 12 months, 31 per cent as compared to the EU average of 22 per cent. Published the same year, TENI's *Speaking from the Margins: Trans Mental Health and Wellbeing in Ireland*, found that 21 percent of trans respondents reported having experienced physical violence, 44 per cent reported experiencing physical intimidation and threats, 15 per cent reported sexual assault, and seven percent reported being raped, all as a direct result of being trans.

Globally, trans people are recognised as being at particular risk of violence, even in comparison to other commonly targeted groups: trans people are more likely to experience hate crime than LGB people.[6] Perry[7] and Moran

---

[2] European Union Agency for Fundamental Rights, *Being Trans in the EU: Comparative analysis of EU LGBT survey data* (FRA 2014) <http://fra.europa.eu/en/publication/2014/being-trans-eu-comparative-analysis-eu-lgbt-survey-data> accessed 26 September 2017.

[3] According to the FRA 2014 report, it is almost impossible to determine the proportion of trans people in the general population: most states do not register trans people and not every person pursues a legal or medical path that would produce a record.

[4] BeLonG To Youth Services, *Review of the Gender Recognition Act 2015* (*Welfare.ie* 2018) <https://www.welfare.ie/en/downloads/GRA%20Review%20Report.pdf> accessed 23 January 2019.

[5] European Union Agency for Fundamental Rights, *Being Trans in the EU: Comparative analysis of EU LGBT survey data* (FRA 2014) <http://fra.europa.eu/en/publication/2014/being-trans-eu-comparative-analysis-eu-lgbt-survey-data> accessed 26 September 2017.

[6] K Browne and J Lim, *Count Me In Too: Lives in Brighton and Hove* (University of Brighton and Spectrum 2008); MA Walters and Jenny Patterson, *Transphobic Hate Crime and Perceptions of the Criminal Justice System* (University of Sussex 2015).

[7] B Perry, *In the Name of Hate: Understanding Hate Crimes* (Routledge 2001).

and Sharpe[8] link high rates of victimisation to visibility, while Human Rights Watch[9] highlight a link to discrimination – forced out of employment, trans people may resort to sex work enhancing their vulnerability. International research points to differences in exposure to violence among trans people based on racialised identity and migrant status.[10] These forms of intersectionality and the potential fluidity of victim and offender statuses can be important to understanding trans people's experiences of policing.

The same transphobia and cisnormativity which generate an increased risk of victimisation for trans people, can also serve as an obstacle to their equal access to the criminal justice system, including among the public's first point of contact – the police. Internationally, trans people's interactions with the police are integrally shaped by gender norms. Experiences with police officers and services are often characterised by apathy, ignorance and in some cases outright hostility.[11] In some national contexts, police themselves perpetrate transphobic violence.[12] Exclusion from the protection of the State is thus both a symptom and a cause of trans people's wider social marginalisation.[13] It is in this context that the research was undertaken. The research was funded by the Irish Research Council under its New Foundations programme, and the Transgender Equality Network Ireland was a partner to the project.

Minoritised communities and the police in Ireland

Access to justice is a fundamental human right protected by a multiplicity of international agreements and conventions. In order to guarantee access, minoritised communities must be provided with both procedural and

8 LJ Moran and AN Sharpe, 'Violence, identity and policing: The case of violence against transgender people' (2004) 4(4) Criminal Justice 395–417.

9 Human Rights Watch, *Sex Workers at Risk: Condoms as Evidence of Prostitution in four Cities* (*Human Rights Watch*, 2012) <https://www.hrw.org/sites/default/files/reports/us0712ForUpload_1.pdf> accessed 3 October 2017.

10 D Meyer, 'Evaluating the Severity of Hate-motivated Violence: Intersectional Differences among LGBT Hate Crime Victims' (2010) 44 (5) Sociology 980–995.

11 LJ Moran and AN Sharpe, 'Violence, identity and policing: The case of violence against transgender people' (2004) 4(4) Criminal Justice 395–417.

12 C Gossett, *QTGNC Resistance, Neoliberalism and social memory* (UCLA Centre for the Study of Women 2010).

13 S Phelan, *Sexual strangers: Gays, Lesbians and the Dilemmas of citizenship* (Temple University Press 2001).

substantive supports to ensure their rights are protected.[14] However, these supports operate on the presumption that the communities in question trust the system to act in their best interests. For minoritised communities this is not always the case. In England and Wales, the approach of the criminal justice system to hate crime was in some ways reconceptualised due to a recognition of the existence of prejudice within the criminal justice system, and an acknowledgment of the effect that this could have on access to justice.[15]

There have been some studies done on relationships between minoritised communities and the police or legal system in Ireland, which without exception demonstrate lower levels of trust in those institutions on the part of such communities than the majority population.[16] Prior to embarking on this research, we were provided with an analysis from the European Social Survey, a cross-national representative survey of attitudes and behaviours which has been conducted in Ireland since 2002.[17] In 2012, 2014 and 2016, all participants were asked to rate their trust on a scale of 1–10 in four key state institutions: the parliament; the legal system; the police; and politicians. All participants were also asked whether they were a member of a group that was discriminated against (referred to here as 'the minoritised population'). When the results for questions relating to group identity and trust were cross-tabulated, the minoritised population expressed consistently lower levels of trust in all four institutions.

When asked to indicate their levels of trust in the legal system on a scale of 0 to 10, with 10 equating to complete trust, for individuals from the majority population the mean score was between 5.29 and 5.5 across the three years (see Figure 1). Average scores for the minoritised population's response to the same question ranged from 4.24 to 4.61 across the same period. Results for trust in the police (see Figure 2) were higher, but again a gap remains between the majority (ranging from scores of 6.69 in 2012

---

[14] D Rhode, *Access to Justice* (OUP 2004). We define a minoritised community as 'a social group with a shared characteristic whose position in society is characterised by relative disadvantage which may be economic, cultural, or political. This position is produced by power imbalances, and maintained by, existing structural inequalities in society.'

[15] N Chakraborti and J Garland, *Hate Crime: Impact, Causes and Responses* (2nd edn, Sage 2015).

[16] A Mulcahy and E O'Mahony, *Policing and Social Marginalisation in Ireland,* Working Paper 05/02 Dublin: (Combat Poverty Agency 2005) 5; A Haynes and J Schweppe, *Policing Beyond the Binary: The Relationship between the Trans Community and An Garda Síochána* (TENI forthcoming).

[17] Analysis of the ESS data was provided to us by the postdoctoral researcher associated to the European Social Survey for Ireland, Dr A Erbe Healy.

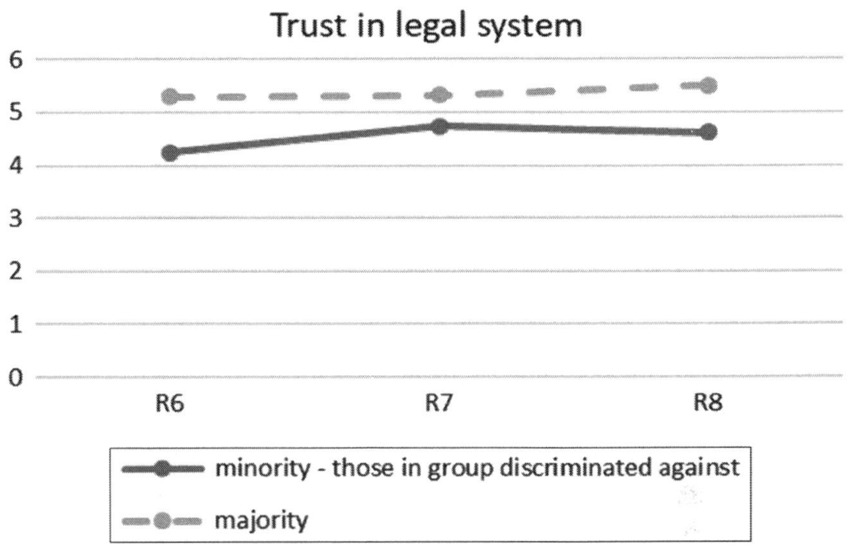

Figure 1: ESS – Trust in the Legal System

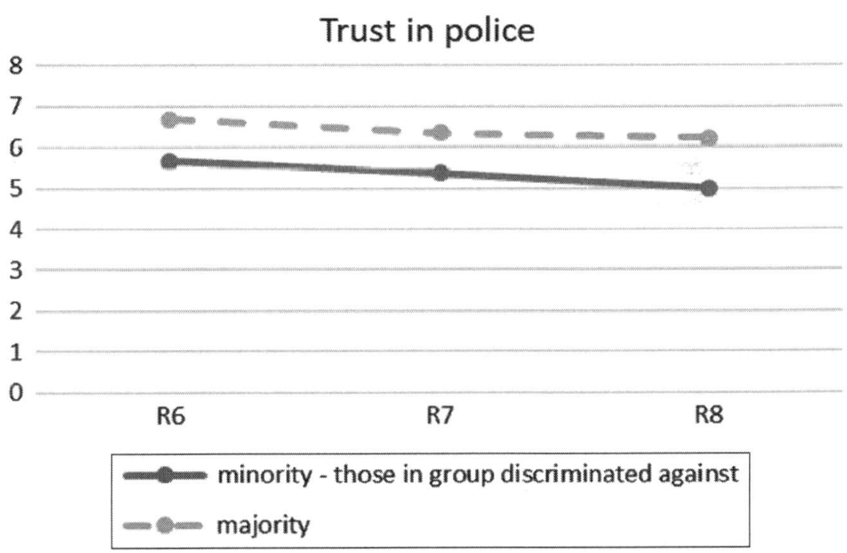

Figure 2: ESS – Trust in police

to 6.23 in 2016) and the minoritised population (ranging from scores of 5.67 in 2012 to 5 in 2016).[18]

Another potential means of determining whether minoritised communities are exercising their rights of access to justice comparably to that of the majority community is through an examination of the first point of contact that victims have with the criminal justice process: the point of reporting crime. The Garda Public Attitudes Survey (GPAS) reveals a very high rate of reporting by victims of crime generally, with 86 per cent of crimes experienced by respondents having been reported to An Garda Síochána in Quarter 2 of 2017.[19] A lower rate of reporting is recorded in the Quarterly National Household Survey Crime and Victimisation Module.[20] Here, 62 per cent of household crime was stated to have been reported to An Garda Síochána, with 54 per cent of crime against individuals reported.[21]

When we examine the reporting rates of victims of hate crime specifically, the figures are demonstrably lower. Our analysis of third party reporting mechanisms found that, of the 143 incidents involving hate crimes reported to ENAR Ireland in 2015, only 24 per cent were reported to An Garda Síochána.[22] Of the 11 hate crimes reported to GLEN in the same year, only three were reported to An Garda Síochána, representing 27 per cent.[23] For members of the trans community, the figures give cause for concern: in 2014, 25 per cent reported their experiences to An Garda Síochána.[24] This dropped to five per cent in 2015, with no reports being made to An Garda Síochána in 2016 by those who logged transphobic crimes with TENI.[25] It is in this latter context that we began to particularly explore the relationship between the trans community and the police.

---

[18] Results for trust in the country's parliament for the majority ranged from scores of 3.63 in 2012 to 3.86 in 2014 to 4.51 in 2016; for the minoritised population the scores ranged from 2.91 in 2012 to 3.11 in 2014 to 3.65 in 2016. Results for trust in the country's politicians for the majority ranged from scores of 3.12 in 2012 to 3.37 in 2014 to 3.76 in 2016; for the minoritised population the scores ranged from 2.8 in 2012 to 2.67 in 2014 to 3.1 in 2016.

[19] An Garda Síochána, *Public Attitudes Survey Bulletin Q2 2017* (An Garda Síochána 2017).

[20] Central Statistics Office, *Crime and Victimisation, Quarterly National Household Survey Q3 2015* (Central Statistics Office 2016).

[21] ibid 2.

[22] J Schweppe and A Haynes, *Monitoring Hate Crime in Ireland: Towards a Uniform Reporting Mechanism?* (HHRG 2016) 16.

[23] ibid 27.

[24] A Haynes and J Schweppe, *STAD: Stop Transphobia and Discrimination Report 2014–2016* (TENI 2017).

[25] ibid.

Research design

The research sought to illuminate the relevance in an Irish context of growing international evidence of difficulties which trans people experience in accessing justice, and of the potential for direct victimisation and revictimisation by police officers. While there have been a number of surveys of the general public's attitudes towards the police conducted in an Irish context, none have included a 'diversity booster' which would allow for the exploration of experiences of minoritised groups, and since 2007, the Gardaí have not conducted any research on the experiences of particular minority communities. In this context, it was important to conduct research with members of the trans community. Given the scale of the task involved in conducting a general population survey, we chose to address trans peoples' experiences, not as a subset of a larger sample, but as direct participants to research designed with and for that community in particular.

In terms of methodology, we utilised a socio-legal approach, which sought to study 'law, legal processes and legal phenomena using social research methods'.[26] We sought to answer our research question by utilising mixed methods, i.e. qualitative and quantitative methods, incorporating focus groups, individual interviews, and an online survey.

In this context, we specifically addressed rates of, experiences in, and obstacles to reporting crime victimisation to An Garda Síochána. However, recognising that An Garda Síochána provide a diverse range of services and that there are a multiplicity of contexts in which members of the public interact with members of An Garda Síochána, the research also addressed everyday interactions in the context of policing public events and processing official documents. Finally, and particularly recognising the growing body of international evidence of the risks to trans people of being misgendered in custody, the research explored the experiences of trans people who are stopped, detained or arrested by An Garda Síochána.

Further, the research sought to produce attitudinal data in line with questions on trust, satisfaction, and perceptions of capability and effectiveness, asked in the Garda Public Attitudes Survey (GPAS) in the same time period to compare attitudes to the police among the trans community to those among the wider population in Ireland. Ultimately, the research provides an evidentiary base for inclusive policing for trans people in Ireland.

---

[26] M Burton, 'Doing Empirical Research: Exploring the decision-making of magistrates and juries' in D Watkins and M Burton (eds), *Research Methods in Law* (Routledge 2013) 55.

II – Methodological Approach and Methods Used

As outlined above, the research employed a mixed methods approach. The primary data for the research was gathered by means of an online survey regarding respondents' experiences with and perceptions of An Garda Síochána. The survey design was informed by qualitative focus groups and interviews on the same topics.

Sampling strategy

Rarely is it possible for a researcher to collect data from every person (or other unit of study) whom they are interested in learning about.[27] Consequently, sampling strategies are employed to identify a subset of the overall group of interest from whom data can be gathered. Approaches to sampling can be divided into two key types, each of which have a different underlying rationale.[28] While probability sampling prioritises establishing the statistical representativeness of the findings, the emphasis in non-probability sampling, employed in our research, is on achieving depth of understanding.[29]

Both focus group participants and survey respondents were recruited using a volunteer sampling strategy.[30] Volunteer samples are often recruited through the advertisement of the research objectives and criteria for inclusion through channels likely to reach suitable participants, requesting people who meet the criteria for inclusion to volunteer to participate in the study. This sampling strategy can be particularly useful when potential participants are dispersed throughout the community or are difficult to access directly.[31] The research was advertised extensively by TENI via email distribution lists, closed and publicly accessible social media, via its website, and directly to peer support group members. The researchers attended community meetings to advertise, and answer questions from potential participants about the research. Perhaps due to increased cultural visibility, the amount of research conducted with Ireland's small trans community has increased

---

[27] Obstacles to collecting data on an entire population relate primarily to resource constraints and accessibility.

[28] A Bryman, *Social Research Methods* (4th edn, Oxford 2012); G Payne and J Payne, *Key Concepts in Social Research* (Sage 2004).

[29] JW Creswell, *Qualitative Inquiry and Research Design: Choosing among five approaches*, (2nd edn, Sage 2007).

[30] V Jupp, *The Sage Dictionary of Social Research Methods* (Sage 2006).

[31] K Elmusharaf, *Qualitative Sampling Techniques Training Course in Sexual and Reproductive Health Research* (RCRU 2012) <https://www.gfmer.ch/SRH-Course-2012/research-methodology/pdf/Qualitative-sampling-techniques-Elmusharaf-2012.pdf> accessed 3 October 2017; K Parahoo, *Nursing Research: Principles, Process and Issues* (Palgrave MacMillan 2006).

significantly in the past couple of years.[32] We completed three focus groups and four one-to-one interviews, across three cities, in preparation for the design of the online survey. The survey itself garnered a total of 61 responses.

Thompson and Phillips maintain that there has been very little exploration of strategies for including 'nonassociative' hard-to-access communities in research. That is; 'those whose members do not normally have contact with other members.'[33] Their research suggests that recruiting potential participants by reaching out through advertising and media can be a highly effective means of including particularly hard-to-reach populations in a sample.[34] Another effective, more policy focused approach which Thompson and Phillips recommend and one which was also used in our research was to link the research with outreach services to include people who may not be in contact with relevant statutory services, an approach we found useful in this research.[35]

Focus groups and interviews

This qualitative phase of the project took the form of three focus groups and four one-to-one interviews. The methodology had originally envisaged four focus groups, one in each of four cities (Dublin, Cork, Limerick and Galway). Ultimately, three focus groups were successfully convened, two in Dublin and one in a regional city, due to an inability to attract a sufficient number of participants to a fourth focus group. Potential participants were offered the choice of a one-to-one interview should this be their preference: four individuals were interviewed using this format. These four one-to-one interviews widened the geographic scope of this phase of the research to a third city and permitted the inclusion of additional participants who could not be facilitated within a scheduled focus group or who did not wish to participate in a group interview. The individual interviews were unstructured in format and adapted the focus group questions to a one-to-one scenario. The unstructured interview has been described as a 'conversation with a

---

[32] See for example: A Higgins, L Doyle, C Downes, R Murphy, D Sharek, J DeVries, T Begley, E McCann, F Sheerin and Si Smyth, *The LGBT Ireland Report: National study of the mental health and wellbeing of lesbian, gay, bisexual, transgender and intersex people in Ireland* (2016); *STAD: Stop Transphobia and Discrimination Report* (2014 TENI); J McNeil, L Bailey, S Ellis and M Regan, *Speaking from the Margins: Trans Mental Health and Wellbeing in Ireland* (TENI 2013).

[33] S Thompson and D Phillips, 'Reaching and Engaging Hard-to-Reach Populations With a High Proportion of Nonassociative Members', (2007) 17(9) Qualitative Health Research 1292.

[34] ibid.

[35] ibid.

purpose'[36] and indeed a goal of the unstructured interview is create a relaxed and informal atmosphere in which the interviewer and interviewee can converse. Interviews are considered one of best methods to elicit information from key informants due to the often effective personal aspect of face-to-face interactions[37] while Kitzinger[38] suggests the focus group is a non-discriminatory means of encouraging participation from people resistant to one-to-one interviews or who feel that they have nothing of significance to contribute to the study.

Focus groups generate data from communication between multiple research participants. Although there may be a reluctance among some researchers to collect information on sensitive topics such as crime via group formats, focus groups can offer advantages in research with minorities; the group format is held to '...provide collective power to marginalised people'[39] and reduce the power imbalance between researcher and participants,[40] amplifying the voice of the participants.[41] The group format provides for mutual support within the group facilitating people '... to speak about uncomfortable and formidable topics'.[42] Successful focus groups require skilled facilitators, however, and training is key.[43] With the approval and assistance of TENI, we were given an opportunity to engage with pre-existing groups, and we found that the dynamics of the group facilitated an open and engaged discussion between members.

According to Duggleby,[44] focus group analysis should follow the same criteria as other forms of qualitative research, the analysis should depend on the methodological approach chosen by the researcher. The analysis of focus group data, however, differs in that it incorporates three levels of data; the individual, the group and the group interaction. Duggleby suggests that group interaction data should be analysed separately from group and individual

[36] M Hennink, I Hutter and A Bailey, *Qualitative Research Methods* (Sage 2011) 109.

[37] S Best, *Understanding and Doing Successful Research* (Pearson 2012).

[38] J Kitzinger, 'Qualitative Research: Introducing focus groups' (1995) 311 (7000) BMJ: British Medical Journal 300.

[39] P Liamputtong, *Focus Group Methodology: Principles and Practice* (Sage 2011).

[40] S Hesse-Biber and P Leavy, *The Practice of Qualitative Research* (Sage 2010).

[41] DJ Warr, '"It was fun ... but we don't usually talk about these things": Analyzing Sociable Interaction in Focus Groups', (2005) 11(2) Qualitative Inquiry 200.

[42] P Liamputtong, *Focus Group Methodology: Principles and Practice* (Sage 2011) 114.

[43] D Stewart and P Shamdasani, 'Focus Group Research: Exploration and Discovery' in L Bickman and D Rog (eds), *Handbook of Applied Social Research Methods* (Sage 1998) 505.

[44] W Duggleby, 'What about focus group interaction data', (2006) 15 (6) Qualitative Health Research 832–840.

data and that the findings should then be integrated with the other data.[45] Data collected from both the focus group discussions and the one-to-one interviews were subject to thematic analysis.

Thematic analysis approaches categorise the most important ideas which occur in the data into specific themes. These themes can be taken from an individual account or, more typically, from a number of participant accounts.[46] The focus group and interview data was used to determine what themes were salient for the community and, in addition to providing unique insights into individual participants' experiences of policing in Ireland, provided an informed basis for developing relevant questions for the online survey.

Survey

An online survey probed the wider relevance of themes arising in the qualitative phase of the research. The Garda Public Attitudes Survey was also consulted to develop questions about policing practices and experiences which would not only document trans experiences, but also provide for comparisons between trans community and majority population experiences of policing in Ireland. The Office for Democratic Institutions and Human Rights recommends allowing for '... meaningful comparisons between the surveys and data recorded by criminal justice agencies'.[47] While our focus was on experiences of policing rather than experiences of crime, we felt that such comparisons would be instructive as to the degree to which the trans communities' experiences of policing might be influenced by cisnormativity. The survey provided the opportunity for people to document unique experiences via 'other' options and included opportunities for respondents to explain their selections via text boxes.

The survey was disseminated online to maximise the opportunity for trans community members across Ireland to participate. As not everyone in the trans community has access to or contact with organisations or support groups, it was felt that using an online survey was the best means of extending the reach of the research. The survey was distributed via EU Survey, and was therefore hosted within the European Union and subject to EU data protection laws. EU Survey is an online survey management system developed by the European Commission to create and publish forms

[45] ibid.

[46] M Barkham, G Hardy, J Mellor-Clark, *Developing and Delivering Practice-Based Evidence: A Guide for the Psychological Therapies* (Wiley-Blackwell 2010).

[47] Office for Democratic Institutions and Human Rights, *Hate Crime Data-Collection and Monitoring Mechanisms: A Practical Guide* (OSCE 2014) 34.

and surveys for distribution to the public.[48] The survey remained live for exactly two calendar months during the summer of 2017. It garnered a total of 61 responses, which we considered a satisfactory result.

III – Challenges and Ethical Considerations

The research study received ethics approval from the Arts, Humanities and Social Sciences Research Ethics Committee (approval number 2016-06-04-AHSS). Given the sensitive nature of the topic, engaging as it does with a marginalised community, on the topics of victimisation and encounters with the State, it was appropriate that the research met the institution's high ethical standards. Research ethics are codified principles concerned with delimiting 'proper practices' for a profession. Their purpose is to ensure the rights and welfare of people, groups and communities who are the subjects of social research. Although each research question raises unique ethical issues, two of the most common and important ethical principles which researchers must uphold are informed consent and confidentiality. Informed consent is the agreement of the individual to participate in the study after being informed of all facts which would be likely to influence his/her willingness to participate.[49] The purpose of informed consent is to allow people to protect their own interests. In relation to the focus groups and interviews, we ensured that participants were fully informed as to the nature of the research by providing them with an information sheet which explained the nature and purpose of the research prior to the engagement, and also providing the participants with consent forms which detailed the research procedures. The survey set out this information on the first page. We made our informants aware before commencing our research that their participation was voluntary and that they could withdraw from the interview or focus group at any time. They were also provided with the contact details of the researchers and given the opportunity to ask questions throughout the entire research process. Potential focus group participants were also offered the choice of a one-to-one interview should this have been their preference.

Voluntarism relates to the participants' freedom to choose to participate in the research. Voluntarism may be threatened where there is an unequal relationship between researcher and potential participant, or between the potential participant and any third party who will have knowledge of and an

---

[48] European Commission, *About EU Survey* (*EU Survey,* 26 July 2017) <https://ec.europa.eu/eusurvey/home/about> accessed 11 September 2017.

[49] JW Creswell, *Qualitative Inquiry and Research Design: Choosing among five approaches,* (2nd edn, Sage 2007).

interest in their participation.[50] Researchers must be particularly cognisant of the manner in which relationships between potential participants and gatekeepers who mediate access may impact upon their capacity to choose participation or non-participation. In this case, the invitation to participate was distributed via an intermediary, TENI, and voluntary participation was emphasised.

Anonymity and confidentiality are often conflated but can be conceptually differentiated. Anonymity is achieved where even the researcher cannot associate the participant with their data.[51] This is realised, in particular, by the use of data collection instruments which can be completed in the absence of the researcher and which do not collect personal data, as in the case of our survey. Confidentiality is achieved where the researcher can connect the identity of the participant with their data but protects the participant's identity, as in the case of our interviews.[52]

Providing for the participants' anonymity or confidentiality is essential to maintaining their privacy and is a fundamental concern of social research. With respect to the online survey, questions regarding personal characteristics were limited to gender identity, gender expression, age and nationality, as these were considered to be potentially significant sources of differentiation based on international and national research.[53] In reporting findings and incorporating illustrative quotes from the online survey and the qualitative phase of the research, we worked closely with TENI to ensure that none of the participants are identifiable.

Participants must be made aware of any limits to the researchers' assurances of confidentiality,[54] including relating to group formats of data collection. From a general perspective, a disadvantage of the focus group format is that the researcher can make guarantees of confidentiality only with regard to their treatment of the data. They can request that each participant respects the privacy of the group interview setting, but they cannot ensure that this will be

---

[50] ibid.

[51] G Crow and R Wiles, *Managing anonymity and confidentiality in social research: the case of visual data in Community research*, ESRC National Centre for Research Methods NCRM Working Paper Series 8/08.

[52] John W. Creswell, *Qualitative Inquiry and Research Design: Choosing among five approaches,* (2nd edn, Sage 2007).

[53] E Vasquez del Aguila and P Franey, *Supporting LGBT Communities: Police ToolKit.* (2013) 17 <http://researchrepository.ucd.ie/handle/10197/4819> accessed 3 October 2017.

[54] S Venkatesh, 'Research: The Researcher's Dilemma' (2006) 24(4) Law and Social Inquiry 987–991.

upheld.[55] In most cases, focus group participants were recruited from peer support groups where participants had previously shared sensitive information and were sensitised to the limits of confidentiality in a group setting. The limits of confidentiality in the focus groups were clearly explained to the participants both in the information letter and at the start of each focus group. On commencing the focus group, participants were also reminded that they were under no pressure to contribute and could decline to answer any question or leave at any time. Participants did vary in the amount to which they contributed. While most participants made detailed contributions, a minority chose to focus on assenting or dissenting to clarifying questions posed to the group, rather than providing individual responses.

IV – Findings

The findings of our research highlighted ongoing inconsistencies in trans community members experiences with An Garda Síochána, in relation to the reporting and recording of crime, access to specialist officers, provision of information on support services, and respectful treatment, and others – which raise structural concerns with respect to, for example, training and policy. The findings of the research show that when we compare findings of Quarter 3 of the Garda Public Attitudes Survey 2017 against those of the Trans Policing Survey 2017 (carried out for the purposes of this research in the same timeframe), there are clear attitudinal differences between the general and trans populations in respect to An Garda Síochána. For example, trans community members responding to the Trans Policing Survey 2017 reported far lower levels of trust in An Garda Síochána than respondents to the Garda Attitudes Survey taken in the same time period. Whilst 43 per cent of the general population categorise themselves as having 'high trust' in An Garda Síochána, only eight percent of respondents to the Trans Policing Survey 2017 feel the same way. Similarly, whilst 69 per cent of the general population categorise themselves as being 'very satisfied' or 'quite satisfied' with An Garda Síochána, only 34 percent of respondents to the Trans Policing Survey 2017 felt the same way.

V – Challenges and Ethical Considerations

Our research on the relationship between the trans community in Ireland and the police in Ireland has produced new knowledge, which we believe will be useful to both parties. The process of conducting the research was immensely satisfying, but also intellectually challenging, requiring us to make

[55] K Kaiser, 'Protecting Respondent Confidentiality in Qualitative Research' (2009) 19(11) Qualitative Health Research 1632–1641; J Kitzinger, 'Qualitative Research: Introducing focus groups.' (1995) 311(7000) BMJ: British Medical Journal 300.

methodological choices which caused us to reflect deeply upon the principles which drive our research. This section documents some of the clarity which we acquired through this process.

Choosing non-probability sampling strategies

In relation to the particular challenges associated with this research, the small sample size posed challenges, as the lack of an appropriate sampling frame can sometimes be seen as counterproductive to the task at hand. Presenting the findings of research undertaken with a more robust sample population would be easier to stand over as probability sampling techniques could be employed which could arguably be perceived as more representative of the community. More generally, the issue as to whether a volunteer sampling approach is methodologically acceptable is one which we grappled with throughout the research, the ultimate question being whether it is possible to rely on data which is collected in this manner. Research which requires the self-selection of participants can introduce participant bias to the research which can produce less randomised findings. However, where the community in question is small, dispersed across the country, and in some cases hidden, it is only through this self-selection process that any research can be carried out. Thus, the typical requirements of 'statistically representative' findings cannot be possible where a community is historically or culturally marginalised, particularly where the research seeks to explore the relationship between that community and an organ of the State.

In this project, we chose to accept that risk because, given the available resources, a survey was the most effective means of reaching more members of a community who remain relatively stigmatised and are geographically dispersed, but who we knew we could reach online via TENI's online platforms. While the survey findings are not statistically representative, they identify a diversity of experiences which in itself points to the need for the development of consistent practices supported by clear policy. Moreover, the data evidences patterns of perceptions and experiences at a level which, particularly among a small population, cannot be readily dismissed as exceptional. A strength of the sample is its inclusion of men/men with a trans history (50 percent, 30 people), women/women with a trans history (18.3 percent, 11 people) and binary/gender fluid/gender queer/androgynous people (23.3 percent, 14 people.[56] Survey responses

[56] One person declined to provide their gender identity while the remaining five participants chose the option of 'other' (8.3 percent).

were analysed using SPSS (statistical analysis software) with a particular focus on descriptive statistics.[57]

We accept that the volunteer sampling strategy we used both in respect to our survey and our qualitative methods of data collection will always be impacted to some extent by self-selection, and can be criticised for that. However, not even TENI had access to a sampling frame which would permit the random selection of a sample. Official membership of TENI is not confined to trans people, while its online platforms reach multiples of its members. It is worth noting that both the survey and the qualitative approaches elicited both positive and negative accounts of policing practices.

Focus groups and power differentials

The focus group format offers many advantages in conducting research with vulnerable communities; ethically it offers peer support to participants while prompting recall and allowing participants to cross-check information through the dynamics of group interaction. Bloor[58] suggests that the use of pre-existing groups is particularly advantageous. Pre-existing groups can consist of acquaintances, social groups, support groups or friendship groups. Such groups can draw one another's attention to details relevant to the research which may have otherwise gone undisclosed. Another advantage of pre-existing groups is that participants in research of a sensitive nature will not have to be over cautious about disclosing a status or characteristics to other group numbers given that the research relates to this characteristic and as such will be shared by all participants.[59] Participation in a group discussion may also appear less daunting if the participants have an existing knowledge of one another.

Research application

The resulting report incorporated specific recommendations for developing trans aware and trans positive policing practices, informed by the research and by international good practice. The report was published by TENI and received and launched by an Assistant Commissioner in An Garda Síochána. In this sense, the research sought not only to produce new knowledge regarding the relationship between the trans community in Ireland and An Garda Síochána, but to use that knowledge to identify actions which would address issues of concern arising. It is our intention that the research be of

---

[57] W Trochim, *Descriptive Statistics* (*Social Research Methods,* 20 October 2006). <https://www.socialresearchmethods.net/kb/statdesc.php> accessed 11 September 2017.

[58] M Bloor, *Focus groups in social research* (Sage 2001).

[59] ibid.

practical use both to organisations advocating for trans people and to An Garda Síochána, as well as adding to international literature in the fields of policing and gender. While we are alive to value of theorisation, and actively contribute to the development of academic knowledge, we believe that there is a particular onus on researchers working with vulnerable communities, who often occupy a position of relative power and privilege to their research participants', to conduct research which is relevant to their research participants' lives. In line with the quality criteria of 'utilization/application/action orientation' advocated by the influential qualitative methodologists Miles and Huberman,[60] we sought to conduct research with the potential to inform recommendations for positive change. While it was not within our capacity to enact that change, we ensured that the research was disseminated to those with that capacity, and in a format, which was both persuasive and accessible. Academic and action-oriented research are not mutually exclusive. In our experience, as researchers committed to translational research, a single study has diverse applications (academic, practical, political), which provides researchers with a 'mandate ... for reporting results in forms tailored, and forums targeted, to specific audiences'.[61]

Positionality

Having moved beyond the presumption that detached objectivity will necessarily produce better research, a rich body of literature has developed addressing the limitations of outsider research and the politics of representation.[62] In our work with the trans community, our personal sensitivity to our outsider status and to issues of power has been buttressed by the cautions available to us from this research literature. We are sensitised to the potential impact of our status on the research, particularly with respect to defining the parameters of relevant experience and their interpretation.[63]

For these reasons, we chose a mixed methods approach to this research. The qualitative methods which were employed in collecting data were selected for the open-endedness and flexibility. They were intended to provide trans participants with the opportunity to identify the practices, processes and policies salient to their relationship with the police, rather than

[60] MB Miles and M Huberman, *Qualitative Data Analysis: An Expanded Sourcebook* (Sage 1994) 280.

[61] M Sandelowski and J Leeman. 'Writing usable qualitative health research findings' (2012) 22(10) Qualitative health research 1410.

[62] cf R Merton, 'Insiders and Outsiders: A Chapter in the Sociology of Knowledge' (1972) 78(1) American Journal of Sociology 9–47.

[63] cf H Gans, 'Toward a Reconciliation of "Assimilation" and "Pluralism": The Interplay of Acculturation and Ethnic Retention' (1997) 31(4) International Migration Review 875–92.

our defining the parameters of the enquiry. The discursive character of the focus group and qualitative interview was also essential to accessing the participants own interpretations of their experiences. These open-ended methods informed the design of the survey instrument which was made available online. Although composed largely of closed-ended questions, we sought to also incorporate in the survey many opportunities for participants to explain their responses to closed-ended questions in their own words.

Insider status is far from a guarantee of access. Given the internal heterogeneity of any community, insider researchers may engender different reactions from different parts of the population, while apparent outsiders may have other points of commonality with potential participants on the basis for example, of ethnicity, class, or gender.[64] Nonetheless, outsider status can present additional challenges not only in securing access, but also in generating rapport, and therefore quality interaction with participants.[65] As we have described TENI acted as an important intermediary in accessing a difficult-to-reach population. It is worth noting that the individual researchers and the research group had a record of working with TENI and supporting trans rights, and self-identify as trans allies. This history may have aided us in recruiting participants and in achieving rapport. We have no doubt that partnership with TENI, and the organisations' endorsement of the researchers, was also influential in these regards. Certainly, we would characterise participants to the qualitative phase of the research as open, generous, and thoughtful.[66]

With respect to interpretation, TENI were available to us as a sounding board during the interpretative process. We drew on their insider perspective where we had any uncertainty about our interpretation. The organisation had an advisory role in finalising the report and its recommendations. As is unsurprising in the context of a body of literature which documents that insider and outsider roles both have methodological advantages and disadvantages,[67] our outsider status, which may have been limiting in some

---

[64] AM Kusow, 'Beyond indigenous authenticity: Reflections on the insider/outsider debate in immigration research' (2003) 26(4) *Symbolic Interaction* 591–599; P O'Connor, 'The conditionality of status: Experience based reflections on the insider/outsider issue', (2004) 35(2) Australian Geographer 169–176.

[65] ibid.

[66] In this context, a single, particularly reticent, focus group participant stands out in our memories as exceptional. The reasons for their reticence are unknown, as we respect every participants' right to choose how much or how little they share.

[67] S Acker, In/out/side: Positioning the researcher in feminist qualitative research (2000) 28 (1/2) Resources for Feminist Research 189.

ways, also proved useful in recognising certain themes. In particular, our outsider status was important to recognising the normalisation of violence, consequent to the greater risk of exposure within the community.

We believe that partnership with TENI was important to the success, but also the ethicism, of the research. We recognise that as researchers and allies we may amplify the voices of our trans participants, but that voice belongs to them.

VI – Conclusion

In presenting this case study, we have sought to underscore the multidimensional complexity of conducting research with vulnerable communities, recounting not just the logistical challenges we encountered, but, more importantly, the political and ethical dilemmas with which we wrestled. In working with TENI, it has always been our objective to adhere to standards which go beyond 'doing no harm', to seeking positive engagement with participants and positive outcomes for the community. Setting aside the limitations of time and resources, our capacity to strive towards these goals, has been shaped most significantly by our active engagement with social research as a field of study in its own right. Our involvement with this field of study takes the form of ongoing training not only in methods of data collection and analysis, but also in procedural and practical research ethics. It takes the form of attendance at seminars and conferences in which common sense understandings of the relationship between the researcher and the researched are disrupted and critiqued. It takes the form of submersion in the rich body of methodological literature, in which other researchers unveil their own struggles to translate the neat principles of 'good' research practices in the context of the messy realities of fieldwork. Frustratingly, these resources highlight that there are no right and wrong answers in social research, only choices whose appropriateness is utterly context dependent. Nonetheless, it is precisely through these resources that we are sensitised to the range of choices we make as researchers, their potential impacts and possible alternatives. The evaluation of our success in applying this knowledge rests with our partner TENI, and those for whom they advocate.

Chapter 8

Capturing Cultures of Control: Some Reflections on Social Research

Claire Hamilton*

I – Introduction

Arriving onto the criminological scene in 2001, David Garland's rich, yet pessimistic, account of the decline of penal welfarism and commensurate growth of popular punitiveness or '*Culture of Control*'[1] — is anything but uncontroversial. Garland's is a masterful analysis of changes in crime control strategies in the United States and United Kingdom from the late 1970s, including soaring rates of imprisonment and dramatic changes in the emotional tone of crime policy. However, his work paid little attention to differences between countries. The question for criminologists thus quickly became, 'does his thesis hold generally?' Among the many works rushing to contest, qualify or indeed build on his arguments, the Irish case has generated a rich body of scholarship on what may be loosely termed 'Hibernian exceptionalism' or Ireland's tendency to buck such putative international trends.[2] Though ultimately less sanguine than some of these accounts, it was undoubtedly in the shadow of the *Culture of Control* and the related literature that I too embarked in 2006 upon my examination of the 'new punitiveness'[3] in three small jurisdictions, namely, Ireland, Scotland and New Zealand from 1976 to 2006. Given the tendency at that

---

* Professor of Criminology, Maynooth University

[1] David Garland, *The Culture of Control* (OUP 2001).

[2] See, for example, S Kilcommins, I O'Donnell, E O'Sullivan and B Vaughan, *Crime, Punishment and the Search for Order in Ireland* (Institute of Public Administration 2004); D Healy and I O'Donnell 'Probation in the Republic of Ireland: Context and Challenges' (2005) 52(1) Probation Journal 56; D Healy, 'Advise, Assist and Befriend: Can Probation Supervision Support Desistance?' (2012) 46(4) Social Policy and Administration 377; D Griffin and I O'Donnell, 'The Life Sentence and Parole' (2012) 52(3) British Journal of Criminology 611.

[3] Punitiveness has been used to refer both to public attitudes towards punishment and state punitiveness (see, for example, H Kury and TN Ferdinand (eds), *International Perspectives on Punitivity* (Universitatsverlag Brockmayer 2008). It should be noted that it is exclusively *state* punitiveness which forms the subject of this book.

time to treat punitiveness (or penal harshness) as a 'one size fits all' phenomenon extending from the US into Europe and beyond, my motivation was to turn the spotlight on criminal justice as it operated in smaller jurisdictions 'on the periphery'.[4] Another motivation for the research derived from what I felt was a disciplinary bias within criminology towards the measurement of punitiveness through imprisonment rates and a focus on sentencing and prisons. What was unique to my study, therefore, was the application across the three sample countries of a multidimensional tool for measuring punitiveness that incorporated a range of variables reflective of the defendant's journey through the criminal justice system. Thus, instead of focusing exclusively on a state's use of prison at the 'back' end of the system, the test also aimed to capture punitiveness at the 'front' end through the exercise, for example, of police powers or restrictions placed on procedural protections for suspects and defendants.

In the context of this edited collection, what I propose to discuss, after some necessary ground-clearing on the aims of the study and methods used, are the challenges that I faced in identifying, collecting, and particularly interpreting and analysing, the quantitative data necessary for capturing, in Garland's terms, a 'culture of control'. Like many lawyers, I felt less than secure in my abilities in this area, not having been professionally trained in statistics or, indeed, the fundamental principles of social research. This insecurity was probably compounded with the complexities attendant on comparative research, moreover, and the challenges which come with interpreting data at a distance. With the aid of some guidance and excellent advice, however, I managed to locate and analyse the data necessary for the purposes of answering the research questions. Challenging, certainly, but not impossible, the message of this chapter is that collection of quantitative data acts as a powerful complement to both qualitative and doctrinal research and, as such, is certainly not something which legal researchers should dismiss out of hand.

II – Research Questions

In line with the theorising of Garland and others, my first research question sought to establish the extent to which a 'punitive turn' had occurred in Ireland, Scotland and New Zealand over the period 1976–2006. This 30-year period was selected in the light of the fact that many commentators, including Garland, appear to have identified these decades as the period

[4] K Aas, 'The Earth is one but the world is not: Criminological theory and its geopolitical divisions' (2012) 16(1) Theoretical Criminology 5.

during which policies and practices have become more punitive.[5] The term 'punitiveness' is often used loosely to describe a plethora of attitudes, policies and practices but usually denotes a 'tougher' approach to the processing and punishment of offenders.[6] Its most obvious manifestation has been in the US where the eightfold rise in the use of imprisonment since the 1970s has resulted in it now having the highest rate of incarceration in the world. As noted above, the distinctive feature of my study was the broad definition afforded to punitiveness, incorporating variables at the 'front-end' of the criminal justice system (police, prosecution) as well as at the 'back-end' (prisons, probation, etc.) (but without, it should be stressed, any pretence to be exhaustive). Up until that point in the early 2000s most criminologists, including Garland, were content to rely on imprisonment rates (numbers imprisoned per 100,000 population) as a convenient, if imperfect, 'ready reckoner' of punitiveness. The second research question was linked to the first and contemplates the effects of this redefinition of the dependent variable (i.e. the variable being tested). Is custody (or for that matter any singular index) an adequate measure of what states are doing in contemporary crime control? Are there better measures? The final part of the investigation involved a shift away from issues concerning definition and measurement towards the explanatory. Borrowing from Tonry's[7] framework of the three candidate determinants of penal policy—risk, protective and non-factors—it was intended to identify the main characteristics of the three states in question which have influenced the direction of criminal justice policy. Additionally, it was hoped to get a sense of the relative influence of the global and the local: do local factors and institutions merely exercise a mediating effect or do they rather constitute the *primary* determinants of crime control policy? What is the role of policy transfer?

III – Methodological approach and Methods used

Although the collation and analysis of quantitative data formed an important part of the research methodology, this strand of the research was also complemented by further documentary analysis, interviews and field visits in order to provide some understanding of the context in which the three criminal justice systems operated, and also richer data to flesh out the quantitative information. The overall research design was therefore

[5] Garland (n 1) 1–2.

[6] M Tonry (ed), *Crime, Punishment and Politics in Comparative Perspective*, vol 36 of *Crime and Justice: A Review of Research* (University of Chicago Press 2007).

[7] ibid.

predominantly linked with the interpretivist paradigm. Denscombe[8] describes this approach as follows: 'the role of social research must always be to interpret social phenomena, recognising that researchers' thinking will be shaped to some extent by their own experiences and identities as members of the social world within which their work takes place'. This paradigm was best suited to many features of the research such as the 'insider' status of the researcher (as an Irish legal academic researching my own jurisdiction), the contested and fluid nature of the subject matter (i.e. 'punitiveness' – see further below) and the highly exploratory nature of the research in all three jurisdictions. In keeping with the interpretivist paradigm, the research took the form of a multiple or collective case study wherein more than one case (in this instance a country) is selected for intensive investigation.[9] In the current study, three countries—Ireland, Scotland and New Zealand—were selected for 'focussed comparison' based on a 'most-similar' design.[10] The countries selected were all similar enough to enable meaningful comparison, including, critically, population size, but also differed considerably in terms of imprisonment rates[11] and other indicators of penal harshness.

As noted, a multi-method or triangulated approach including both qualitative and quantitative methodologies was adopted in order to attempt to more accurately grasp the punitiveness of each of the three countries. As Brannen observes, one of the major advantages of a triangulated approach is 'its ability to confront contradictions and highlight the fragmented and multi-faceted nature of human consciousness.'[12] It was felt that using a variety of research methods was particularly appropriate in a study exploring a complex and protean concept such as punitiveness given the many different ways in which a state can be punitive.[13] Further, by triangulating the methods employed to include both qualitative and quantitative methodologies, the weaknesses of one set of methods can be offset against the strengths of the other. For example, it is difficult to operationalise the local historico-political

[8] M Denscombe, *The Good Research Guide: For Small-Scale* Social *Research Projects* (McGraw-Hill Education 2014) 2.

[9] RE Stake, *The Art of Case Study Research* (Sage 1995); RK Yin. *Case Study Research, Design and Methods* (Sage 2003).

[10] F Pakes, *Comparative Criminal Justice* (Routledge 2014) 17.

[11] In 2006, Ireland's imprisonment rate was 75 per 100,000 population, Scotland's was 140 and New Zealand's 186.

[12] J Brannen, 'Combining qualitative and quantitative approaches: An overview' in J Brannen (ed), *Mixing Methods: Qualitative and Quantitative Research.* (Aldershot 1992) 31.

[13] D Gordon, 'The topography of criminal justice: A factor analysis of the 'get tough' policy trend' (1989) 3(2) Criminal Justice Policy Review 89.

factors which have so often proved to be critical determinants of penal policies[14] and it is precisely these issues that can be explored through field trips, desk based research and elite interviews. In particular, a detailed analysis of the relevant criminological literature in each jurisdiction, together with the interview data, were critical to forming a sufficient understanding of the extent of penal change over the period.

Data were collected and applied to a 34 variable multidimensional test for state punitiveness which incorporated seven indices, namely, (A) Policing, (B) Procedural Protections, (C) Use of Imprisonment, (D) Juvenile Justice, (E) Prison Conditions, (F) Post-Release Control and (G) Death Penalty. Raw data relating to policing, crime, the use of imprisonment and the operation of juvenile justice were first of all collected and then adjusted for population changes over the period. In practical terms, this meant collecting population data from government agencies such as the Central Statistics Office in Ireland and then dividing the data (e.g. number of prisoners) by the total population of the country in question. In order to avoid working with tiny decimals, statisticians usually multiply this by 100,000 and give the result as a rate per 100,000 people. This was considered important as the population in both New Zealand and Ireland has increased significantly over the study period (Scotland's population has remained fairly static). A scoring system was then applied whereby each of the 34 variables identified in the Table 1[15] was given a score of 10, 20 or 30 denoting low or less than moderate punitiveness; moderate punitiveness; and more than moderate or high punitiveness. A score was awarded based on the punitiveness of the states at the end of 2006 but consideration was also given to how policies and practices had evolved over the 30-year study period. The scores for all the variables in each index were totalled and divided by the total number of variables to get overall punitiveness scores (OPSs).[16] Finally, a mean OPS score for all the indices (the sum of the OPSs for each index divided by seven) was calculated for each of the countries.

In relation to the qualitative data, approximately 8–9 interviews were held with key criminal justice stakeholders in each jurisdiction, including civil servants, academics, lawyers, politicians, crime editors and at least one current or former Minister for Justice. These interviews were conducted

[14] J Neapolitan, 'An examination of cross-national variation in punitiveness' (2001) 45(6) International Journal of Offender Therapy and Comparative Criminology 691, 696.

[15] Please see Table 1 below: 'Indices and Variables Used in *Reconceptualising Penality* study'.

[16] B Kutateladze. *Is America Really so Punitive?: Exploring a Continuum of US State Criminal Justice Policies* (LFB Scholarly Publishing 2009).

mostly during the course of an extended visit to the jurisdiction in question, an experience which was invaluable in itself for the light it shed on each criminal justice system's 'ethos' or ideology.

IV – Challenges

Challenges in carrying out the research came in many forms but in relation to the quantitative aspects of the study can perhaps most usefully be divided into the following categories: (i) operationalisation; (ii) collection of quantitative data; (iii) interpretation of quantitative data; and (iv) analysis of quantitative data.

(i) Operationalisation

One of the early challenges faced in the research was that of operationalising (i.e. defining the measurement of a phenomenon that is not directly measurable) such a protean (and indeed contested)[17] concept as punitiveness. While it is to imprisonment rates that researchers look most frequently in drawing conclusions as to state punitiveness, as already observed, the research sought a more comprehensive understanding of the concept beyond this measure. In this regard, it was influenced by a small yet growing literature pointing to the need to incorporate several other dimensions of the criminal justice system.[18] Most influential, however, was the work of Australian criminologist, Lyn Hinds[19] who had drawn attention to the possibility of increased punitiveness in law enforcement or what she termed the 'front end' of the criminal justice system. In a comparison of punitiveness in the US, Australia and Europe, Hinds broadened the scope of her inquiry to include 'police rates' (the number of police employees per 1,000 population) and police expenditure as well as the conventional measure of imprisonment rates. Her findings suggested the existence of a 'crime control continuum', with Europe and Australia choosing to focus on social control at the 'front end' of the criminal justice system and states in the US (particularly the South) exhibiting a preference for custodial control or the 'back end' of the criminal justice system. Hinds's work, (like that of Diana Gordon[20] before her), points to the importance of taking a holistic

[17] See, for example, R Matthews, 'The myth of punitiveness' (2005) 9(2) Theoretical Criminology 175.

[18] Such as the work of K Pease, '*Cross-national* imprisonment rates: Limitations of method and possible conclusions' (1994) 34(5) British Journal of Criminology 116; B Kutateladze. *Is America Really so Punitive?: Exploring a Continuum of US State Criminal Justice Policies* (LFB Scholarly Publishing 2009) and M Tonry (ed), *Crime, Punishment and Politics in Comparative Perspective*, Vol. 36 of *Crime and Justice: A Review of Research* (University of Chicago Press 2007).

[19] L Hinds, 'Crime control in Western countries: 1970 to 2000' in J Pratt et al (eds), *The New Punitiveness: Trends, Theories, Perspective* (Willan 2005).

[20] Gordon (n 13).

view of a state's crime control policy together with the need to recognise that states exhibit different 'national signatures' in the way they deal with the problem of crime.

Drawing on the above arguments, a 34 variable multidimensional test for state punitiveness was developed across seven indices as indicated above. These indices reflected the broader conceptualisation of punitiveness underpinning the study, beginning at the moment of identifying a suspect and ending at the point of this person's death. It is important to stress that the above test does not claim to advance the selected variables as objective phenomena which unproblematically reflect the 'real' world, but rather as proxies for the punitiveness of the criminal justice system.[21] Still less does it pretend to be an exhaustive measure of the punitiveness or harshness of a state towards its citizens. Several obvious measures of 'system punitiveness' such as the number of searches, arrests and prosecutions, for example, were discounted from the beginning of the study, owing to anticipated difficulties in accessing and interpreting such data (front-end decisions are usually not as well documented as those at the back-end).[22] The test was also confined to variables measuring the harshness of the *criminal justice* system. While convincing arguments may be made for the inclusion of broader mechanisms of social control in a test for state punitiveness,[23] the inexhaustibility of the subject of social control necessitates some selectivity. In this case the compromise struck was a focus on the objects of the criminal justice system only. The test does, however, have a number of advantages over those currently employed. The first of these concerns transparency and the fact that the definition and measurement of punitiveness is given much greater consideration than it is usually accorded. Secondly, in addressing the current bias towards 'back-end' system outcomes, it seeks greater alignment of the punitiveness test with the experience of the offender.

---

[21] For a discussion see Maureen Cain and Janet Finch, 'Towards a rehabilitation of data' in P Abrams, R Deem, J Finch and P Rock (eds) *Practice and Progress: British Sociology 1950–1980* (Allen and Unwin 1981).

[22] In many countries data on arrests, prosecutions and convictions are unavailable. Even if such data are available, it may be unreliable. Pease (n 17) observes a number of anomalies such as data from the Third UN World Crime Survey where some countries recorded more people convicted than were prosecuted which he attributes to the particular characteristics of the criminal process in many countries.

[23] E O'Sullivan and I O'Donnell, '*Coercive confinement* in the Republic of Ireland: The waning of a culture of control' (2007) 9(1) Punishment and Society 27.

(ii) Collection of quantitative data

To the uninitiated, accessing basic data on the operation of a given jurisdiction's criminal justice system may appear a deceptively simple task. In reality, however, it can represent one of the most burdensome aspects of quantitative criminological research, particularly in smaller jurisdictions. A good illustration of this is the gap in the data available on the number of committals (entries) to prison and committals under sentence in Ireland between 1994 and 2000, owing to the absence of Annual Reports on Prisons during this period. Detention rates of juveniles in Ireland are also very difficult to ascertain, primarily owing to the way the statistics are presented. With respect to prisons, in the Annual Reports up until 2005 attention is focused on those under 21 rather than those under 18 so that a definitive account of the juvenile rate of detention is not available for this period.

The situation in New Zealand was also very challenging, with basic information concerning the number of committals to prison and committals under sentence seemingly unavailable on initial inquiry. While I was very fortunate in that the Department of Corrections kindly agreed to compile this information for me from their own data warehouse, there remained considerable gaps in the data provided, such as the number of committals to prison between 1991 and 1997. Accessing crime data in New Zealand also proved problematic in that information on the various categories of crime was only publicly available from the New Zealand Statistics office for the previous 10 years (1996–2006) with earlier data available from the New Zealand Police on a commercial basis. In order to complete the data set I therefore had to pay the police for their time in compiling the information. Scotland was by far the jurisdiction with the most complete records of crime data and data on the penal system, although even there I experienced difficulties in the continuity of the data series owing to the fact that from 1987 onwards penal statistics were presented by financial, rather than calendar, year. While some of these difficulties were surmountable, others were not so that, having exhausted all possible avenues of inquiry, often the only option was to highlight and explain gaps and inconsistencies in the data where they appear.

Before moving on to the difficulties in interpreting the data, it's worth dwelling a while on the problem of over—as well as under—supply of sources of criminal justice data. While this doesn't seem like an obvious problem, challenges can arise when multiple data sources appear to contradict one another. In New Zealand this was the case with the prison population data supplied to me by the Department of Corrections and data which appeared in official reports published by the Ministry of Justice. In this situation it's helpful to consider the methodology employed in the compilation of both sets of data and to speak to the statisticians responsible for its collection if possible. Again, I was very fortunate in that the Department of Corrections was happy to assist in this regard, outlining that the discrepancy may have arisen from the difference between their data sources (musters reconstituted from court sentences and Parole Board orders as stored in their databases) and recorded data held by the Ministry for Justice. It may also help to consult secondary sources such as the academic literature so as to arrive at a satisfactory conclusion about the relative reliability of the two data sources.

(iii) Interpretation of quantitative data

As indicated above, even official sources of criminal justice data offering the advantage of convenience and validity should be approached with circumspection. Jacob puts it well when he likens official statistics to 'the apple in the Garden of Eden: tempting but full of danger for the unwary researcher'.[24] This is all the more so when one considers the many issues to be considered when interpreting statistical data, particularly longitudinal criminal justice data which may be affected by legislative changes, computerisation, changes in counting and recording practices.[25] In an Irish context, the best example of the impact of computerisation is probably the changeover from manual recording of crime to an electronic system (PULSE) in 1999. As Kilcommins et al[26] have noted, the 20 percent increase or 'tidal wave of crime' which followed the introduction of PULSE in 2002 is more than likely a result of the more comprehensive recording resulting from the introduction of that system rather than any change in the underlying rate of victimisation. Similar issues arose with the (less dramatic) increase in the Scottish prison population deriving from the change from manual statistical returns to a computerised recording system in the Scottish penal statistics in 1996.[27] For researchers, particularly those who may not be familiar with the criminal justice system they are examining, changes in recording practices are generally detectable when there has been a dramatic shift in crime or prison rates compared to adjacent years, particularly if the shift continues in future years.[28] In this regard, it is vitally important to keep contemporaneous notes which are as detailed as possible and to draw on these when contextualising trends in prison or crime statistics. Aside from changes in the

[24] H Jacob, *Using Published data: Errors and Remedies* (Sage 1984) 9.

[25] For an overview of these difficulties in relation to the interpretation of criminal justice statistics see Hale et al *Criminology* (3rd edn, OUP 2013), ch 3.

[26] S Kilcommins, I O'Donnell, E O'Sullivan and B Vaughan (n 2) 110.

[27] The Scottish prison population went from 110 per 100,000 population in 1995 to 117 in 1996.

[28] J Neapolitan, *Cross National Crime: A Research Review and Sourcebook* (Greenwood Press 1997) 17.

manner of recording of criminal justice statistics, my experience of comparative research has also underlined the need to be cautious when interpreting crime statistics and, in particular, never to lose sight of these statistics as social constructs which are heavily influenced by institutional targets and priorities. A good illustration of this is provided by the sharp increase in the number of assaults in New Zealand, from 741 in 1987 to 3,128 in 1996, often drawn upon to suggest changes in the underlying levels of violent crime, and corresponding need for harsher penal policies, but which was in fact largely attributable to the semi-mandatory arrest policy adopted in relation to domestic violence cases by the police after 1992.[29]

Of course, comparative research presents an additional layer of complexity for the researcher in that differences in definitions, counting practices, and criminal procedure can present significant obstacles to cross-national comparison, even when the reliability of a data series is not in doubt. As regards definitional problems, comparability varies across the range of crimes with traditional crimes such as murder and theft demonstrating the greatest consistency in terms of the way they are defined and categorised across jurisdictions, and drugs and sexual offences the most likely to differ.[30] Comparative researchers generally deal with such difficulties when they arise by collapsing various crimes into broad categories (indeed, this is the approach taken by Interpol and the UNCS). This creates its own problems, however, as important intra-category variations may be concealed. Lynch[31] gives the example of robberies in the US, 33 percent of which involved firearms, compared to robberies in the UK, of which 8.6 percent involved firearms. Moreover, definitional problems are not confined to crime categories. In relation to imprisonment rates, what look to be comparable rates are often not, owing to differences in the way that the figures are calculated and varying approaches to the inclusion in the calculations of certain groups such as juveniles, illegal immigrants and those on temporary release/parole. In Ireland, it is estimated that the omission of those on temporary release may significantly underrepresent the numbers of those imprisoned, particularly those from the 1990s,[32] but in other jurisdictions such as Scotland this may be less significant.

---

[29] M Brown and W Young, 'Recent trends in sentencing and penal policy in New Zealand' (2000) 10 International Criminal Justice Review 1.

[30] Neapolitan (n 27) 16.

[31] J Lynch, 'Crime in international perspective' in JQ Wilson and J Petersilia (eds), *Crime* (Institute for Comparative Studies Press 1995).

[32] See I O'Donnell, 'Putting prison in its place' (2005) 5(2) Judicial Studies Institute Journal 54.

Counting practices are also capable of significantly distorting the crime statistics. One Swedish study,[33] for example, estimated that for certain offences Swedish data would require an adjustment of up to 50 percent to render them comparable with other European countries. The same study drew attention to the following three elements of the rules governing the production of crime statistics as warranting scrutiny: (1) at what point during the processing of offences the crimes are registered, (2) whether or not the principal offence method is applied, and (3) whether serial offences are counted as a single offence or as several offences. The first issue is clearly significant in that a count taken at the early stages of the criminal process prior to an investigation will be higher than a count of crimes which have actually been established as such. The latter two counting rules both relate to the way in which police record multiple offences. A country which is offence rather than incident based will record many more offences as the latter approach mandates that only the most serious offence per incident or victim is recorded. The combined effect of these differences can be very powerful indeed, particularly given that some countries such as New Zealand do not apply any of these 'hierarchy rules' whatsoever in respect of multiple offences.[34] Again, the issue of counting rules does not apply only to crime. Counting practices in the three jurisdictions in relation to entries to prison differed quite considerably, as did the terminology, with variance in relation to issues such as whether existing prisoners are counted as fresh committals after being either convicted (i.e. a change in status from remand to convicted prisoner) or reconvicted (due to the imposition of a further sentence of imprisonment).

In light of these difficulties, the best advice for researchers engaging in this form of analysis is to consider abandoning absolute comparison in favour of comparing changes over time.[35] This involves treating the start point of the study, namely, 1976 as an index year and observing changes relative to that date and then comparing changes relative to that point across the jurisdictions. For me, this had the added benefit of shifting the focus of the research to the onset of a *new* rather than pre-existing punitiveness in each of the three jurisdictions given the claims of Garland and others of a profound transformation in the nature of criminal justice. The technique

33 Brottsforebyggande radet (brå), *Cross-National Comparison of Crime Statistics: An Empirical Study of the Effect of Different Statistical Rules* (Brottsforebyggande radet (brå) 1999). Available from: <http://www.bra.se/extra/pod/?module_instance=11> accessed 9 September 2008.

34 W Young and M Brown, 'Cross-national comparisons of imprisonment' in M Tonry (ed) *Crime and Justice: A Review of Research*, Vol 17 (University of Chicago Press 1993) 27.

35 G Barclay and C Tavares, *International Comparisons of Criminal Justice Statistics 2001* (Home Office 2003).

works, of course, on the assumption that other factors will have remained constant over the period so careful note should be taken of factors potentially interfering with the time series such as those observed above. Care should also be taken in each case to ensure that the index or baseline year, in this case 1976, was not an outlier year by examining data for the years immediately preceding it.

Finally, it should be noted that, while providing an important overview of the criminal justice terrain and its development over the period, the weaknesses of descriptive statistics relate to the lack of background information on local conditions and practices. Clearly, quantitative data can only represent abstractions from complex interactions, divorced from their context. As Lynch[36] has observed: 'if ... it is the very foreignness of nations that complicates cross-national studies, then the most important attribute of a study is to "get things right" – that, is, policies and outcomes are accurately characterized in and across nations.' In this study the limitations of the quantitative investigation in decontextualising the criminal justice systems of the three countries were compensated for by the use of the qualitative methods such as desk top reviews, elite interviews and field visits, a point we shall return to later.

(iv) Analysis of quantitative data

Having collected and cleaned the empirical data relating to the three jurisdictions, the next issue involved the use to which these data would be put. Following Hinds,[37] I considered carrying out inferential statistics testing to examine whether changes in penal trends in, for example, the 1990s and 2000s represented significant changes from previous decades. I was surprised to learn from the Statistics Advisory Unit in Dublin Institute of Technology (where I then worked), however, that longitudinal whole population data does not lend itself to inferential analysis and that there remains quite some controversy in the research literature concerning the appropriateness of applying significance tests to whole populations. An additional complication stems from the fact that the observations (namely, data relating to given years) were not viewed as sufficiently independent of one another for the purposes of carrying out inferential testing. In light of these considerations, I was advised to simply present the data descriptively and for this purpose a worksheet in the Microsoft Excel work programme proved sufficient rather than a software analysis package such as SPSS (Statistical Package for the Social Sciences – only available commercially) or R (free statistical package).

---

[36] Lynch (n 30) 14.
[37] Hinds (n 18).

Data that were relied on as part of my analysis of punitiveness in each jurisdiction included: police expenditure per head of population; police numbers per 100,000 population; prison population per 100,000 population; convicted prisoners per 100,000 population; committals to prison per 100,000 population; sentenced committals per 100,000 population; number of offenders committed to prison receiving sentences of two years or more; number of prisoners per 1,000 violent crimes; number of prisoners per 1,000 burglaries; and number of prisoners per 1,000 thefts. While the latter variables required the correlation of crime and prison data, this could be done easily in Excel through linking spreadsheets and the inputting of simple formulas. Graphs illustrating patterns in the data were also easily generated using Excel.

It is notable that out of a maximum possible overall score of 30 (scores ran from 10 to 30) all the countries obtained mean Overall Punitiveness Scores (OPSs) below the moderate punitiveness level of 20. The results also clustered within a relatively narrow range: Scotland received the most favourable mean OPS at 15 points, Ireland scored 15.8 points and New Zealand 16.7 points. While the suggestion that Scotland may have resisted more punitive trends is far from new,[38] the homogeneity implied by the results was surprising given the suggestion in the research to date of a mild penal climate in Ireland and an increasingly populist tone in New Zealand.[39]

The key to understanding this is what Kutateladze[40] refers to as the 'multi-level' and 'contradictory' nature of punitiveness or, more prosaically, the fact that all three countries possess both exacerbating and ameliorating features. These aggravating and mitigating features tended to cancel each other out as the level of aggregation increased. For example, over the period New Zealand experienced significant increases in its prison population (Index C) and has introduced stringent post-release measures to control serious offenders (Index F) although this should be considered against its progressive system of youth justice and strong procedural protections (Indices B and D). Indeed, on Index B (Procedural Protections) New Zealand obtained the lowest scores of the three jurisdictions. This cancelling out effect was also observable in Ireland which attained its highest punitiveness scores in relation to two indices (C and E) and relatively low scores on the

[38] See, for example, L McAra, 'Modelling penal transformation' (2005) 7(3) Punishment and Society 277.

[39] On Ireland, see the 'Hibernian exceptionalism' literature referenced at n 2 above. On New Zealand, see for example, J Pratt and M Clark, 'Penal populism in New Zealand' (2005) 7(3) Punishment and Society 303.

[40] Kutateladze (n 15).

remainder. Scotland was more consistent in its scores across the six indices, although even in this jurisdiction scores for Indices E and F were higher than those for the other indices.

While researchers must remain alive to this issue both in determining the optimal number of variables and also in interpreting their results, disaggregating the scores by index may go a long way towards identifying these effects and may also reveal some interesting nuances in the data. Thus, despite the similar final scores achieved by Ireland and New Zealand in the multidimensional test (15.8 and 16.7 respectively), the differences in the distribution of moderate-high scores across the indices is suggestive of a more punitive approach gaining momentum across a number of different sectors of New Zealand's criminal justice system (four out of six). Additionally, the fact that Scotland failed to attain a score of above 20 in relation to any of the indices serves to reinforce its position as the least punitive state. The emphasis which researchers may choose to place on either score or interpretation (aggregated/disaggregated) clearly raises difficult theoretical questions relating to the nature of the underlying relationships between the variables and whether it is possible (or indeed desirable) to view punitiveness in one sector as 'offsetting' punitiveness in another. From a more technical perspective, in a study incorporating a bigger dataset (i.e. more jurisdictions) it would of course be possible to run statistical tests such as correlation analysis or factor analysis in order to test for relationships between the variables. In his research, Kutateladze[41] used correlations testing to show the weak to moderate relationship between the variables, consistent with the argument that states vary in the ways in which they can be punitive. In the instant case—reflecting once again the complex nature of the phenomenon under discussion—what may be said is that a more complete understanding of developments in the three jurisdictions can be achieved by approaching the issue from a variety of different perspectives. Important insights may be gained from *both* aggregated scores and disaggregated scores by index in order to capture the dynamic of differences across the indices.

V – Ethics

As a member of the British Society of Criminology, the research was conducted within that organisation's ethical guidelines. Interviewees were asked to read and sign a consent form prior to the interview which explained the purpose of the research, provided the name of my supervisor and relevant contact details and which drew attention to the voluntary nature of their

[41] ibid.

participation. Given that confidentiality was a key issue for elite interviewees, all interviewees were provided with assurances regard to the confidentiality of interview recordings, notes and transcripts. As regards anonymity, respondents were informed that, although parts of the interview may be used in my thesis and in publications arising from it, under no circumstances would their name be associated with any direct quotations included in the research nor would any identifying information be revealed.

VI – Reflections

Writing about the challenges associated with comparative research, Downes[42] has warned of the need to avoid doubts about cross-national study morphing into 'methodological impossibilism'. As he goes on to observe, however, there is cause for optimism in light of the thriving body of comparative criminological research which has emerged in the last twenty years or so. A similar degree of optimism can also be expressed about socio-legal research which ventures beyond traditional doctrinal analysis into realms more commonly occupied by social scientists. As Brants[43] astutely observes, it is at least as difficult to approach criminal justice from different disciplinary perspectives as it is to examine differences cross-nationally, but these challenges, as has been briefly discussed above, are not insurmountable. Suggestions outlined in relation to the collection of quantitative data include: triangulation of data sources (gathering data from as many sources as possible); the keeping of detailed contemporaneous notes with data; reading data in conjunction with the academic literature so as to draw the correct inferences; and the possibility of abandoning absolute comparison in favour of comparing percentage changes over time. Beyond the pragmatic, perhaps the most important lesson for the legal researcher engaged in such analysis is to resist the temptation to regard such data uncritically and to acknowledge both its limitations and the empirical reality within which rules function. As revealed by my own investigation into criminal justice in Ireland, Scotland and New Zealand, while criminal justice statistics shed much important light on the punitiveness or harshness of the system (and indeed cross-sectoral variation within it) they are necessarily limited in the amount of information they can provide on the important qualitative dimension to punishment concerning policy intentions and system ethos. In all three jurisdictions the interview data served to complicate (yet also illuminate)

[42] D Downes, 'Comparative criminology, globalization and the "punitive turn"' in D Nelken (ed), *Comparative Criminal Justice and Globalization* (Ashgate 2011) 28.

[43] C Brants, 'Comparing Criminal Process as Part of Legal Culture' in David Nelken (ed), *Comparative Criminal Justice and Globalization* (Ashgate 2011).

any simple conclusions which could be drawn from the quantitative data. Scotland provides the best example, with its strong welfarist ethos yet high rate of imprisonment and with many respondents struggling to square this circle when asked whether they considered their country to be a punitive one. Interview data was similarly robust in its finding that criminal justice had achieved a different level of embeddedness in New Zealand political life than in the other two countries, despite similar OPS scores. As with social research more broadly, there is a need to consider each case on its own terms and to (cautiously) engage with the views of local actors about what they believe is happening, prior to 'reading off' certain interpretations from the statistics.[44]

Table 1: Indices and Variables Used in *Reconceptualising* Penality study

Indices of Punitiveness	Variables
A Policing:	Zero-tolerance policing, police expenditure, strength of police service, police powers, number of police complaints, strength of the private security sector.
B Procedural Protections for Defendants:	Right to silence, rule against double jeopardy, evidential exclusionary rules, use of civil law to control criminal behaviour, law relating to bail.
C Use of Imprisonment:	Presumptive or mandatory sentences, use of alternatives to custody, imprisonment rates, convicted prisoner rates, prison admission rates, convicted prisoner admission rates, imprisonment rates using different types of crime as a base, length of prison sentences.
D Juvenile Justice:	Age of criminal responsibility, compliance with human rights instruments, sanctions and alternatives to detention, detention rates.

[44] See further, C Hamilton, *Reconceptualising Penality: A Comparative Perspective on Punitiveness in Ireland, Scotland and New Zealand* (Routledge 2014) 109–113.

E Prison Conditions:	Respect for human rights, deaths in prison, size of institutions, overcrowding, rehabilitative programmes, medical services and food.
F Post-release Control:	Sex/drug offender notification schemes, shaming schemes, post-release supervision, reintegration, and expungement of criminal records.
G Death Penalty:	Date of abolition, date of last execution.

CHAPTER 9

Using Methodological Triangulation to Understand Illicit Drug Markets

Johnny CONNOLLY*

I – INTRODUCTION

The objective of this research was to investigate an area that has been largely neglected in academic criminological study, namely the impact of illicit drug markets and drug law enforcement strategies on local communities.[1] The purpose of the study was to explore the phenomenon of illicit drug markets in Ireland, and to examine in particular how drug markets in four specific locations interacted with and impacted upon their local 'host communities'.[2] It sought to understand the thinking behind drug law enforcement and to describe the activities engaged in by An Garda Síochána drug units as they attempt to counteract local drug markets. Ultimately the aim of the study was to assess this activity from the perspective of garda members, those involved in drug markets as sellers and buyers, and also from the perspective of the residents of the respective communities.

II – RESEARCH QUESTION

Background

There is a great deal of debate about the merits of the so-called 'war on drugs'. The impact of the illicit drug trade in Ireland has been well documented and led to major criminal justice reform, mostly of a draconian nature.[3] The failure of prohibition to significantly reduce drug use and availability, the resilience and adaptability of illicit drug markets in the face of

* Dr Johnny Connolly, Irish Research Council/Irish Council for Civil Liberties research fellow, University of Limerick.

[1] J Connolly and A Donovan, *Illicit Drug Markets in Ireland* (National Advisory Committee on Drugs and Alcohol 2014).

[2] The term 'Host community' is derived from T May, M Duffy, B Few and M Hough, *Understanding Drug-selling in Communities: Insider or Outsider Trading* (Joseph Rowntree Foundation 2005).

[3] J Connolly and A Percy, 'Illicit Drugs, Criminal Justice and Harm Reduction: Getting the Balance Right' in Deirdre Healy, Claire Hamilton, Yvonne Daly and Michelle Butler (eds), *The Routledge Handbook of Irish Criminology* (Routledge Taylor and Francis Group 2015).

highly-resourced drug law enforcement (relative to drug treatment services), coupled with the negative consequences that can arise from drug law enforcement has led to calls for a fundamental re-examination of the international system of drug prohibition.[4] Advocated policy options range from changes to the legal status of drugs, whether through direct legalisation or some form of decriminalisation,[5] to a realignment of the balance between criminal justice and harm reduction approaches and the promotion of approaches that can facilitate recovery from addiction.[6]

This research arose from a concern about the dearth of knowledge we currently have about these drug markets that apparently concern us so much. We know even less about why or how the vast resources expended by the State through criminal justice and policing responses are utilised. We also have limited knowledge about the impact such activity has on these markets or on the safety of the communities in which they tend to develop. This study was premised on the belief that until we know more about these matters, debates, for example, about the future legal status of drugs will remain built on sand, and efforts to enhance the safety of those communities where drug sale and use have had the most pernicious effects will remain under-informed and under-developed. The aim of this study, in a time when policy is supposed to be evidence-based, was to provide some context to these issues and debates, and to provide a basis for a more informed set of policy responses. The first National Drugs Strategy 2001–2008 set out detailed actions and key performance indicators across four pillars of supply reduction, prevention, treatment and research.[7] The research pillar sought to develop an evidence base through the establishment of the National Advisory Committee on Drugs to inform policy responses across the various pillars.[8] Howevèr, a concern that motivated this research was that there was limited research evidence supporting the relevance or impact of the various legislative measures introduced in relation to the supply reduction pillar.

---

[4] ibid.

[5] In 2017, the Irish Government launched its National Drugs Strategy, titled 'Reducing harm, Supporting recovery: a health-led response to drug and alcohol use in Ireland 2017–2025'. In November 2017, Junior Minister with responsibility for the strategy Catherine Byrne, TD, set up a working group to consider alternative approaches to the possession of drugs for personal use.

[6] R Room and P Reuter, 'How well do international drug conventions protect public health?' (2012) 379 (9810) Lancet 84–91.

[7] Department of Tourism Sport and Recreation, 2001.

[8] See the Health Research Board National Library on Drug Use which is a receptory for all research conducted in this area: <www.ndc.ie>.

In order to bring some cohesion to various ideas that I had been working on since the early 1990s and prior to conducting the research, I conducted two overviews of the available research evidence in Ireland in relation to drugs, crime and illicit drug markets. The first of these focussed on what we knew about illicit drug markets.[9] The second focused on the available research on the relation between drugs misuse and crime.[10] This latter study reached the conclusion that the development of an effective crime-reduction strategy in relation to drugs must begin with a greater appreciation of the complexity of the drugs-crime nexus, and that such a strategy must move beyond individual explanations for such crime and to addressing the environmental context in which both drug use and crime occur. The overview of illicit drug markets concluded that, although 'knowledge about how the illicit drug market operates was an important prerequisite for effective interventions and responses to it', it remained an 'aspect of Irish society which has suffered from an almost total absence of in-depth research and analysis'.[11] On the basis of this work I was invited, in my role as Research Officer with the Health Research Board,[12] by the National Advisory Committee on Drugs (NACD), established as part of the National Drugs Strategy, to conduct the study. The study was funded primarily by the NACD, with partial funding provided by the Department of Justice and Equality.

Conceptualising the research

The overall conceptual approach adopted here, rather than focusing on the supposed pathologies of those who buy and sell drugs, was to emphasise the dynamics and processes of illicit drug markets *as markets* and the roles, strategies and activities of those involved in them, whether as dealers, drug users or law enforcement personnel. This approach informed the methodology used in this study. Illegal drugs are commodities that are produced and distributed in markets and therefore, one would presume, subject to laws of supply and demand and other normal market influences. Although the general concept of the market is familiar and such matters should appear to be self-evident, as Babor et al observe, 'policy discussions show a strange unwillingness to apply this understanding of markets when the commodity is an illicit drug'.[13] Perhaps the most important distinction between legal and

---

9 J Connolly, *Illicit drug markets in Ireland* (Health Research Board Overview series 2005).

10 J Connolly, *Drugs and crime in Ireland* (Health Research Board Overview series 2006).

11 ibid, 100.

12 The Health Research Board is the lead funding agency for health research in Ireland. It also manages the National Drugs Library and is the Irish Focal point for the European Monitoring Centre for Drugs and Drug Addiction, based in Lisbon, Portugal.

13 T Babor, J Caulkins, G Edwards, B Fischer, D Foxcroft, K Humphreys, I Obot, J Rehm, P Reuter, R Robin, I Rossow and J Strang, *Drug Policy and the Public Good* (OUP 2010) 63.

illegal markets is that participants in the latter have 'no recourse to the system of property rights and dispute resolution offered by the civil courts and legal system'.[14] This has important consequences for the way in which drug markets are organised and the way in which business is conducted for example, in terms of the role that violence performs in drug transactions.[15]

III – Methodological approach and Methods used

Socio-legal research and methodological triangulation

This research adopted a socio-legal approach to the study of illicit drug markets. Socio-legal research sees law as a social phenomenon. It seeks to consider the social, economic and political context in which law is formed. It also examines the operation of law, in both formal (court) and semi-formal (policing on the street) contexts for example. It also recognises the need to analyse the experience of those affected by processes of law. As a consequence socio-legal research adopts an inter-disciplinary and mixed methodological approach to the study of law and legal phenomena. Ritter, a clinical psychologist, from a review of five disciplinary approaches to studying drug markets—ethnographic and qualitative approaches; economic approaches; behavioural and psychological research; population-based and survey research; criminology and law enforcement evaluation—suggests that a good theoretical model in this area would be one that can depict the dynamic relationships between drug users, their environment, the operation of the market and interventions (that is, law enforcement, treatment, harm reduction). The study of such markets is, she suggests, ripe for 'inter- and trans-disciplinary' approaches that would seek to synthesise and integrate different disciplinary approaches thereby leading to new concepts and ideas.[16] Dwyer and Moore, responding to Ritter and drawing from ethnographic and sociological accounts of illicit drug markets, reveal them as complex and fluid phenomena. Interventions made in response to them must also, they suggest, be suitably nuanced.[17] Taking its lead from Ritter, this study combined ethnographic, qualitative, economic, quantitative, survey-based and criminological and law enforcement evaluation approaches.

---

[14] ibid 64.

[15] For further discussion of the role of violence in the illicit drugs trade see J Connolly 'Illicit drug markets, systemic violence and victimization' (2017) 68(4) NILQ 415–32.

[16] A Ritter, 'Studying illicit drug markets: disciplinary contributions.' (2006) 17 International Journal of Drug Policy, 17: 221–8: 216.

[17] R Dwyer and D Moore, 'Understanding illicit drug markets in Australia: Notes towards a critical reconceptualization' (2010) 50 British Journal of Criminology 82–101.

Methodological triangulation enables the obtaining of information on the same phenomena using two or more different methods, by using the strengths of one method to overcome the deficiencies of another, which achieves a higher degree of validity and reliability.[18] The research incorporated such a mixed methodological approach, involving both qualitative and quantitative data sources.

Ethnographic and qualitative approaches involved semi-structured in-depth interviews with both former and active drug users and street sellers, as well as a number of imprisoned convicted drug suppliers and drug couriers. These latter interviews were conducted in order to obtain an insight into higher-level drug supply activities. No research has been conducted in Ireland on this important dimension of the drug trade, although research in the United Kingdom is of interest given the proximity and probable links between the British and Irish markets.[19] Further interviews were conducted with experienced members of dedicated Garda drug units in the four study sites and with senior members of the Garda National Drugs Unit. This data provided, for the first time in Irish research, a comprehensive account from active drug law enforcement personnel of their strategies and activities. Further semi-structured interviews were conducted with care workers and public health professionals.

Comprehensive criminal justice data on drug searches, drug arrests and seizures, and the profile of offenders and the circumstances of their arrest were also compiled using the Garda Síochána PULSE (Police Using Leading Systems Effectively) information technology system. This is the first study where this data has been accessed by independent researchers in Ireland. Access to PULSE data was facilitated by the member of the Garda National Drugs Unit (GNDU) represented on the Research Advisory Group, which was established to assist with and oversee the research. Accessing this data involved the researcher working with the garda member in the headquarters of the GNDU in Dublin Castle and transferring data from PULSE to an encrypted password protected research computer, using a numerical coding system. This ensured that no data that could potentially identify suspects or offenders left the garda station.

Economic approaches to the study of drug markets sometimes rely on drug price and drug purity data and this was also gathered as part of this study. A comprehensive forensic analysis of drug seizures in the study sites was

---

[18] S Sarantakos, *Social Research* (Palgrave Macmillan 1998).

[19] Matrix Knowledge Group, *The illicit drug trade in the United Kingdom* (London: Home Office 2007).

conducted by the Forensic Science Laboratory as part of the research. Again, the level of data analysed for this study was unprecedented. Where such data has been compiled it is seldom made publicly available.[20] Finally, a street survey of approximately 200 residents in each of the research locations was conducted. Although crime surveys have been conducted in Ireland previously, no survey on this topic or on this scale had been conducted.

Methodological triangulation is particularly suitable to the study of hidden activities such as those involved in the illicit drug trade, whether from the perspective of drug dealers or, indeed, drug law enforcement officers. When studying illicit activities, for example, some participants might exaggerate or downplay their activities. Others, such as dependent drug users whose lifestyle might be quite chaotic, might forget or confuse information. Consequently, interviews with dependent drug users and also street survey interviews were structured to include internal reliability checks. During the course of an interview, questions would be repeated in a modified form to check for inconsistencies. Another triangulation technique employed involved sequencing fieldwork interviews with drug sellers on the one hand and professionals on the other, so that inconsistencies could be checked. Likewise, the street survey data were validated using a pre-determined series of logical or validation checks.

Research locations

In order to develop an understanding about community impact, empirical research was carried out within four particular local communities in Ireland; two sites in urban areas, one in a suburban area and one in a rural area. These sites varied considerably in terms of population and geographic location. The basic selection criteria was that the areas should be sufficiently varied to provide a cross section of illicit drug markets in Ireland. The electoral divisions (ED) within the study sites chosen were those where deprivation levels were high (based on proportion of over-15s unemployed, proportion of population in social class 5 [Semi-skilled] or 6 [Unskilled], proportion of households with no car and proportion of rented or local authority housing). The Small Area Health Research Unit (SAHRU) deprivation index was used to determine the level of material deprivation in the Electoral Divisions (EDs).[21] Data on the proportion of residents who had served prison sentences for drug offences were also used as an indicator. This data was derived from a combination of 2006 Census data and data

[20] Connolly, Illicit drug markets in Ireland (n 9).

[21] The index was calculated by the Small Area Health Research Unit at Trinity College, Dublin.

from the Irish Prison Service computer-based record system (PRIS), which facilitated the mapping of the distribution of prisoners released in 2004 after serving sentences for drug offences. The identities of these sites were concealed so as not to consolidate their reputation as illicit drug market locations. Site A in the original study is located within a suburban satellite town with a population of approximately 40,000. Site B is a rural site encompassing just two ED's – one representing the town, with a small population of 2,000–3,000 and the second representing the population of the rural hinterland, with a population of 10,000–11,000. Site C is an urban site encompassing 20 EDs, with a population of 30,000. Site D is an urban site with 19 EDs and a population of some 60,000.

IV – Methods used

Literature review

A literature review was initiated as part of the preparation of the original research tender. The review initially focused on the study aims and objectives and ultimately served a number of functions. First, by indicating the extent to which the topic was already researched, it enabled the siting of the study within a wider body of existing knowledge about drug markets. Second, it helped identify specific study themes and topics. Third, it enabled the selection of the most appropriate methods of data collection and analysis and assisted in the development of data-collection tools – including surveys, interviews and criminal-justice data sources. Finally, collaboration with colleagues with experience of researching illicit drug markets meant that the research team was informed of previous methodological limitations that could be avoided.[22] The literature review consisted primarily of a purposive iterative search using key drug market and policing studies. International and national websites were accessed on a regular basis while a wide range of international journals was also reviewed regularly. Available Irish data sources were accessed through the monthly online newsletter of the Health Research Board National Drugs Library (available at www.ndc.ie), an invaluable source of information in this area.

---

[22] The approach was largely modelled on that taken by Tiggey May and colleagues (n 2). I am grateful to Tiggey May and Mike Hough for their assistance. The prison interviews, which sought to access higher-level drug dealers, were informed by the approach taken by the Matrix Knowledge Group (n 19). I am also grateful to Laura Wilson for her assistance in this respect. Consulting with experienced colleagues can also be a valuable research technique.

Qualitative data methods

Interviews were conducted with the following:

- Thirty-five former and active drug users and street sellers;
- Sixteen individuals serving prison sentences of more than seven years for drug supply;
- Twenty experienced members of dedicated Garda drug units in the four study sites and senior members of the Garda National Drugs Unit;
- Six drug-treatment workers and one public health specialist; and
- One focus group with a community-based family support group.

Individual, face-to-face, in-depth interviewing was carried out with all interviewees. Former and active drug users and sellers were selected in order to obtain information about the operations of illicit drug markets in the study sites. It became apparent however that because these participants were accessed via drug treatment centres, all were street level dealers. Following contact with the Irish Prison Service and the Governor of Mountjoy Jail, a number of interviews were conducted with individuals serving prison sentences of more than seven years for drug supply to obtain information on higher-level drug trafficking (See below). Interviews were also conducted with a number of female drug couriers in the Dóchas Centre, a women's prison in Dublin. Most of these were of African origin but spoke fluent English (see below).

In interviews with drug users/sellers, a semi-structured interview schedule was used, which focused on the following key areas of interest:

> Socio-demographic profile/Initiation into alcohol and illicit drug use/ Personal drug-use pattern and purchasing practices/Entry into drug-selling and selling practices/Market knowledge – price, purity and structure of local market/Experience with local police/Risk management/experience of drug-related violence/Criminal history.

Individual, face-to-face, in-depth interviews were also conducted with experienced members of dedicated Garda drug units to obtain information about the operations of local illicit drug markets and policing responses to market activity. Again, a semi-structured interview schedule was used, which focused on:

> Description of community and drug activity/Involvement of young people in drug-selling/Drug-related criminal activity/Policing response to drug markets/Relationship with local community/Additional resources needed.

Following the completion of the interviews with local Garda units, a further three interviews were conducted with three senior members of the Garda National Drugs Unit (GNDU). The primary purpose of these interviews was to gain an insight into the GNDUs role and strategy and to obtain their views on a number of issues which had arisen during the course of the study. Another reason why these interviews were conducted was because some senior garda members were concerned about comments made by junior members, due to a perception that opinions expressed by frontline garda members on some issues might not have fully reflected garda policy. It would obviously have been entirely unethical to dilute or amend the views expressed by their junior colleagues, so in order to address their concerns, garda management were invited to participate so as to provide a senior policy perspective. Dilemmas such as this must be confronted and negotiated on an ongoing basis by the researcher, particularly where the research is dependent on gatekeepers providing access to key data and sensitive data sources. Furthermore, this study was a new departure for the statutory bodies involved: the Department of Justice, An Garda Síochána, Customs Drug Law Enforcement and the Irish Prison Service.

Individual, face-to-face, in-depth interviews were also conducted with drug-treatment workers to gather supplementary information on the impact of drug-selling in communities. A semi-structured interview schedule was used to explore the following key areas of interest:

> Description of community and drug activity/Involvement of young people in drug-selling/Relationship with law enforcement.

Sampling strategies and data collection

Purposive and snowballing sampling procedures were used to select participants for qualitative interviewing. In a purposive sampling procedure, study participants are chosen because they have particular features or characteristics which will enable detailed exploration of the research objectives.[23] Participants in the study were selected on the basis of their

[23] C Robson, *Real world research: a resource for social scientists and practitioners* (Blackwell 2002).

knowledge of the operation of the illicit drug market. The initial participants were recruited through existing contacts, drug users' forums, and treatment, probation, police and prison services. Thereafter, a snowballing technique was used, whereby the initial participants recruited new interviewees who fit the research criteria through their own networks and contacts.[24]

In order to be eligible to take part in the study, all drug-using and/or drug-selling participants had to self-identify as a drug user and/or drug seller. All participants had to be at least 18 years of age. Although young people under the age of 18 are involved in drug-selling, the numerous ethical issues involved when interviewing minors were beyond the scope of the study. It was also beyond the scope of the study to involve non-English speakers although a number of non-native drug couriers who spoke English fluently were interviewed in the Dóchas Centre. Drug service providers acted as gatekeepers and made contact with individuals deemed appropriate for interview, based on their knowledge of the local drug market. Potential participants were informed about the study, or were provided with leaflets explaining the background and objectives of the study in accessible language, before meeting interviewers. Interviews took place in the premises of drug services or in suitable public locations such as cafes and community centres. Many of the interviews with drug users/sellers were organised through treatment or social services in the different sites. As many of these individuals were dependent drug users, their experience of the illicit drug market was generally limited to street-level dealing.

In order to get an insight into higher-level dealing, interviews were organised with people serving lengthy prison terms for drug supply. Data on the number of male prisoners serving sentences for supply were obtained from the Irish Prison Service. Obtaining access to the prisons proved to be time consuming. Approximately 50 individuals serving sentences of more than seven years in one Irish prison were contacted by the researcher by mail. Ten of these individuals responded and expressed a willingness to participate in the research. With regard to the male prisoners interviewed, although all of those who expressed an interest were interviewed, only data from prisoners who were from the areas under study were included in the study. Once ethical approval was obtained from the Irish Prison Service, six interviews with female prisoners were conducted in the Dóchas Centre women's prison in Dublin. Most of these women had been convicted of importing drugs into Ireland through Dublin airport.

---

[24] ibid.

Data analysis

Except in the case of a number of prison-based interviews where detailed handwritten notes were taken, interviews were recorded, with the consent of participants, using a digital recorder.[25] Recorded interviews were transcribed verbatim. The interviews were analysed by study site, and the QSR NVivo software package was used to manage data. Each interview was coded in line with the themes in the topic guide; these represent 'nodes' in NVivo. Sub-themes were identified within themes and coded as 'sub nodes'. The interviewees' experiences were described under each theme, and the similarities and differences highlighted where relevant.

Quantitative data methods

Street survey

A street survey of 800 local residents and business people was carried out to gather information about the local community in each study site and its experience of illicit drug use. A questionnaire with mainly pre-coded answers was designed to investigate the following areas of interest:

> Attitude to locality/Drug use and its impact on the area/Policing in the locality in relation to drug activity.

The fieldwork for the survey was carried out by a private company, *Evidence Led Solutions*. Interviews were conducted in a variety of locations (supermarkets, post offices, schools, retail and business districts) and at varying times (early morning, afternoon and evening) to capture a cross-section of residents and workers.

Non-probability quota sampling logic was used to select respondents.[26] In each study site a sample was achieved that was proportional to the local population in terms of age and gender. Eight-hundred and eleven interviews (approximately 200 respondents in each location) were completed, with a response rate of 37 percent for the entire sample in terms of the number approached. Overall, the response rate was the same for both males and females (37 percent). Not all survey respondents answered every question, for example, where the respondent did not have the time to complete the full survey. Survey data were entered into the Statistical Package for the Social

[25] Initially interviews were not recorded due to a delay in approval for entering the prison with a recording device.

[26] The sample was selected on a first to agree to respond basis until each allocated quota by age and gender was filled for each area.

Sciences (SPSS). The data were validated using a pre-determined series of logical or validation checks. The survey data were analysed by study site using proportions to describe the respondents' opinions, beliefs or experiences.

Drug offence data – Garda PULSE system

Drug offence data can provide an indication of the operation of different market levels, whether the offence is related to drug supply or simply drug use. For example, information in relation to seizure size by drug type and location enhances understanding of drug use and police activity at a local level. Drug offence and search data in relation to each of the study sites for a six-month period were obtained from PULSE incident reports. The Garda PULSE system was introduced in late 1999 primarily to service the internal operational activities of the Garda Síochána. Generally, an alleged offence is entered into the PULSE system shortly after it has been allegedly committed or become known to the garda member. Thus, PULSE includes information on the number of drug seizures in an area, the profile of offenders and the circumstances of arrest. The PULSE data collected for the study related to the seven primary offences prosecuted under the Misuse of Drugs Act 1977.[27]

Data on over 1,200 cases were analysed from 12 Garda stations throughout the study sites. The recorded drug-specific offences or incidents in this analysis exclude drug offences that occurred in a prison located in the study site, because not all study sites had a prison located in the area and not all prisoners would normally be resident in the area. All other recorded drug-specific offences or incidents were included in the analysis regardless of the outcome; it is not known how many of these incidents led to legal proceedings and/or resulted in convictions. PULSE data were entered into SPSS, and the data were then analysed by study site. Frequencies, medians, means, ranges and cross-tabulations were used to describe patterns in the data. Estimates of drug prices and profits were made through a combination of PULSE data and interviews with drug users/sellers.

Drug purity analysis – forensic science laboratory

Systematic purity testing of drugs seized at all market levels can provide useful information on market dynamics and profit margins. Forensic analysis

[27] s 3 – possession of any controlled drug without due authorisation (simple possession); s 15 – possession of a controlled drug for the purpose of unlawful sale or supply (possession for sale or supply) and s 21– obstructing the lawful exercise of a power conferred by the Act (obstruction). Drug importation contrary to s 20; permitting one's premises to be used for drug supply or use contrary to s 19; the use of forged prescriptions (s 18); and the cultivation of cannabis plants (s 17).

of seized drugs can also provide information on the types of adulterant used to bulk up drugs for street sale, a factor that can have important health consequences for drug users.

Samples from drug seizures made by Gardaí based in the four study sites over a six-month period were submitted to the Forensic Science Laboratory (FSL) for analysis. Qualitative analysis was performed to identify the presence of illicit substances (i.e. those scheduled under the Misuse of Drugs legislation). Quantitative analysis (drug purity) was then performed on powders and tablets containing specific drugs, namely amphetamine, cocaine, diamorphine (heroin) and MDMA, to determine the levels of purity of the illicit substances present. The analysis also identified the other substances found in the samples, giving an indication of the typical bulking agents used within the illicit drug market. The data were analysed by study site. Frequencies, medians, means and ranges were used to describe patterns in the data.

V – Ethical considerations

Ethical approval for this study was received from the Drug Treatment Centre Board and, for the prison-based interviews, from the Research Ethics Committee of the Irish Prison Service. The principle of 'informed consent' was followed throughout the research and confidentiality and anonymity were afforded to all participants. Drug users and drug sellers who were interviewed were compensated for their time with a €20 An Post voucher. No payments were offered to professionals working in drug or police services or to respondents in prison. Data were kept securely on encrypted storage devices and were anonymised – all identifiers that could link the data with the participants were removed. All recordings were made on a digital recorder; interviews were then uploaded to the website of the transcription service. Access to these interviews was password protected. Once the transcription was received by the research team, original recordings were deleted in line with the research ethics protocol, to ensure complete anonymity. Transcriptions were then entered into NVivo as described above. The four study sites are identified only by the type of location, so as to prevent any of the sites from developing or consolidating a reputation as a drug market.

VI – Challenges

A study of this scale and on such a sensitive topic is bound to face challenges. For example, the aim was to describe, as best we could, the operation of illicit drug markets in the four areas. Rates of recruitment of eligible drug users and drug sellers varied in the different study sites. The sample of drug sellers is unlikely to be representative of drug sellers across Ireland. Many service providers reported that suitable individuals were apprehensive of participating in an interview which would probe their illegal activities, albeit at a general level. For ethical reasons, people under the age of 18 were not interviewed yet other respondents' claimed that young people performed important roles in some of the drug markets studied. This also became apparent from PULSE data where young people had been arrested for drug selling.

Although extensive efforts were made, obtaining access to treatment-workers proved difficult in some study locations. This was possibly due to the nature of the study and concerns that their participation might in some way have a negative impact on their relations with their clients, an often 'hard-to-reach' group in these locations. Consequently, follow-up contact was made with three harm-reduction specialists on specific issues which arose during the study. These included a senior public health specialist, a member of a family support group and a representative of the Irish College of General Practitioners (ICGP).

The prison-based interviews with those convicted of drug supply were organised at an advanced stage of the research as we realised that such higher-level sellers were under-represented. Obtaining access to the prison proved extremely time-consuming. Also, although a number of non-Irish prisoners were interviewed, for ethical reasons, we confined our interviews to only those respondents with a proficiency in English. It also needs to be acknowledged that prison-based interviews only provide access to those people who have been apprehended by law enforcement, thereby providing us with limited information on those who evade detection.

Research challenges such as these also arose during the street survey. Not all street survey respondents answered every question. This may have occurred, for example, where the respondent did not have the time to complete the full survey. Although the survey enabled the research to access a large sample of local residents, street surveys also have certain limitations. For example, open street-level interviews are not the best place to discuss sensitive matters such as local drug-related crime. Poor weather can be a hindrance to survey completion and the nature of the survey does not allow for in-depth responses. However, while such surveys can be skewed in favour of the opinionated or those with time on their hands, the survey team found that respondents were generally very generous with their time and that most of those approached were prepared to answer the questionnaire. The survey therefore can be said to provide a reasonable indication of local concerns about drug-related crime.

It is important to note that the PULSE system is an operational database and its main function is to record Garda activity. There are therefore limitations to the use of such a system for research purposes. Obviously, not every drug offence comes to the attention of An Garda Síochána. Furthermore, even when crimes are reported, they are not always recorded. A number of problems have been identified, not only with the system itself, but how it has been used. Deficiencies noted in the PULSE data by the Garda Inspectorate include the classification and reclassification of crimes, the recording of actions taken or evidence collected and the rationale for deeming cases to be closed.[28] Nor is it possible to quantify the amount of reported crime in the study sites that was drug related. Drug-related crime includes crimes such as burglary, vehicle theft, mugging and assault that occur due to the business of buying and selling illegal drugs. It is therefore safe to assume that the PULSE system underestimates the amount of drug related activity and its impact. It is also important to note that drug seizures are an indirect indicator of the extent of drug use in an area. They should be regarded primarily as an indicator of police enforcement activity. Since the completion of the study, the recording of data by An Garda Síochána has come in for intense scrutiny and criticism by the Garda Inspectorate, among others.[29] At the time of writing, the Central Statistics Office refuses to publish this data due to concerns about its reliability.

Notwithstanding these various issues, I am confident however that, even in locations where the level of participation in the study by drug sellers was low, a reasonably accurate and reliable picture of the local drug markets was achieved for the purpose of this study through a combination of street survey, interview and criminal justice data.

The research would not have been possible without the significant funding provided by the National Advisory Committee on Drugs and Alcohol and the Department of Justice. Access to data heretofore unavailable to researchers was also facilitated through the participation of stakeholders on the Research Advisory Committee, such as the Garda National Drugs Unit, Revenue and Customs Drug Law enforcement and the Forensic Science Laboratory. It is unclear whether this unprecedented access occurred because the research was conducted under the auspices of the Health Research Board, a Non Commercial Semi-State Body (NCSSB). The involvement of such statutory bodies acted as an enabler for the research. On the other hand, a number of challenges also arose when it came to publishing the findings of the research.

---

[28] Garda Síochána Inspectorate *Crime Investigation* (Garda Síochána Inspectorate 2014).

[29] ibid.

The terms of the research contract prevent me from going into detail as to the nature of these issues.

VII – Reflections and Conclusion

Drug law enforcement activities may have contributed to the relative containment of illicit drug use, and the authorities have had some success in disrupting drug markets and dismantling organised crime groups. However, there is little evidence in Ireland or internationally that such strategies have halted the expansion of the illicit drug market or reduced the criminal activities associated with it for any sustained period of time.

Reuter argues that the absence of an adequate understanding of the effectiveness of the drug prohibition regime in deterring drug use and/or dealing is a consequence of the way in which drug control has become politicised:

> It is hard … to say what good policy would look like, because one consequence of politicians' treating drug control as a moral crusade has been an absolute disinterest, bordering on gross negligence, in assessing the consequences, good or bad, of the emphasis on punishment … there is no credible basis for describing a policy that would reduce, in any important dimension, the extent of (drug problems) …[30]

Where drug policy aims to alleviate drug-related harms to individuals and society, it must be informed by an understanding of how those harms are unevenly distributed throughout society. Similarly, control systems need to be developed, not in an atmosphere of moral panic, but through an understanding, developed through empirical research, of how current drug laws actually operate in relation to the markets they are seeking to affect and the communities whose problems they are purportedly designed to alleviate. A group of leading drug scholars, in an analysis of international drug control efforts stated:

> We conclude with one over-riding analytical observation: supply control interventions absorb the bulk of drug control spending in most nations, even nations that have a reputation for tolerating drug use. The evidence base concerning these interventions is distressingly weak …. Governments are still flying blind (in the war on drugs). (Babor et al 2010)[31]

---

[30] P Reuter, 'Why can't we make prohibition work better? Some consequences of ignoring the unattractive', Vol 141: 263–275 (Proceedings of the American Philosophical Society 1997).

[31] T Babor, J Caulkins, G Edwards, B Fischer, D Foxcroft, K Humphreys, I Obot, J Rehm, P Reuter, R Robin, I Rossow and J Strang J, *Drug Policy and the Public Good* (OUP 2010).

The research described above was groundbreaking, in terms of the data accessed and the methodological approach adopted. It offers a distinctive perspective on an issue that is characterised by vigorous opinion and emotive public debate but that is notably bereft of empirical research. Through the combination of and triangulation of research methods it synthesises original data across a range of dimensions of the illicit drug trade, drug law enforcement and at a local community level. In doing so, it brings new evidence to bear on an old issue, using research techniques and instruments and accessing data sources not heretofore utilised. It represents the first occasion that such a wide range of data sources have been used for the analysis of illicit drug markets and responses to them in Ireland. The findings derived from the research have certain implications for policy makers. First, the complete removal of illicit drug markets through drug law enforcement is not an achievable goal in the foreseeable future. Second, not all drug markets are equally harmful. For example, some are more violent than others and open markets cause more disruption to communities than closed ones. Third, law-enforcement interventions that focus on the particular harms associated with an individual market have the potential to have an impact on those harms and they may also lead to a more effective and economically viable use of public resources.

Chapter 10

Crossing the Line: Ethnographic Fieldwork on Crime and Justice

Jonathan Ilan*

I – Introduction

It was a series of unplanned but fortunate events that saw me 'crossing the line' to undertake an ethnography of young people, street crime and juvenile justice in an inner-city Dublin community.[1] First, I had the fortune of being accepted onto a funded PhD programme at the Dublin Institute of Technology in 2003. Second, I was assigned Dr Karen Lysaght, an anthropologist and ethnographer as my supervisor. She encouraged me to cross lines—between research and everyday life, participant and researcher and between academic disciplines—to embed myself close to the people and issues I was studying for an extended period of time. Third, I had the support of institutions and individuals who were unstintingly generous in providing access, time and insight to my project. This chapter provides a personal, reflexive account of how this particular research project was conceived and ultimately completed (if research does ever finish). This narrative requires some explanation of ethnographic methods (research through immersion in a culture) and the qualities that make it distinctive. The issues that any piece of social research must consider from design and sampling, to analysis and ethics will all be considered in that context. Ultimately, this chapter traces the journey of a

* Senior Lecturer in Criminology, Department of Sociology, City, University of London, UK.
The PhD research from which this article is drawn was conducted as part of the Young People's Experience of Crime Project at the Dublin Institute of Technology, funded by the Department of Education and Science (Ireland) under Strand III.

[1] See: J Ilan, *Still playing the game: an ethnography of young people, street crime and juvenile justice in an inner-city Dublin community* (Dublin Institute of Technology 2007); J Ilan, 'If You Don't Let Us In, We'll Get Arrested': Class-cultural Dynamics in the Provision of, and Resistance to, Youth Justice Work' (2010) 10(1) *Youth Justice* 25; Jonathan Ilan, 'Reclaiming Respectability? Class-culture, crime, community and governance in inner-city Dublin' (2011) 48(6) *Urban Studies* 1137; Jonathan Ilan 'Street Social Capital in the Liquid City' (2013) 14(1) *Ethnography* 1; J Ilan, 'Scumbags! An ethnography of the interactions between street-based youth and police officers' (2018) 28(6) *Policing and Society* 684.

naïve law-graduate, to a somewhat less naïve criminologist. Crossing disciplinary and methodological lines was a hugely rewarding process. Amongst those inner-city residents who exist at the sharp end of the issues I study, I found myriad relationships and insights that challenged my middle-class subjectivities and prejudices. Additionally, my experiences amongst welfare and justice professionals challenged some of my political biases, highlighting the difficulties of providing straightforward solutions to multi-faceted social problems.

II – Research Question

In undertaking my project, I set the following primary research question, together with a secondary question and a long list of sub-questions that I thought would help me to answer it: 'What is the nature of the *Northstreet* young offenders' interaction with wider society that results in their persistent involvement with the criminal justice system?'[2] Whilst this might seem vague, it is common for ethnographers to engage in 'progressive focusing' – or practically refining research questions as one researches.[3] Given that one cannot really know what is relevant to participants until one gets to know them and their world, this technique demonstrates a concern with 'grounded theory'[4] or prioritising the explanation of the social phenomenon observed over testing pre-existing theories.

My vision was to undertake for the first time in the Republic of Ireland, the kinds of ethnographies of offending youth I had read voraciously in preparation.[5] Ultimately, the way in which the research unfolded meant that I produced something different, involving neighbours and professionals to a greater extent than I initially thought I might. The flexible research design at the heart of an ethnographic approach allowed me to snatch success from the jaws of failure and ultimately make a virtue of the fact that I was able to access some parts of the field better than others. It is fair to say that when I began fieldwork in May 2004 (which continued until October 2005) I was certain only of the fact I had a year and some contingency time in which to undertake my research and that I was seeking to understand the culture of youth crime and responses to it more deeply. This 'getting out there and seeing what one can find' approach is typically ethnographic and thus to

---

[2] Ilan, *Still playing the game* (n 1) 40.

[3] M Hammersley and P Atkinson, *Ethnography: Principles in Practice* (3rd edn, Routledge 2007).

[4] B Glaser and A Strauss, *The Discovery of Grounded Theory: Strategies for qualitative research* (Aldine 1967).

[5] See, e.g. H Parker, *View from the Boys: A Sociology of Downtown Adolescents* (David and Charles 1974).

understand how formal academic research can come from such an approach it is important to gain an overview of this methodology.

III – Methodological Approach and Methods Used

> 'Ethnography is the study of people in naturally occurring settings or "fields" by means of methods which capture their social meanings and ordinary activities … to collect data in a systematic manner'.[6]

Ethnography is most commonly associated with 'participant observation' (studying people through taking part in their everyday lives and keeping a systematic diary of what occurs for later analysis) but more accurately might be understood as a general approach to research that privileges the lived experiences and perspectives of participants over the theoretical concerns of the researcher.[7] With roots in anthropology, it has tended to involve a researcher living amongst participants for an extended period of time (traditionally over a number of years although this is becoming increasingly rare). The goal is to develop a deep understanding of how participant communities live and see the world. This approach is particularly useful in the study of crime, justice and marginalised communities. Those involved in crime can be reasonably assumed to be secretive and difficult to identify and access. Criminologists tend to spend relatively little time speaking to actual offenders and when they do, they tend to find them in prisons or through the police: in other words, they find it difficult to research criminals who evaded detection and to study in natural as opposed to institutional settings.[8] An important ethnographer of crime[9] warned against becoming 'jailhouse or courthouse sociologists' where criminological research is directed according to the lens of criminal justice and to the benefit of its administration. There is much that can be gained by approaching criminological research from a less determined perspective.

Crime ethnography is interested in understanding 'criminological *verstehen*'[10]—the subjective experience of breaking the law—what does it feel like? What does it mean to those involved in it? This generates a range

6 J Brewer, *Ethnography* (Open University Press 2000) 10.

7 Atkinson and Hammersley (n 3).

8 M Maguire, 'Researching "Street Criminals": A Neglected Art' in R King and E Wincup (eds), *Doing Research on Crime and Justice* (OUP 2008).

9 N Polsky *Hustlers Beats and Others* (Aldine 1967) 145.

10 J Ferrell, 'Criminological Verstehen: Inside the Immediacy of Crime' in J Ferrell and M Hamm (eds), *Ethnography at the Edge: Crime, Deviance, and Field Research* (Northeastern University Press 2008).

of insights otherwise unavailable to those who would make policy on issues of crime control and prevention. It can furthermore contribute to a more humanistic view of the 'criminal' that views them as fully-formed humans as opposed to pathological 'monsters'. On a more practical level, the trust that develops over the course of ethnographic engagement allows for a more accurate understanding of criminal matters. Crime statistics are notoriously difficult to trust in their own right. If one was to picture a researcher administrating a survey to an individual who has been involved in crime, it is very difficult to imagine that full and frank information would be provided. A researcher who has invested a year or more getting to know individuals, who becomes embedded within everyday life locally and can raise issues in casual conversations later recorded in field notes, may well fare differently. Disadvantaged communities that have had mixed experiences of research and the arms of the state/municipality may also be less likely to engage with remote researchers who visit only briefly. The researcher who stays only for a short while can miss a lot of what is revealed only in time, at alternative times, or to those who have achieved enough of an 'insider' status.

The operation of justice and policing, although part of the machinery of the state, is nevertheless 'low visibility'[11] often occurring away from the gaze of those who would hold power accountable. The individuals involved in such processes may have cause to defend themselves politically and can be skilled in obfuscating problems where identified. Criminal justice institutions moreover can point to the law, rules and regulations in response to questions about their practices and procedures, where unwritten rules, informal actions and powerful organisational cultures can have significant influence without necessarily being apparent. For these reasons ethnographic research has served to provide a more fulsome and nuanced picture of the operation of policing[12] and the law in general[13] than other research methods might typically achieve.

This is not to say that ethnographic methods would suit every research project or are without their disadvantages. Ethnographic studies are time consuming and emotionally draining, restricting their viability for academics tied to institutional duties.[14] Crossing the line and becoming a presence in the lives

---

[11] R Reiner, *The Politics of the Police* (OUP 2000) 219.

[12] See e.g. Nigel Fielding, *Joining Forces: Police training, socialization and occupational competence* (Routledge 1998).

[13] See e.g. P Ewick and SS Silbey, *The Common Place of Law: Stories from everyday life* (University of Chicago Press 1998).

[14] D Hobbs, 'Peers, Careers and Academic Fears: Writing as Field-Work' in D Hobbs and T May (eds), *Interpreting the Field Accounts of Ethnography* (Clarendon Press 1993).

of active offenders can create ethical dilemmas for individual researchers, not to mention academic institutions. Researchers 'must make the moral decision that in some ways he will break the law himself' – either directly or through acquiring the 'guilty knowledge' of crimes that have occurred that perhaps will go undetected and unpunished.[15] Ethnographers of crime and justice are at risk, not just from what they might observe, but what might occur to them in terms of physical and emotional harm. University ethics committees have arguably become aware of these risks; and also what are perceived as reputational risks to universities themselves; and have thus been implicated in restricting the kinds of criminological research that might be undertaken.[16] Researchers and universities concerned about the legal risks of crime ethnography can be proactive rather than fatalistic about the prospects of conducting this kind research safely.[17] Despite these issues, quality ethnographies of crime are continuing to be produced internationally.

There are also a number of more epistemological criticisms that might be made about ethnographic research. As a form of qualitative research *par excellence*, and indebted to philosophical principles of interpretivism, the approach is open to being labelled as a glorified form of journalism on the one hand, and impossibly postmodern and relativistic on the other.[18] Ultimately, ethnographic studies tend to be undertaken in-depth with small groups of individuals. 'Sample' sizes are inherently small and whether research findings are specifically local or more generally applicable remain a constant query. Ethnographic studies are impossible to replicate, being unique to the individuals who undertake them, their specific positionality and biography[19] and the ways in which they are received and reacted to by their participants, and within a specific time and place. Nevertheless, scholars of hidden, complex social phenomena (in this example, urban deprivation but applicable more generally) have been happy to trade positivism and generality for depth and empathic insight:

> … [D]isadvantages (of ethnographic methods) are counterbalanced by an intimate view of slum life which gains in validity what it lacks in representativeness. When observing from a great distance one is apt

[15] Polsky (n 9) 138.

[16] See P Adler and P Adler, 'Foreword: Moving Backward', in J Ferrell and M Hamm (eds), *Ethnography at the Edge: Crime, Deviance, and Field Research* (Northeastern University Press 2008).

[17] See T Elliott and J Fleetwood, 'Law for Ethnographers' (2017) 10(1) *Methodological Innovations*.

[18] See Hammersley and Atkinson (n 3).

[19] See J Okely, 'Anthropology as Autobiography: Participatory and Embodied Knowledge' in J Okely and H Callaway (eds) *Anthropology and Autobiography* (Routledge 1992).

> to invent all sorts of irrational mental mechanisms to account for the behaviour of slum residents. When observing close at hand, we are made all the more aware of how our own ideals have blinded us to the practicality of slum residents.[20]

Ultimately every ethnography turns on the connected lives of researcher and participants. The story of the research itself becomes essential context for how the findings produced are to be understood. The reader can mull this description over and make decisions around the reliability of various data and interpretations. Future researchers, moreover, can perhaps take some comfort in reading about predecessors struggling, making mistakes and yet nevertheless completing research more or less successfully. Much of the chapter below provides the story of how my particular project unfolded.

I was lucky to be introduced to the youth worker I came to call 'Gerry'. I refer to participants and where they live/work with false names to protect their anonymity. He ran *The Club*, a youth justice project in what I would come to call *Northstreet*, an area of disadvantage in inner-city Dublin. In an act of great faith, he agreed to host me for a year. I was to act as a volunteer on his programmes and in return I would have access to *Club* clients and an introduction to their wider community. The Gardaí, who funded *The Club*'s work, after some negotiation not only granted me access to it but asked me to observe policing practices in the area to gain their perspective. Quite quickly, I learned the boundaries and layout of my 'field': *Northstreet*, and also began to get a sense that I had found the 'sample' that was most useful to my research: *The Crew*, a fluid offending youth group, with eight core and a rotating array of peripheral members.

For the young people, I surmised that in dress, accent, education and interests, I seemed indistinguishable from the myriad of youth, community, welfare and social workers that operate in the inner-city. This became increasingly apparent. Whilst I was spending full working days in *Northstreet* five days a week, my relationship with *The Crew* in particular remained stalled by their reluctance to be too frank with what they perceived to be an agent of officialdom. Even if I chose to identify myself as a researcher, 'writing a book' (as I called my PhD) on inner-city youth offending, subjects in the field tend to assign an identity to the ethnographer in a way that makes sense to themselves.[21] I had crossed lines in wanting to know about the real, lived

[20] G Suttles, *The Social Order of the Slum* (University of Chicago Press 1968) 12.

[21] See Hammersley and Atkinson, 2007 (n 3).

experiences of urban crime, but with my assigned identity I had lines left to cross.

IV – Challenges

It had become increasingly clear to me that I needed to get to know *The Crew* in the context of their street lives. I spent as much time as I could accompanying them as they 'cruised' (walked) around their area. I leaned my back against walls with them and eagerly became a passive observer of their conversation culture. Over the fieldwork my relationship with *The Crew* fluctuated. Some members came to trust me, whilst others did not. I had the opportunity to fruitfully interview some of them, whilst others became increasingly hostile to my presence. Ultimately it was difficult to maintain a field-persona whereby I could balance being a trusted confidant to the young men, whilst also clearly associated with the world of adult respectability in which youth and social workers operated. Indeed, as I spent afternoons quietly present, listening and observing as the young men constructed and smoked joints, it became understandably confusing that I could not to permit them to behave similarly when in *The Club*. Certain *Crew* members would use the cannabis itself to highlight our differences – waving joints in front of my mouth and explaining that everyone who wanted to be part of their group should smoke it. I consistently refused. Some lines could not be crossed.

Ultimately confused by what I was encountering I realised that there were a number of differences between my community of study and what I had previously read in literature. *The Crew* were not 'street elites',[22] nor were they a working class youth culture with deep ties to their community of origin. Rather, they were viewed by key members of the community as 'blow ins', unconnected to the area and its long-term residents. They were viewed as particularly troublesome, poorly presented and beneath the expectations of how historically working-class communities should behave in the 'renewed' inner-city of (then) Celtic Tiger Dublin.[23] The ways in which the residents of *Northstreet* articulated their understandings of local crime issues significantly differed furthermore. Some identified high-level drug dealing taking place on the estate whilst others claimed that *The Crew* were the sole local offenders. What determined these different views was a deep-seated community schism that opened during the emergence of Dublin's heroin epidemic and attempts by grass-roots activists to end it. I could not have known to even ask about these matters before I began fieldwork and indeed

[22] See J Katz, *Seductions of Crime: Moral and sensual aspects of doing evil* (Basic Books 1988).

[23] Ilan, 'Reclaiming Respectability?' (n 1).

it took the full duration of my time in the community to understand the meanings underpinning the conflicting accounts.

Time and trust made these nuanced findings possible and these qualities themselves were generated by blurring the boundaries between research and life. Ultimately, my existing middle-class presumptions about the population of council flat complexes had been significantly overturned. I had not previously understood the extent to which distinct hierarchies existed within such communities and how individuals, groups and families were far from homogenous. I learned that attitudes towards marginality, the law and state authority varied and had complex roots and drivers. I gained a significant empathic insight into how the marginalised struggle, not just for material security but to carve out a sense of worth, when wider society can view the urban poor as relatively worthless. The sheer volume of time spent in the company of *Crew* members, from whom I variously experienced protection and support, put-downs, suspicion, and at a final point, threats, demonstrated the extent to which the humanity and complexity of offenders should be highlighted. Criminals are neither 'monstrous' nor 'romantic', but complex and multifaceted. The same young people who could embody cold toughness could show remarkable tenderness to their young relatives. Much of *The Crew*'s day was dedicated to relatively typical teenage male pursuits.

My access to *Northstreet* had been very hard-won, in stark contrast to the rapid manner that I was accepted by youth/community/social workers and later the Gardaí at the local station, most of whom accepted my project and endeavoured to be both open and helpful. The assistance of various workers opened alternative avenues when my attempts to get closer to the community were floundering. I was drawn into useful networks, attending relevant meetings and learning more about the people and area I was studying. After researching within the *Northstreet* community for a year and some months, my transition to researching alongside the Gardaí was noticed and disapproval set in for various different participants. Specifically, *The Crew* made it clear that I was a suspected 'rat' and *persona non-grata*. This was disappointing. I had thought that I had been consistently laying the groundwork for my move – frequently mentioning that much like I was 'hanging out' with them, I wanted to do the same thing with the Gardaí. On the other hand, *The Crew* (and street groups like them) tend to construct the police as their enemy[24] and I had violated their taboo against speaking to police. I had thus crossed a line into a separate phase of the research.

[24] Ilan, 'Scumbags' (n 1).

When I reported to the *Northstreet* Garda station to begin research, this stage of the ethnography required a gearshift. First, I felt that I needed to project something of a more professional persona given that I was to be accompanying men and women in uniform engaging in more formal work than I had been used to observing. I eschewed my regular clothing in favour of slacks and smart shirts and was more forthright about taking notes and requesting interviews. Embedded first within a 'neighbourhood' and later a 'regular' unit, I felt that a relationship of mutual respect grew between myself and Garda participants. Approval was expressed at my approach of 'shadowing' members for entire shifts, sharing their anti-social hours, busy schedules and takeaway meals. For my part, I gained an appreciation of how difficult policing is, physically and emotionally. Interestingly, ideological misgivings that might be expected to develop between a leftist researcher and inner-city police division did not manifest. Rather, I felt included within a culture of deep solidarity and camaraderie that sustains Gardaí through the rigour and dangers of their job. I was surprised how open my participants were about some of the harsher and muscular approaches that can be taken to policing inner-city residents and felt gratitude with the extent to which my participants readily placed their bodies in front of mine when danger arose.

Every day, I kept a fieldwork diary of what I encountered and observed: incidents and conversations that stood out – whether as particularly noteworthy to me or my participants. At first these often took the form of surface observations; in time I was able to apply my existing knowledge to record deeper insights. The idea was to record concrete detail factually and to supplement it with notes about my feelings to maintain a reflexive perspective. In other words to try and be aware of how my moods might be affecting my records. My time in *Northstreet* and with the Gardaí yielded books full of handwritten fieldnotes and later typed files – together with folders full of transcribed interviews. This data was manually, thematically analysed. This entailed days of reading this data over, different coloured highlighters in hand, dividing the words into themes, quotes and insights. Of course, I had already crossed the line into analysis whilst fieldwork was underway. My experiences of fieldwork and deep knowledge of the participant groups and their circumstances would inherently inform the intuitive way in which the salient themes were identified.

V – Ethical Considerations

The entire research had been designed with a deep sense of ethics and had been cleared by the ethics committee at my institution. Informed consent was sought from participants both younger and older – parental consent was additionally sought to work with participants under the age of 16. Near-total confidentiality was guaranteed to every participant, whether young person, community member or professional – the only proviso (expressly communicated) was that confidentiality would be broken should disclosure of intention to hurt self or another take place. I recorded interviews using a tape recorder (digital not having become the norm yet) or by hand if that made the participant more comfortable. Some participants remained suspicious and asked to view my scratchy notes for signs of incriminating evidence, whereas others pointed out that they know what a signed confidentiality agreement meant and used the time to unburden themselves of what seemed like pent up feelings. Access negotiation did not just centre on interviews and indeed became an ongoing process where periodically participants made judgements about what would be shared with me.

Ultimately, the ethical framework I adopted called for more than expressly agreeing all principles in advance with participants and signifying this through obtaining a signature on a consent form (although this was done for all interviews – whilst 'passive consent' or informing participants of the research and carrying it out in the absence of objection was deployed in observation situations when interrupting the flow of the field would have been inappropriate). I was dedicated to representing participants in a fair and balanced manner, recognising that they had been generous in allowing me to study in their world, and that the power relations in our relationship would invert once I left the field and became an academic arbiter of how particular communities might be viewed[25] It was difficult to wring order out of accounts that were often conflicting. Part of the *Northstreet* adult community seemed to trust me and to open up about life in the area, past and present, whereas another section of the community did not seem to go beyond certain stock statements about improvements locally. I highlighted ambiguity and controversy where it existed and attempted as best as I could not to 'take sides', however much my relationships were better with certain participants than others. I strictly avoided involvement in offending behaviour and made every effort to suspend moral judgements and to neutrally observe participants without favour, whether they were young people in conflict with the law, members of the broader *Northstreet* community, Gardaí or social/youth workers.

VI – Reflections

Although lasting just two months, the police fieldwork was intense. Together with earlier material considering the role of youth justice workers, an analysis demonstrated the difficulties in simply dichotomising between progressive

[25] See Hobbs (n 14).

notions of welfarism, and regressive punitivism. Garda motivations, and their attitudes to inner-city residents varied between units and individuals. A significant number expressed their desire to help and their actions bore this out. Others were quite open in complaining about their duty to police recalcitrant criminals, 'scumbags' and 'gougers'.[26] Overall, there was a sense that the Gardaí constructed their mission as defending the values of the decent, law-abiding citizen (of which they could locate many within the inner-city) against the encroachment of this undesirable element. Their enthusiasm for this task and indeed sincere honesty could overspill into inappropriate remarks and actions that did little to improve frayed relations with the Irish urban poor that have a long historical legacy.[27]

Across the line, exposed to the lived experience of policing and being policed, the ways in which criminal justice operates 'on the ground' became clearer. The notion of a bureaucratic and legalistic system operating according to strictly rationalistic and evidence-based procedures did not hold up to what was recorded in my field notes. Rather, both officers and those who attempt to evade their attention are emotionally invested in their interactions, following cultural scripts built by social class and cumulative memory, and driven through masculinist prerogatives to triumph over the other side.[28] Many of the inner-city residents identified as 'decent' would say that the Gardaí had a distance to go to provide the level of service and protection that they would want, whereas those identified as 'rough' would tend to view the Gardaí as illegitimate oppressors. The dynamics of inner-city policing were furthermore complicated by urban renewal and rising property values, the reconstitution of class identities and the tendency of community schisms to leave particular groups and individuals open to censure as the local 'crime problem'.[29] The research produced findings that located the production of criminal behaviour within a 'dyadic' class-cultural dynamic[30]: the urban poor are exposed to structural conditions that can precipitate criminal activity, whilst at the same time the policing of their behaviour is underpinned by a set of meanings that treats the general behaviour of the urban poor as suspicious.

Even the more progressive and welfarist project of youth justice work showed evidence of class-cultural dynamics where, with echoes of Victorian

[26] Ilan, 'Scumbags' (n 1).

[27] A Mulcahy and E O'Mahony, *Policing and Social Marginalisation in Ireland* (Combat Poverty Agency 2005).

[28] Ilan, 'Scumbags' (n 1).

[29] Ilan, 'If you don't let us in' (n 1).

[30] J Young, *The Exclusive Society, Social Exclusion, Crime and Difference in Late Modernity* (Sage 1999).

reformism, clients were to be rescued from becoming socialised into a ghetto culture, through a pedagogy that equates citizenship and inclusion with a more middle-class subjectivity.[31] Hardworking and caring youth justice workers precipitate change through cultivating human relationships, slowly gaining the trust of their clients who may not be in a position to action the lessons they are learning for some years. Throughout the research, change seemed possible when lines were crossed and middle-class professionals and marginalised young people, offending or at risk of, could respect and understand each other. Such moments proved to be relatively rare and fleeting as the leviathan of social structures urged individuals in different directions. Indeed, as my PhD finished, and a career in academia developed, it was to do the same to myself and my young participants, some of whom were developing significant criminal records.

Although I still consider this research to be one of the most worthwhile experiences of my life, it was not without its difficulties. I was always regretful that my hard-won relationships with various individuals in *Northstreet* deteriorated. I had gotten to know many residents and those working close-by well. Even the relationships that endured eroded with time. The *Crew*'s rejection of me weighed particularly and I wondered whether I should have conducted the policing research in a different part of the city. On the other hand, I had gained the opportunity to observe my own participants from different sides of the criminal justice system directly interacting. It is difficult to say whether I would have done anything differently. For sure I made numerous mistakes (for example being over ambitious in my attempts to establish research relationships early) but these were most apparent in hindsight. The exceptional training and support I received from my supervisor were complemented most effectively by what I learned from my mistakes and some of her lessons only made sense to me in light of them. Personally, I had become significantly less naïve about what producing deep insight entails and how the complex realities of urban marginality and crime evade simplistic solutions. Ultimately I learnt the value of ethnographic work that blurs the lines between life and research, researcher and participant, academic theory and authentic accounts of life at the margins.

---

[31] Ilan, 'If you don't let us in' (n 1).

Chapter 11

Researching Domestic Violence: The INASC Project

Conor Hanly*

I – Introduction

This chapter describes the methodology employed by Irish researchers from *Safe Ireland* and NUI Galway to document the response of the criminal justice system to incidents of domestic violence. This research was part of a wider pan-European study known as the INASC project – an acronym for *Improving Needs Assessment and Victims' Support in Domestic Violence-related Criminal Proceedings*. Organisations from five European countries—Austria, Germany, Ireland, the Netherlands, and Portugal—attempted to determine the experience of victims of domestic violence within the criminal justice system in each country, and the extent to which the needs of such victims were being assessed and met by law enforcement agencies.[1] The project received funding from the Criminal Justice Programme of the European Union.[2]

II – Research Question

In 1997, the Task Force on Violence against Women identified the key elements of domestic violence:

> Domestic violence refers to the use of physical or emotional force or threat of physical force, including sexual violence, in close adult relationships. ... The term 'domestic violence' goes beyond actual physical violence. It can also involve emotional abuse, the destruction of property, isolation from friends, family and other potential sources

---

* Dr Conor Hanly, Lecturer in Law, NUI Galway: The reflections in this chapter are those of the author alone and do not necessarily reflect the views of the other researchers involved in this project or of Safe Ireland.

[1] See <www.inasc.org> accessed 12 March 2019., where all outputs from the project may be reviewed.

[2] Grant number JUST/2013/JPEN/AG/4591. This programme is implemented by the Justice Directorate General. For information on the programme, see <http://ec.europa.eu/justice/grants1/programmes-2014-2020/justice/index_en.htm> accessed 12 March 2019.

> of support; threats to others including children; stalking; and control over access to money, personal items, food, transportation and the telephone.[3]

Unlike other jurisdictions, domestic violence is not itself a crime under Irish law, but many of its forms—especially those involving physical or sexual violence—have long been prosecutable: assault, sexual assault, rape, threats to kill, criminal damage, etc. Other forms of domestic violence, such as taking steps to isolate another person from support networks or controlling his or her access to money and other items (today referred to as coercive control[4]) were not prosecutable until very recently.[5]

The prevalence of domestic violence in Ireland is unclear, but all indications suggest that it is a problem of considerable proportions. In 2017, for example, the courts dealt with almost 16,000 applications for orders under the Domestic Violence Act 1996.[6] This figure underrepresents the true scale of the problem: table 1 sets out the findings of several prevalence studies conducted in or relevant to Ireland.[7] Each of these studies indicates that a large number of people in Ireland suffer domestic violence in some form.

---

[3] Task Force on Violence against Women, *Report* (Office of the Tánaiste 1997) para 3.1.

[4] See, for example, Stark, *Coercive Control: How Men Entrap Women in Personal Life* (Oxford University Press 2009).

[5] The Domestic Violence Act 2018, in s 39, makes it an offence for a person to knowingly and persistently engage in controlling or coercive behavior that has a serious effect upon that person's spouse, civil partner or intimate partner, and is such that a reasonable person would consider this effect to be likely. A serious effect is one that causes the victim to fear that violence will be used against him or her, or causes the victim serious alarm or distress that has a substantial adverse impact on his or her day-to-day activities. The 2018 Act came into effect on 1 January 2019.

[6] Courts Service, *Annual Report for 2017* (Courts Service 2018) 61-2. These orders are explained in n 23. The District Court, which deals with the vast majority of such applications, granted just over half of them (8,927 out of 15,962). The Circuit Court issued a further 51 orders under the same legislation. ibid.

[7] Note that each of these studies classified the forms of domestic violence differently, and had different eligibility criteria.

Table 1: Prevalence Studies applicable to Ireland

Study	**N=**	**Physical Violence (%)**	**Sexual Violence (%)**	**Controlling Behaviour (%)**	**Emotional or Psychological Violence (%)**
Women's Aid, 1995[8]	575	10	4	____	13; 9; 2[9]
Bradley et al, 2002[10]	1692	39[11]	____	69	____
Watson & Parsons, 2005[12]	3077	6.5 (+7)	5	____	5 (+20)
Fundamental Rights Agency, 2014[13]	1567	24	8	23	31[14]

These findings suggest that the scale of the domestic violence problem in Ireland is huge. Using the 2011 census figures and extrapolating from the FRA findings, for example, some 385,000 women have suffered physical

[8] Kelleher and Associates and O'Connor, *Making the Links* (Women's Aid 1995). A total of 677 women completed questionnaires, of whom 575 either were currently, or had been, in an intimate relationship.

[9] The figures presented here are in respect of mental cruelty, threats of physical violence, and damage to pets, property or other items, respectively.

[10] Bradley, Smith, Long & O'Dowd, 'Reported Frequency of Domestic Violence: cross sectional survey of women attending general practice' (2002) 324 BMJ 271–74. Self-completion questionnaires were given to 2,615 women attending 22 general practitioner practices. A total of 1,871 responded, but the survey analysis was limited to the 1,692 women who were currently or had been involved in an intimate relationship.

[11] The definition of violence in this survey included forced sex (i.e. rape).

[12] Watson and Parsons, *Domestic Abuse of Women and Men: Report on the National Study of Domestic Abuse* (National Crime Council, 2005). The research team conducted telephone interviews with a nationally representative sample of 3,077 men and women aged 18 or over. The researchers distinguished between those who had suffered minor or isolated acts of abuse, and those who had suffered severe domestic abuse. The figure in brackets is the former group. There were no minor acts of sexual violence.

[13] Fundamental Rights Agency of the European Union, *Violence Against Women: An EU-wide Survey* (Publications Office of the European Union 2014). This study involved interviews with 42,000 adult women across all 28 Member States of the EU, with at least 1,500 in each country (aside from Luxembourg in which 908 women were interviewed). The figures presented here are lifetime experiences since the age of 15. An interactive survey map setting out the results in each country is available at <http://fra.europa.eu/en/publications-and-resources/data-and-maps/survey-data-explorer-violence-against-women-survey> accessed 12 March 2019.

[14] This figure includes any form of psychological violence, including controlling behavior, economic violence, abusive behavior, and threats to children. The separate figure for controlling behavior is set out for comparison purposes.

violence at the hands of an intimate partner.[15] Watson and Parsons estimated that 213,000 women and 88,000 men have suffered severe domestic abuse at some point in their lives.[16] This abuse can lead to homicide: the Women's Aid Femicide Monitoring Project has tracked 209 women who died violently between 1996 and 2016 in Ireland.[17] In the cases that were resolved, over half the women died at the hands of a male intimate partner, and another third were killed by a male relative.[18]

All victims of crime require law enforcement agencies to vindicate their rights by arresting the perpetrator and prosecuting him through the criminal justice system. Victims of domestic violence, however, by definition are caught up in an ongoing situation. The nature of domestic violence as a pattern of behaviour rather than an isolated event is well-recognised by academic researchers,[19] by government officials,[20] and by An Garda Síochána.[21] A victim of a theft or even a robbery is unlikely to be in a similar position again. A victim of domestic violence, on the other hand, is almost certain to face a similar or worse situation unless preventative steps are taken. Bradley et al found, for example, that of the 651 women in their sample who had suffered violent behavior at the hands of a current or previous partner, nearly one-third (201) had suffered eight or more violent

[15] These figures are derived from the 2011 Census, which found a total of 1,605,052 females in Ireland aged between 18 and 74, the age parameters for the FRA study. For the 2011 Census figures, see <https://www.cso.ie/px/pxeirestat/Statire/SelectVarVal/Define.asp?maintable=CD202&PLanguage=0> accessed 12 March 2019.

[16] Watson and Parsons, op cit, 169.

[17] See Women's Aid, *Behind Closed Doors: 20 Years of the Women's Aid Femicide Monitoring Project 1996–2016* (Women's Aid Dublin 2016) available at <https://www.womensaid.ie/download/pdf/20161129124652.pdf> accessed 12 March 2019. Women's Aid report that another eight women died in 2017. Women's' Aid, *Femicide Watch 2017*, 2018, available at <https://www.womensaid.ie/download/pdf/womens_aid_femicide_watch_2017.pdf> accessed 12 March 2019.

[18] Women's Aid, *Behind Closed Doors*, op cit, 7. The figures given are 89 (54 percent) and 54 (33 percent), respectively. What constitutes a 'resolved' case is unclear, but the term appears to refer to a case in which the identity of the perpetrator is known.

[19] See, for example, Watson and Parsons, op cit, 38 ('a pattern of physical, emotional or sexual behavior between partners in an intimate relationship that causes, or risks causing, significant negative consequences for the persons affected.').

[20] See, for example, Task Force on Violence against Women, op cit, para 3.9.

[21] An Garda Síochána, *Domestic Violence Policy* (An Garda Síochána, 1996) at para 10.7 ('domestic violence crimes are repeated, systematic and dangerous crimes, often against the same victim'). This policy has since been revised, but the nature of domestic violence as an ongoing phenomenon continues to be recognised: see An Garda Síochána, *Domestic Abuse Intervention Policy 2017* (An Garda Síochána 2017) at para 3.14 (noting that domestic abuse tends to follow three phases, and once it has begun it 'not only continues, but over time tends to increase in both frequency and severity'.).

episodes.[22] In addition to vindication, therefore, domestic violence victims also have ongoing protection needs. Traditionally, these needs have been met through the civil courts: the Domestic Violence Act 1996, for example, empowers the courts to issue a range of protective orders,[23] a breach of which constitutes a distinct offence.[24] Increasingly, however, assessments of these ongoing needs are being integrated into the criminal justice system itself, and this is especially true following the enactment of the EU Victims' Directive.

The Victims' Directive

The European Union began to legislate on behalf of crime victims from the beginning of the twenty-first century.[25] The European Commission explained that doing so grew from the Union's objective to 'offer its citizens an area of freedom, security and justice in which their freedom of movement is ensured.'[26] Without common minimum standards of treatment for victims of crime, citizens would be unable to trust the legal system in other Member States, and that absence of trust would interfere with free movement.[27] In 2012, the EU adopted the Victims' Directive, which came into effect in November 2015.[28] The Directive requires Member States to enact legislation to give effect to a variety of rights that crime victims should enjoy throughout the European Union. Of particular interest is art 22(1):

> Member States shall ensure that victims receive a timely and individual assessment, in accordance with national procedures, to identify specific

---

[22] Bradley et al, op cit, at 272.

[23] Broadly, the courts may issue barring orders or safety orders. A barring order removes the abuser from the family home. A safety order prohibits the abuser from engaging in violent conduct towards the victim. The courts may also issue a protection order, which is effectively a temporary safety order, or an interim barring order, which temporarily removes the abuser from the family home. Virtually all applications for orders under the 1996 Act are dealt with in the District Court: see n 6.

[24] Domestic Violence Act 1996, s 17. The penalty for breach of these orders is a fine or imprisonment for up to 12 months. Under s 18, members of An Garda Síochána may arrest without warrant anyone they believe with reasonable cause to have breached an order made under the Act.

[25] See, for example, Council Framework Decision 2001/220/JHA on the standing of victims in criminal proceedings, and Council Directive 2004/80/EC relating to compensation for victims of crime. The 2001 Framework Decision was a milestone in that it represented the first '"hard-law instrument" concerning victims of crime at the international level'. Groenhuijsen and Pemberton, 'The EU Framework Decision for Victims of Crime: Does Hard Law make a Difference?' (2009) 17 E J Crime, Crim L and Crim Jus 43–59, 43.

[26] Communication from the European Commission, COM (2011) 274 final, 18 May 2011.

[27] ibid.

[28] Directive 2012/29/EU of the European Parliament and of the Council of 25 October 2012 establishing minimum standards on the rights, support and protection of victims of crime, OJ L 315/57.

protection needs and to determine whether and to what extent they would benefit from special measures in the course of criminal proceedings, as provided for under Articles 23 and 24,[29] due to their particular vulnerability to secondary and repeat victimisation, to intimidation and to retaliation.

The assessment should consider in particular the victim's personal characteristics, the type or nature of the crime, and the circumstances of the crime.[30] Member States should pay particular attention to 'victims whose relationship to and dependence on the offender make them particularly vulnerable.'[31] Assessments should be 'carried out with the close involvement of the victim and shall take into account their wishes'.[32] The Justice Directorate General (DG) considers art 22 to be 'one of the major achievements' of the Directive.[33] The DG noted that good practice indicates that either police or victim support services are best placed to conduct the needs assessment.[34] The core of the INASC project focused on the extent to which assessment procedures and victim-protection mechanisms were in place in five European jurisdictions immediately prior to the Directive coming into force. The project was designed to help improve understanding of victims' experiences and the manner in which domestic cases were dealt with by criminal justice agencies.

---

[29] Art 23 requires Member States to ensure that victims with special protection needs can avail of various measures to ensure a sympathetic interview, to give evidence without being physically present, to prevent unnecessary questions about the victims' private life, and that court hearings will not be open to the public. Art 24 provides for further measures to be taken when dealing with a child victim.

[30] Victims' Directive, art 22(2).

[31] ibid, art 22(3). See also Recital 18, which notes that violence committed within a close relationship 'could cover physical, sexual, psychological or economic violence and could result in physical, mental or emotional harm or economic loss. Violence in close relationships is a serious and often hidden social problem which could cause systematic psychological and physical trauma with severe consequences because the offender is a person whom the victim should be able to trust. Victims of violence in close relationships may therefore be in need of special protection measures.'

[32] ibid., art 22(6).

[33] *DG Justice Guidance Document related to the transposition and implementation of Directive 2012/29/EU*, December 2013, at 44. This document can be accessed online at <https://e-justice.europa.eu/content_victims_of_crime_in_criminal_proceedings-66-en.do> accessed 12 March 2019.

[34] ibid at 45. The Guidance Document does not make clear what kind of expertise victim support services should have, but presumably such groups should not be involved in victim assessments without demonstrable relevant experience.

III – Methodological Approach

The INASC project was conceived, designed and implemented by non-governmental organisations in five EU jurisdictions.[35] The project timeline was from February 2014 until March 2016, and focused on intimate partner violence (IPV) against adult women by their male partners. The INASC project was built around four workstreams:

- Workstream 1 – A report on the legal and policy frameworks within which cases of domestic violence are dealt;
- Workstream 2 – A quantitative analysis of 70 domestic violence files from either the public prosecutor's office or from the courts, to identify needs and risk assessment indicators;
- Workstream 3 – A series of qualitative interviews with criminal justice agencies and victim support services;
- Workstream 4 – The production of a 'toolkit', to include a set of criteria for the establishment or improvement of protection needs assessment mechanisms, a booklet on case typologies, and a pack for evaluating the impact of assessment procedures.

The Irish research team consisted of five members from Safe Ireland (three of whom were directly involved in the research process), two from NUI Galway, and three NUI Galway PhD students recruited as research assistants. The NUI Galway team was involved primarily in Workstream 2, and it is with this element of the INASC project that this chapter is concerned.

To complete Workstream 2, all five participating countries were required to conduct a quantitative analysis of 70 recent and completed official prosecutorial domestic violence files.[36] The purpose of this analysis was agreed at an early meeting:

> [T]he analysis will focus on relevant indicators, namely those arising from the approach contained in Article 22 of the Directive 2012/29/EU regarding the individual assessment components. The type and quality of

[35] The participant organisations were CESIS (Centre for Studies for Social Intervention) in Portugal, the Institute of Conflict Research in Austria, the German Police University and Zoom (the Society for Prospective Developments) in Germany, the Verwey Jonker Instituut in the Netherlands, and Safe Ireland in Ireland.

[36] The files needed to have been completed as we were interested in recording outcomes as well as needs assessments.

> proofs as well as evidence on the activation of support services essential for ensuring the victim's protection will also be covered. The analysis will also highlight the use by the judicial system of different forms of protection measures and/or protection procedures.[37]

Thus, the analysis was to collect information on the personal characteristics of the victims, the type and circumstances of the crimes being prosecuted, the proofs offered, the use of assessment processes and the protection procedures implemented, if any. This analysis would paint a detailed picture of the way in which each of the jurisdictions involved deal with domestic violence cases on the eve of the transposition of the Victims' Directive. The final output for this Workstream would be a comparative analysis of the national reports, and to assist in that process each of the national teams was required to base their reports on an instrument specially developed by the German Police University.[38]

IV – Challenges

The Safe Ireland/NUI Galway team contacted both the Office of the Director of Public Prosecutions and An Garda Síochána for permission to access files that involved allegations by an adult female of non-sexual and non-lethal violence that occurred in a domestic context.[39] Most such offences would be prosecuted as assault under ss 2 or 3 of the Non-Fatal Offences against the Person Act 1997. By virtue of the DPPs General Direction No 3, issued under s 8 of the Garda Síochána Act 2005, members of An Garda Síochána may prosecute summary offences and many indictable offences other than those reserved for the DPP.[40] Section 2 of the 1997 Act is a summary offence, while s 3 can be tried either way but the DPP has elected generally for summary trial.[41] Thus, An Garda Síochána will have responsibility for prosecuting most domestic violence cases without reference to the DPP, and the Office of

[37] 'Initial Sketch: Draft National Selection Criteria and Outline of Research Design for Workstream 2', agreed at INASC Meeting, 16 July 2014 (on file with author), at para 1.0.

[38] The German Police University drafted the instrument and then sent it to each participating team for comments. The NUI Galway team made suggestions for significant alterations which were incorporated into the final version of the instrument.

[39] Sexual offences and homicides tend to attract special attention from investigators and were placed outside the INASC parameters as their inclusion might skew the results.

[40] General Direction No 3, dated 8 November 2011, at ss 1 and 2. The General Direction is available at <https://www.dppireland.ie/filestore/documents/General_Direction_No._3.pdf> accessed 12 March 2019. Those offences reserved for prosecution by the DPP include homicide, sexual offences and many offences under the Non-Fatal Offences against the Person Act 1997, especially ss 4, 5, 10, 13 and 15 (causing serious harm, threats to kill, harassment, reckless endangerment, and false imprisonment, respectively).

[41] General Direction No 3, at s 4(1)(a).

the DPP confirmed that as a result they could offer little assistance to Workstream 2.[42]

Garda involvement

Safe Ireland requested An Garda Síochána to permit access to their domestic violence files for analysis, and the NUI Galway team met with representatives of the Garda Research Bureau to refine the details of the research. In particular, it was agreed that the project analysis would be more robust if the data were drawn from a representative sample of domestic violence files, and the INASC partners agreed that we could proceed on that basis. Thus, we sought access to a representative sample of files flagged by An Garda Síochána as domestic violence cases that met the following criteria:

a) The offender and victim were involved in a relationship (spouses, civil partners or cohabitants sharing a principal private residence);

b) Files with male victims should be excluded;

c) Files involving allegations of homicide and sexual offences should be excluded;

d) Incidents should have occurred since the start of 2010 (if more than one incident was on a file, then the most recent incident should meet this criterion);

e) Files should have been concluded in their entirety by the end of 2013 (either a decision not to prosecute, or if a prosecution had been initiated, then a resolution by that date with no outstanding appeal).[43]

While these negotiations continued, the Garda Inspectorate published its *Report on Crime Investigation*.[44] The Inspectorate was highly critical of An Garda Síochána's handling of domestic violence cases: inadequate monitoring and supervision by senior officers, incorrect recording and categorisation of many domestic violence cases, non-implementation of the Garda Domestic Violence Policy (especially in terms of arrests and follow up), and negative

[42] Communication dated 19 September 2014; copy on file with author.

[43] Communication dated 12 November 2014 to Garda Research Bureau; copy on file with author.

[44] Garda Inspectorate, *Report on Crime Investigation* (Garda Inspectorate 2014) published on 11 November 2014. The Report is available at <www.gsinsp.ie> accessed 12 March 2019.

attitudes towards domestic violence policy held by some Garda officers.[45] Two months after the publication of this Report, An Garda Síochána declined to participate in the INASC project, citing data protection concerns.[46] The NUI Galway team made suggestions to overcome this issue: in particular, we proposed to release project funds to the Garda Research Bureau to hire a researcher who would work fulltime on extracting data from the files, which would then be handed to the NUI Galway team for analysis.[47] Ultimately, An Garda Síochána again declined to participate, noting that a variety of changes were being implemented on foot of the Inspectorate's Report. These changes would be beyond the INASC study's parameters and the resulting analysis therefore would not reflect the new Garda approach to domestic violence cases.

Revision of Workstream 2 in Ireland

Without access to official files, the Irish research team was unable to contribute directly to the comparative element of the INASC project. To assist the project, however, and to fulfill obligations to the European funders, the project leaders (the Portuguese team) consented to the Irish team putting into operation a revised Workstream 2 that focused on securing information from victims of domestic violence. To keep the Irish contribution in line with the contributions of the other partners, the team agreed to use the research instrument drawn up by the German Police University as a template. That instrument had to be adapted, however, to take account of the differences between the methodology being followed by the other partners and that being followed by the Irish team. From the template, the team produced a survey instrument that contained both quantitative and semi-structured qualitative questions. The survey (both quantitative and qualitative questions) would be administered during individual face-to-face interviews between participants and one of two members of the research team. Adopting this interview method brought several benefits, not least the likelihood of better responses through the development of a rapport between the surveyor and the participant.[48] The researchers were also able to explain questions to the participants, an important point bearing in mind that for some participants,

[45] The Inspectorate's findings with respect to the investigation of domestic violence incidents are set out in the Summary of Findings at 17–18.

[46] Letter dated 5 January 2015, copy on file with author.

[47] Communication to Garda Commissioner, dated 12 February 2015; copy on file with the author.

[48] Mayhew and Van Dijk, 'Assessing Crime through International Victimization Surveys', in Gadd, Karstedt and Messner, eds, *The SAGE Handbook of Criminological Research Methods* (SAGE 2012) 253–67, at 255 (see Box 17.1 summarising the benefits of different victimisation survey methodologies).

English was not their first language. Further, the researcher would be able to assess the participant's demeanour, and to take immediate action if the survey caused the participant to become distressed. Our choice of interviewers was also important. Both were experienced in interviewing victims of violence, and both were women. It was felt, on the basis of similar prior projects, that female victims of domestic violence would be more comfortable speaking to a female interviewer.[49] It was hoped that this would lead to a greater level of disclosure. In the SAVI study, for example, the telephone surveys were conducted by fourteen women; the only male researcher discontinued in that role as he was only half as successful as the female researchers in eliciting participation in the study.[50] Nevertheless, a male member of the INASC team was ready to conduct interviews if that was the participant's preference —no such request was made by any of the participants.

We conducted two pilot interviews to test the survey instrument, and made some alterations to it based on this experience. The final instrument sought information on the following matters:

a) Characteristics of the first, the first reported, and the most violent reported incidents;

b) Reasons for reporting to the Gardaí, and the timing in doing so;

c) Victim expectations of the criminal justice system;

d) Garda response to domestic violence complaints and their subsequent investigations of those complaints;

e) Garda use of needs and risk assessments, and

f) Outcomes of the Garda investigation and any prosecution that was brought.

---

[49] McGee et al, *The SAVI Report: Sexual Abuse and Violence in Ireland* (Liffey Press 2002), at 53. See also Smith, 'Enhancing the Quality of Survey Data on Violence against Women: A Feminist Approach' (1994) 8(1) Gender and Soc. 109–27, 116 (noting that interviewers involved in projects focused on violence against women are invariably female).

[50] McGee et al, op cit. See also Sorensen et al, 'The Prevalence of Adult Sexual Assault: The Los Angeles Epidemiologic Catchment Area Project' (1987) 126 American J Epidemiology 1154–64 (finding that participants were more likely to disclose a sexual assault to female interviewers than to male interviewers).

The quantitative results were input into a specially designed matrix that generated descriptive statistics. Particular care was taken in inputting the data into the matrix, and this was done by one member of the research team to ensure consistency. Members of the research team transcribed the qualitative material which was subjected to a thematic analysis.[51]

Sample

Given the temporal and financial constraints of the project, domestic violence providers associated with Safe Ireland were asked to identify female participants who met the following criteria:

a) They had experienced domestic violence at the hands of a male partner;

b) They had reported at least one incident of domestic violence to the Gardaí between 2010 and 2013;

c) They were aged at least 18 at the time of that report; and,

d) They had sufficient understanding of the English language to be able to answer the survey questions.

The sampling involved therefore was subject to two primary limitations. First, the participants were identified by domestic violence agencies, which thus exercised a form of 'gatekeeper' power. The research team had no way of knowing the basis on which individual participants were selected. Second, our methodology made no attempt to select a random, representative sample, adopting instead a purposive sampling method. In other words, participants were selected on the basis of characteristics that fit the purpose of the study. This form of sampling was deemed appropriate for the purpose of this study, but care would obviously have to be taken in extrapolating more generally from the results.

Participants were sought from around the country in proportions that roughly replicated the spread of the national population:

[51] Safe Ireland published the results of the Irish research under the title, *In Search of Justice: Women and the Irish Legal System* (Safe Ireland 2016), available at <https://www.safeireland.ie/policy-publications/> accessed 12 March 2019.

Area	No of Participants	Area	No of Participants
Dublin	9	Rest of Munster	9
Rest of Leinster	9	Galway	4
Cork	4	Rest of Connacht	1
Limerick	4	**TOTAL**	40

The participants ranged in age from 20 to 62, with an average age of just over 40; half were in their twenties. Thirty-five were either Irish or citizens of the European Union, and almost all had children. Over half held third-level qualifications, but over half worked in the home—only one-third were employed. For over two-thirds of participants, social welfare payments constituted their main source of income.

V – Ethics

The INASC project was conducted externally to NUI Galway, and accordingly formal university ethics approval was unnecessary. Nevertheless, given the sensitive nature of the issues under discussion, the researchers paid particular attention to ethical considerations in designing the research. The team was concerned especially with protecting confidentiality, informed consent, minimisation of distress, and the storage of sensitive information.

Confidentiality

All participants were assured of as much confidentiality as the law permits, and each participant was assigned a random name, which was used throughout the final report. It is not always possible to lawfully maintain complete confidentiality, however. In particular, the Criminal Justice (Withholding of Information on Offences against Children and Vulnerable Persons) Act 2012 makes it an offence for a person to fail to disclose information of material assistance to the punishment of those who have committed scheduled offences against children or other vulnerable persons.[52] When researching issues such as domestic violence, there is always the possibility of uncovering information about the commission of such offences, and the research team

[52] s 2 applies to offences listed in sch 1 committed against children; s 3 applies to offences listed in sch 2 committed against vulnerable persons as defined in s 1 (persons with a mental disorder or an intellectual disability, or a physical impairment, that severely restricts the person's ability to guard against serious exploitation or abuse). Scheduled offences include homicide, rape and sexual assault, incest, serious assaults, threats to kill, endangerment, false imprisonment, and child abduction.

would be under a legal obligation to disclose that information to the Gardaí. All participants were expressly made aware of this fact.

Informed consent

Each participant was provided with a document that explained the nature of the research and its importance. Participants signed a consent form that emphasised that participation was entirely voluntary, and that individual questions could be skipped if the participant felt uncomfortable answering them. Further, the form required participants to affirmatively indicate that the nature of the research had been explained to them, that they understood that they could withdraw at any time, and that they agreed to take part in the research.

Minimisation of distress

The researchers who conducted the surveys were women: as noted earlier, experience in other studies involving sensitive issues indicates that research participants tend to be more comfortable speaking with female researchers. Further, the surveyors were both experienced in dealing with victims of violence. The research team leaders also drew up a comprehensive Distressed Participant Protocol for use in the event of the survey provoking a distressed response from a participant. The Protocol stated that the emotional wellbeing of the participants superseded the collection of data, and that the interview should be suspended if a participant exhibited signs of distress. The participants were to be offered breaks whenever it seemed necessary. Finally, the survey interviewers were equipped with a list of local support agencies to which a distressed participant could be referred.

Access to data

The information disclosed in the interviews was inherently sensitive, and care was taken to restrict access to that information. The completed surveys were stored securely in locked cabinets, to which only members of the research team had access. The materials were removed only for the purpose of analysis, and then only by researchers on the team. All research assistants recruited to transcribe the qualitative answers were also required contractually to sign and to abide by a confidentiality agreement.

VI – Reflections

This project raised several methodological issues, some relating to design and others to practical problems that arose during the project. Perhaps the most important design issue concerned the focus on female victims of domestic violence. A second design issue concerns the use of victim interviews to capture factual court-related information. On the practical side, the size of the sample deserves a comment, as does the difficulty in accessing official files.

Gender symmetry in domestic violence

The INASC project focused on the experience of women who have suffered interpersonal violence at the hands of male partners. This focus on the experience of female victims derives from the feminist male control theory of interpersonal violence (IPV), which holds that due to the gender inequalities inherent in the patriarchal nature of society, IPV is invariably committed by men as a means of maintaining control within a family structure.[53] This view of domestic violence informs most international instruments. The Istanbul Convention, for example, makes reference in its Preamble to violence against women being a 'manifestation of historically unequal power relations between women and men'.[54] Domestic violence is stated to affect women disproportionately, and accordingly falls within the definition of gender-based violence.[55] By art 2(2), signatory States are obligated to 'pay particular attention to women victims of gender-based violence in implementing the terms of the Convention.'

As a research methodology, focusing on women's experiences is a perfectly valid approach—innumerable studies have focused on the experiences of particular social subgroups. Nevertheless, some thought should go into a decision to focus on women. Numerous studies have shown a high incidence of female-perpetrator domestic violence. In Ireland, for example, in a report to the Irish Department of Health, McKeown and Kidd identified 13 prevalence studies carried out in four common-law countries between 1972 and 1999, that were based on representative samples and which included

[53] See, for example, Dobash and Dobash, *Violence against Wives: A Case against the Patriarchy* (Open Books 1979) and 'Women's Violence to Men in Intimate Relationships: Working on a Puzzle', (2004) 44 Brit J Criminol. 324–49; Pagelow, *Family Violence* (Praegar 1984); Fagan and Browne, 'Violence between spouses and intimates: Physical aggression between women and men in intimate relationships', in Reiss and Roth, eds, 3 *Understanding and Preventing Violence* (National Academies Press, 1994) 115–292; Smith, 'Patriarchal Ideology and Wife Beating: A Test of a Feminist Hypothesis' (1990) 5 Violence and Victims 257–73.

[54] Council of Europe Convention on Preventing and Combating Violence against Women and Domestic Violence, 2011. The Convention came into force in 2014, and Ireland signed it in November 2015. The text of the Convention is available at <http://www.coe.int/en/web/istanbul-convention/text-of-the-convention> accessed 12 March 2019.

[55] Art 3(d) of the Istanbul Convention defines gender-based violence as 'violence that is directed against a woman because she is a woman or *that affects women disproportionately*' (emphasis added).

both male and female experiences of domestic violence.[56] This research showed that, at least over the year prior to that in which the studies were conducted, women were more likely than men to engage in violence to their spouses or partners.[57] A recent British study of over 1,000 university students found that women were more physically aggressive to their partners than men, and that there was no substantial difference between the sexes in controlling behavior.[58] Internationally, Martin Fiebert at California State University has compiled a list of 286 scholarly investigations, including 221 empirical studies, that demonstrate that women are at least as physically aggressive as men to their partners.[59] Many of these studies utilised the Conflict Tactics Scale (CTS), which records participants' responses to domestic conflict, from reasoned discussion, through psychological aggression and into physical violence, both minor and severe. This instrument, developed in the United States in the 1970s by Murray Straus,[60] has become the dominant mechanism to measure the prevalence of domestic violence.[61] Notwithstanding its popularity, the CTS has attracted criticism.[62] Some critics suggest that women might employ violence defensively against her male

[56] McKeown and Kidd, *Men and Domestic Violence: What Research Tells Us* (Department of Health and Children 2002) which is available at <http://www.lenus.ie/hse/bitstream/10147/288412/1/MenDomesticViolence.pdf> accessed 12 March 2019. The countries in question were Great Britain, the United States, Canada and Australia.

[57] Supported by 12 of the studies; only one study came to the opposite conclusion. When measured against a lifetime, however, the opposite picture emerged: men were more likely than women to have engaged in interpersonal violence.

[58] Bates, Graham-Kevan and Archer, 'Testing Predictions from the Male Control Theory of Men's Partner Violence' (2014) 40(1) Aggress. Behav 42–55.

[59] See <http://web.csulb.edu/~mfiebert/assault.htm> accessed on 12 March 2019.

[60] Straus, 'Measuring intra-family conflict and violence: The Conflict Tactics (CT) Scales' (1979) 41(1) J Marriage and Fam. 75–88. The revised version of the instrument—the CTS2—is traceable to Straus et al, 'The Revised Conflict Tactics Scale (CTS2): Development and Preliminary Psychometric Data' (1996) 17(3) J. Family Issues 283–316.

[61] Straus asserts that between 1979 and 2005, over 600 peer-reviewed papers and 10 books using the CTS were published, and in the 10-year period between 1995 and 2005, about 5 CTS-based papers were being published each month. Strauss, 'Conflict Tactics Scales' in Jackson, ed, *Encyclopedia of Domestic Violence* (Routledge 2007) 190–97, 195. Langhinrichsen-Rohling considered the development of the CTS among the most important in the field of IPV-research because the instrument 'allowed researchers to quantitatively study events that … typically took place in private.' Langhinrichsen-Rohling, 'Top 10 "Greatest Hits": Important Findings and Future Directions for Intimate Partner Violence Research' (2005) 20 J Interpersonal Violence 108–118, 109.

[62] Strauss dismisses much of this criticism as ideologically inspired, because CTS-based studies frequently contradict the feminist theory that partner violence is almost exclusively committed by men as a means to dominate women. Strauss, 'Conflict Tactics Scales', in Jackson, ed, *Encyclopedia of Domestic Violence*, op cit, at 193.

partner's aggression, a factor that the CTS might have difficulty detecting.[63] Others argue that the CTS 'treats a slap, a push, or a shove by a man as equivalent to the same acts by a woman and fails to measure the damage or consequences of those acts'.[64] Such apparent equivalence fails to take into account the far greater damage that male violence does due to a man's greater size, weight and strength. Watson and Parsons make this point in the context of the ESRI study in Ireland: they found that 29 percent of women and 26 percent of men had experienced domestic abuse in their lifetime.[65] Nevertheless, women were more likely to suffer severe abuse: the authors summarised their findings thus:

> [W]omen are over twice as likely as men to have experienced severe physical abuse, seven times more likely to have experienced sexual abuse, and almost three times more likely to have experienced severe emotional abuse.[66]

Findings like these justify giving prominence to women's experience of domestic violence, for the same reason that we tend to worry more about murders than about assaults. Nevertheless, just as our concern with homicides should not lead us to ignore assaults, it is difficult to dispute McKeown and Kidd's contention that 'domestic violence can no longer be treated as an exclusively women's issue; domestic violence is a relationship issue which affects men as well as women, both as victims and as perpetrators'.[67]

Limitations of victim surveys

Because the Gardaí declined to participate in the study, we were forced to adopt a different methodology based around victim surveys. This change in methodology caused some difficulties in terms of fitting the Irish results into the wider European study. Nevertheless, we obtained a great deal of interesting information, especially as regards the victims' impressions of the criminal justice system and criminal justice agencies. Our findings confirm that the Gardaí have rarely undertaken needs assessments, and that Garda reaction to

---

[63] Debbonaire and Todd, 'Respect Response to Dixon, et al (2012) "Perpetrator programmes for partner violence: Are they based on ideology or evidence?"' (2012) 17(2) Legal and Criminological Psych 216–24, 219.

[64] Johnson, 'Rethinking Survey Research on Violence against Women', in Dobash and Dobash, *Rethinking Violence against Women*, (SAGE 1998) 23–52, 27.

[65] Watson and Parsons, op cit, at 53, Table 2.1.

[66] ibid, at 24. McKeown and Kidd agree, noting that 'it needs to be emphasised that the outcomes of domestic violence in terms of physical and psychological injuries are considerably more negative for women victims than for men victims.' McKeown and Kidd, op cit, at 12.

[67] ibid, at 12.

domestic violence tends to be a bit of a lottery. We also attempted to obtain accurate information from the participants as to the outcomes of the judicial processes in which they had been involved, but failed due to confusion among many of the participants as to these outcomes. The data we collected on these points were too unreliable to be used. This is not a criticism of the participants, but rather points to a limitation of using victim surveys to obtain this kind of information. Many domestic violence victims have been involved in multiple court visits for a variety of purposes, and it would be difficult for anyone to keep straight the details of these court cases. Added to that is the inherent complexity of the criminal justice and judicial systems, and the fact that few victims of domestic violence are likely to have any experience in dealing with them. Factual information about court outcomes (as opposed to impressions of the court processes) should be obtained from official documentation, and for that the involvement of official agencies will be essential. This is a matter of research design—a victim survey is not the best methodology to obtain information of this sort. Our experience illustrates the importance of researchers choosing the methodology most appropriate to achieve the purpose of the project. In our case, external factors forced us to make use of victim surveys, and sometimes circumstances will make using suboptimal methodologies unavoidable. In such cases, the researchers can only do their best, and may have to alter the nature of the project to suit those circumstances.

Access to material

Sometimes a research opportunity will present itself unexpectedly, and researchers will not have time to arrange access to the necessary materials before agreeing to participate. This is what happened with the INASC study. We made every effort to secure access to official Garda files as soon as possible, but the decision by the Gardaí not to participate caused considerable difficulty. Workstream 2 was supposed to culminate in a comparative report on the processes in use in the different jurisdictions. Ultimately, we were unable to participate in this comparative review, although the project still made good use of the information that we obtained. This experience underlines the need for researchers to ensure, whenever possible, that they will have access to the data they need *before* beginning the research.

Size of the sample

Finally, the size of our sample—40 participants—resulted in several limitations. Much of the data collected was quantitative in nature, but with only 40 responses we were precluded from engaging in advanced statistical analyses. More fundamentally, such a small sample is unlikely to be representative of the total population of female victims of domestic violence. Further, the time and financial constraints of the study meant that we were forced to rely on non-governmental agency participant nominations, and this further skewed the representativeness of the sample. Accordingly, we accepted that our results could not be considered definitive. Rather, we suggested that our results should be treated as establishing hypotheses that can be tested in larger and more representative studies.

VII – Conclusion

Published official statistics on domestic violence are limited, and those that do exist must be approached with caution. The Garda Inspectorate censured An Garda Síochána for failings in its categorisation and recording of domestic violence cases.[68] Furthermore, the Central Statistics Office has officially placed Garda statistics 'under reservation', meaning that the statistics do not meet the standards normally required by the CSO.[69] Nevertheless, these statistics, when combined with studies conducted by academics and by non-governmental agencies, allow us to begin to develop a picture of domestic violence in Ireland. Further studies will clarify this picture, and the burden of this chapter has been to highlight some pointers arising from the INASC experience.

Researching domestic violence is notoriously difficult. Wherever possible, researchers need to ensure that they will have access to the necessary materials—especially official materials—before beginning the study. Criminal justice agencies are not averse to assisting researchers but the agencies must balance a host of competing concerns that will sometimes limit the access they can offer. The inability of the INASC research team to access Garda files limited the contribution that they were able to make to the wider project. When conducting victim surveys, researchers must keep in mind the violence that victims have suffered, in many cases over a long period of time. The effects of this violence and the inherent sensitivity of the subject matter mean that victims who agree to participate must be treated carefully and with due regard to their psychological wellbeing. These limitations also mean that some methodological compromises might be necessary in order to locate victims willing to assist in the research. Researchers should not be shy in approaching non-governmental agencies involved in the area, but the limitations and dangers that arise from such approaches must be borne in mind and highlighted in the final report. Finally, the study must also be designed with some care: in particular, lazy assumptions about victims and perpetrators need to be avoided. Limiting a study on domestic violence to women's experiences is entirely valid, but the experiences of male victims are also worth consideration.

---

68 Garda Inspectorate, *Report on Crime Investigation*, op cit.

69 See <https://www.cso.ie/en/statistics/crimeandjustice/> accessed 12 March 2019.

Chapter 12

Mixed Methods Inquiry in Law: Exploring the Temporal Burdens of Medical Negligence Litigation

*Mary-Elizabeth Tumelty**

I – Introduction

It is widely accepted that the traditional approach to legal research is the doctrinal or 'black letter law' approach.[1] Despite the potential of empirical research to provide 'more complex answers to what can still remain distinctly legal problems',[2] law students and early career researchers typically have limited exposure to such methods.[3]

This chapter aims to illustrate the rationale and benefits of using a mixed methods approach in legal research, and to demonstrate how such an approach is relevant to exploring legal phenomena. Drawing on a research project which explored the existence and causes of delay in medical negligence litigation in Ireland, this chapter aims to provide insights into the benefits and challenges of conducting mixed methods research.[4] In doing so, the chapter answers several questions surrounding the use of a mixed methods approach. For instance, why employ mixed methods? What type of questions are suitable to a mixed methods approach? How does one design and conduct this form of inquiry?

---

* Dr Mary-Elizabeth Tumelty, Lecturer in Law at the School of Law, University College Cork.

[1] See, for example, T Hutchinson and N Duncan, 'Defining and describing what we do: Doctrinal legal research' (2012) 17 Deakin L. Rev. 83; R Watt and F John, *Concise Legal Research* (6th edn, The Federation Press 2009).

[2] D O'Donovan, 'Socio-Legal Methodology: Conceptual Underpinnings, Justifications and Practical Pitfalls' in L Cahillane and J Schweppe (eds) *Legal Research Methods: Principles and Practicalities* (Clarus Press 2016) 108.

[3] M Burton, 'Doing empirical research: exploring the decision-making of magistrates and juries' in D Watkins and Mandy Burton (eds) *Research Methods in Law* (Routledge 2013) 55.

[4] Broadly speaking, when looking at empirical sociological research methods, there are two schools: qualitative and quantitative.

By exploring and answering these issues, I hope that students and early career researchers will be better able to place mixed methods within the context of legal research, and to see their wider application in the field of law.

II – The Research Question

As is the case with most research, legal research is conducted to investigate or explore a specific problem or issue. The research methodology and the methods employed will then be guided by the research question.[5] Thus, the first step in planning or designing research is to formulate a research question and/or objective(s) having identified the broader problem or issue. It is necessary to have specific and measurable research questions, as Chui observes, '[i]f research questions are not specific and answerable, it is very likely that the remaining research activities will be fruitless and meaningless'.[6]

Background to the case study: the duration of medical negligence litigation

The project which forms the basis for discussion in this chapter was part of my PhD research which investigated the financial, temporal, and emotional burdens of medical negligence litigation. I have chosen this aspect of my doctoral research for discussion, as it was one of the more challenging elements – but it also provided me with rich data, which formed an important part of my PhD. In sharing and discussing these challenges, I hope to illustrate some of the obstacles researchers can encounter when conducting mixed methods research, and also, the potential of such an approach.

Before proceeding to discuss the particularities of the research, it is first necessary to briefly contextualise the phenomenon which was investigated: the duration of medical negligence litigation. The narrative of the dynamic of medical negligence litigation in Ireland is constantly evolving. Criticisms of the length of the process are frequently made by the mainstream media, practitioners, and academics in the area.[7] However, evidence of the duration of medical negligence litigation is virtually non-existent in this jurisdiction, and reasons for delay remain unexplored. This is problematic as if the reasons

[5] R Burke Johnson and AJ Onwuegbuzie, 'Mixed Methods Research: A Research Paradigm Whose Time Has Come' (2004) 33(7) Educational Researcher 14, 17.

[6] Wing Hong Chui, 'Quantitative Legal Research' in McConville and Chui (eds) *Research Methods for Law* (Edinburgh University Press 2007) 53.

[7] A Sheikh, 'Clinical negligence litigation: A need for change today' (2014) 20(1) Medico-Legal Journal of Ireland 2; D Cott, 'Bad medicine and worse resolutions: Why the HSE should embrace mediation as a response to medical negligence claims' (2012) 12 University College Dublin Law Review 89; Reid, 'Slow dance of litigation in medical negligence cases benefits no one' *The Irish Times* (Dublin, 8 January 2014).

could be identified and addressed where possible, the length of the process could potentially be reduced.

Accordingly, the research questions for this element of my research were as follows:

- How long do medical negligence cases take to litigate?
- What factors contribute to the length of these cases?

III – Methodological Approach

As previously noted, the methodological approach employed will depend on the research question(s). For example, if you are asking 'how many', or 'how much?' questions, then you will be likely to employ a quantitative approach. In contrast, and as Genn explains, when you get to 'why do people do the things that they do?' or 'what are the factors that influence choices?' a qualitative approach will be more appropriate.[8] Those who want to know the answer to both, will have to employ a mixed methods approach. Mixed methods, or the combination of quantitative and qualitative strategies, is a useful approach to answer questions which cannot be answered using one method in isolation. Nielsen notes that a mixed methods approach is particularly useful when exploring closely related phenomena.[9]

As my research questions sought insights into the length of claims and factors which contribute to delay in this context, a mixed methods approach was adopted 'for the broad purposes of breadth and depth of understanding and corroboration.'[10]

There are a number of justifications for employing a mixed methods approach. For example, mixed methods are particularly useful to test the consistency of findings obtained through different instruments, to clarify and build on the results of one method with another, and for 'explanation' purposes, whereby one method is used to help explain the findings which are generated by another.[11] In the context of this research (i.e. investigating the temporal nature of medical negligence litigation), quantitative methods were employed to

[8] H Genn, 'Hazel Genn and Paths to Justice' in S Halliday and P Schmidt (eds) *Conducting Law and Society Research: Reflections on Methods and Practices* (Cambridge University Press 2009) 227.

[9] LB Nielsen, 'The need for multi-method approaches in empirical legal research' in P Cane and HM Kritzer (eds) *The Oxford Handbook of Empirical Legal Research* (OUP 2010) 1086.

[10] R Burke Johnson and others, 'Towards a definition of mixed methods research' (2007) 1(2) Journal of Mixed Methods Research, 112, 123.

[11] A Bryman, *Mixed Methods* (Sage Publications 2006).

investigate the duration of medical negligence litigation, and qualitative methods were employed to explore factors contributing to the length of these claims. This approach enabled the research to investigate gaps between policy and practice, and answer the overall research question(s).

IV – Methods Used

Having decided upon a research question(s) and identified a suitable methodological approach, it was then necessary to consider the data gathering instruments or the methods which would need to be employed. Although quantitative and qualitative methods can be employed in tandem, this research study was sequential; with the quantitative analysis taking place in the first stage of the research, and the qualitative research being conducted in the second stage.

Stage one: quantitative methods

Generally speaking, quantitative research deals with numbers, statistics, and/or hard data.[12] In the context of the case study, quantitative methods were employed to investigate the duration of medical negligence litigation in Ireland. Creswell explains that quantitative methods are most useful when research seeks to explain the relationship among variables which can be measured and analysed 'using mathematically based methods, in particular statistics.'[13] This element of the research involved ascertaining the average duration of medical negligence litigation in Ireland. As quantitative research is essentially concerned with collecting numerical data to explain a particular phenomenon, it was identified as a suitable method to answer this research question.

Research site

Quantitative methods most commonly employ surveys, questionnaires, or examine pre-existing statistical data.[14] In the context of the case study, surveys and/or questionnaires would not be able to answer the research question in an accurate manner. Thus, this part of the research examined pre-existing statistical data.

---

[12] J Creswell, *Research design: qualitative, quantitative, and mixed method approaches* (3rd edn, Sage Publications 2009).

[13] J Creswell, *Research design: qualitative, quantitative, and mixed method approaches* (3rd edn, Sage Publications 2009) 4.

[14] W Hong Chui, 'Quantitative Legal Research' in M McConville and W Hong Chui (eds) *Research Methods for Law* (Edinburgh University Press 2007) 46.

Information relating to medical negligence litigation is published in annual reports by the State, under the auspices of the National Treasury Management Agency (NTMA). The NTMA was established in 1990 to manage the assets and liabilities of the government.[15] Following the enactment of the National Treasury Management Agency (Amendment) Act 2000, the management of clinical negligence claims against the State was delegated to NTMA. When performing this role the NTMA is known as the State Claims Agency (SCA).[16] The stated objectives of the SCA are:

> to ensure that the State's liabilities in relation to personal injury and property damage claims, and the expenses of the SCA in relation to their management, are contained at the lowest achievable level; and
>
> To implement targeted personal injury and property damage risk work programmes to mitigate litigation risk, in State authorities and healthcare enterprises, in order to reduce the costs of future litigation against the State.[17]

Accordingly, the reports published by the NTMA were selected for analysis as they were identified as a rich data source with the capacity to provide insights into the length of medical negligence litigation in Ireland. Limitations, however, were encountered when this research was undertaken which related to the quality and quantity of data provided in the NTMA reports. For example, in its 2015 report, the NTMA states that it resolved 100 percent of medical negligence claims 'within 3 years of the start of legal proceedings'[18] however no further details are given. This was a significant challenge for the research as it was anticipated that such information would be readily available. I felt that I needed to interrogate this statement by the NTMA given the dissonance between the assertion by the NTMA and the general discourse on the temporal nature of medical negligence litigation. In an attempt to surmount this limitation, I submitted an FOI request which sought information relating to how this figure was ascertained. However, this request was denied on the basis that, as a 'partially included' agency,[19] the NTMA are entitled to refuse access to records concerning:

[15] National Treasury Management Agency, 'About the NTMA' <www.ntma.ie/about-the-ntma> accessed 29 March 2017.

[16] National Treasury Management Agency (Amendment) Act 2014, s 33 (1).

[17] State Claims Agency, 'About us' <www.stateclaims.ie/about-us/> accessed 31 January 2017.

[18] National Treasury Management Agency, *Annual Report and Accounts* (2015) 38.

[19] Freedom of Information Act 2014, sch 1, pt 1.

> 'The performance of its functions under Part 2 of the National Treasury Management Agency (Amendment) Act 2000, other than in relation to records concerning the general administration of those functions.' [20]

The 'performance of its functions' refers to the function of the NTMA when operating as the SCA, and include resolving the claim expediently,[21] investigating the claim,[22] retaining professional services,[23] and representing the State in court where necessary,[24] and the agency refused access to this information on this basis.

Given the limitations encountered with the NTMA reports, it was necessary to identify an appropriate research site which could answer this research question. The Medical Negligence Unit (MNU) was identified as such a site, as the case files there belonged to a certain population, i.e. those who had previously been involved in medical negligence litigation. The MNU is a specialised unit within the Legal Aid Board.[25] The Unit was established in 2006, following recognition by the State of the specialised nature of medical negligence, and realisation that every Legal Aid law centre could not provide the requisite expertise.[26] The MNU deals with medical negligence claims from those who are eligible for legal aid. In order to obtain legal aid for civil matters in Ireland a prospective client must have an annual disposable income not exceeding €18,000.[27] Therefore, it should be noted that this element of the study does not capture data from plaintiffs who accessed private legal advice, as access to such data was unavailable.

Data collection and analysis

In order to ascertain the average duration of medical negligence litigation, closed case files belonging to the Medical Negligence Unit (MNU) were analysed.[28] It was necessary to delimit the setting from which a sample for the study was drawn, in order to ensure consistency and accuracy. In order to achieve this, only medical negligence cases which were litigated by the

[20] Freedom of Information Act 2014, sch 1, pt 1 (w) (ii).

[21] National Treasury Agency (Amendment) Act 2000, pt 2, s 6 (1)(a)(i).

[22] National Treasury Agency (Amendment) Act 2000, pt 2, s 6 (1)(a)(ii).

[23] National Treasury Agency (Amendment) Act 2000, pt 2, s 6 (1)(a)(iii).

[24] National Treasury Agency (Amendment) Act 2000, pt 2, s 6 (1)(a)(iv).

[25] The MNU is one of 30 Legal Aid Law Centres in Ireland.

[26] Legal Aid Board, *Value for Money and Policy Review of the Legal Aid Board* (October 2011) wherein it is noted that in 2006, all existing medical negligence files in individual legal aid board law centres were transferred to the MNU. This analysis includes transferred case files.

[27] Civil Legal Aid Act 1995, s 28; For more information see, FLAC, *Report on Civil Legal Aid in Ireland Forty Years On* (2009).

[28] A case file is a collection of legal documents relating to a particular case.

MNU, i.e. cases in which proceedings had been issued and had reached resolution through settlement, mediation or trial, during the period of 2006 to 2015, were identified and analysed. This was necessary as only claims which had reached conclusion would be capable of answering the research question. For example, a claim which had not reached settlement or trial would provide little insight into the duration of the litigation process. The period 2006 to 2015 was chosen as the MNU was established in 2006, and this research was conducted in November 2015. Therefore, it was anticipated that the data from this time period would provide the most accurate and detailed insights. A total of 14 claims met these criteria.

The data extrapolated during the analysis of closed case files was subjected to quantitative analysing techniques (statistics) in order to ascertain the average duration of a claim. This was achieved by inputting the numerical data (date of issuance of proceedings to date of settlement) into a Microsoft Excel document, which generated the average duration of a medical negligence claim.

Stage two – qualitative methods

The second phase of the research involved the employment of qualitative research methods. As previously noted, qualitative methods are necessary where the research seeks to explore and understand the phenomenon based on lived experiences and perspectives.[29] Common methods of qualitative research include participant observations, interviews, and case studies. These approaches typically focus on people or environments, as opposed to quantitative methods, which as we have seen, generally focus on numbers, statistics, and facts.

In addition to ascertaining the duration of medical negligence claims, I also sought to explore factors contributing to the length of claims. It was therefore necessary to employ qualitative methods to gain insights and understanding into this phenomenon. As de Londras surmises:

> 'any research that is interested in effectiveness, implementation, diagnosis of the problem, reform, meaningful comparison, and policy change is likely to need to engage in some way in participatory research in order to be successful.'[30]

[29] D Mertens, 'Mixed Methods and the Politics of Human Research: The Transformative-emancipatory perspective' in Abbas Tashakkori and Charles Teddlie (eds), *Handbook of Mixed Methods in Social and Behavioral Research* (Sage Publications 2003).

[30] F deLondras, 'Participatory research: some provocations for doctoral students in law' in L Cahillane and J Schweppe (eds) *Legal Research Methods: Principles and Practicalities* (Clarus Press 2016) 151.

Interviews were selected as a method, as it was recognized that interviews are a fundamental way to learn about the experience of others. There are many types of interview technique a researcher can choose from, including: structured, semi-structured or unstructured interviews.[31] The type of style the researcher should choose will generally depend on the level of depth needed, the degree of control required by the researcher, and the nature of the research question.[32] In the case of this research, a semi-structured interview format was employed, due to its flexible nature. As Wengraf explains:

> 'semi-structured interviews are designed to have a number of interview questions prepared in advanced but such prepared questions are designed to be sufficiently open that the subsequent questions cannot be planned in advance, but must be improvised in a careful and theorized way'.[33]

It is, as Walker notes, a particularly effective interviewing technique because it enables the researcher to gather the information required to satisfy the aims of the research project while also allowing the participant to freely describe and clarify situations.[34] Thus, the semi-structured interview offers a degree of flexibility, wherein the participant can freely discuss their viewpoint, whilst contemporaneously providing the researcher sufficient control to ensure the research questions can be answered.[35]

Prior to commencing this stage of the research, an aide-memoir (interview guide) was designed.[36] Interview questions were guided by the overall research question, and, in some instances, derived from key concepts which emerged during the literature review.[37] Open-ended questions were posed to

---

[31] J Creswell, *Qualitative Inquiry and Research Design: Choosing among five* approaches (3rd edn, Sage 2013); S Qu and John Dumay, 'The qualitative research interview' (2011) 8(3) Qualitative Research in Accounting and Management 238.

[32] J Creswell, *Qualitative Inquiry and Research Design: Choosing among five* approaches (3rd edn, Sage 2013).

[33] T Wengraf, *Qualitative Research Interviewing: Biographic narrative and semi-structured methods* (Sage 2001) 5.

[34] W Walker, 'Hermeneutic Inquiry: Insights into the process of interviewing' 18(2) (2011) Nurse Researcher 19.

[35] W Walker, 'Hermeneutic inquiry: insights into the process of interviewing' (2011) 18(2) Nurse Researcher 19, 21.

[36] See appendices.

[37] JA Maxwell, 'Designing a qualitative study' (2008) 2 The SAGE Handbook of Applied Social Research Methods 214; HJ Rubin and IS Rubin, *Qualitative Interviewing: The Art of Hearing Data* (2nd edn, Sage 2011).

facilitate the collection of rich, detailed data.[38] Questions were also based on issues which emerged from the quantitative research undertaken. Thus, qualitative methods (interviews) were used to interrogate the findings of the quantitative study.

The selection of research participants

Qualitative inquiry is concerned with the collection of rich data, therefore, all researchers need to consider whom may be able to speak to the phenomenon under investigation, and therefore, appropriate to interview. De Londras usefully outlines three guiding questions to employ when deciding upon research participants:

> '1. What do I need to know?
>
> 2. What do I want to achieve?
>
> 3. Who has the relevant power by reference to questions (1) and (2) above?'[39]

There are a number of sampling techniques a researcher can choose from; I used purposive and snowball sampling.[40]

Patton has noted that purposive sampling is particularly useful, as through the identification of 'information-rich' participants, the research can provide understanding of a complex issue.[41] Similarly, Merriam has highlighted the importance of purposive sampling, and asserts:

> '...since qualitative inquiry seeks to understand the meaning of a phenomenon from the perspectives of the participants, it is important to select a sample from which most can be learned.'[42]

---

[38] P Gill and others, 'Methods of data collection in qualitative research: Interviews and focus groups' (2008) 204(6) British Dental Journal 291.

[39] F de Londras, 'Participatory research: some provocations for doctoral students in law' in L Cahillane and J Schweppe (eds) *Legal Research Methods: Principles and Practicalities* (Clarus Press 2016) 155; She defines 'power' as 'knowledge, influence, experience, ability to bring about change, ability to recruit other participants to the project and so on'.

[40] For a full discussion of qualitative sampling techniques see, G Guest, M Mitchell and E Namey (eds) *Collecting Qualitative Data: A Field Manual for Applied Research* (Sage 2013) 41.

[41] M Patton, *Qualitative Research and Evaluation Methods* (3rd edn, Sage Publications 2002) 45.

[42] S Merriam, *Qualitative Research in Practice: Examples for discussion and analysis* (Jossey-Bass Inc Pub 2002) 12.

The sampling strategy for this section of the research was based on the potential for collection of rich data, i.e. those who could provide insights into the phenomenon under study. Accordingly, the sampling strategy was guided by the research questions as to what sources needed to be the focus of attention and therefore, sampled.

A purposive sampling strategy was identified as most suitable, as this sampling strategy is one in which the questions raised by the research are 'placed at the forefront of sampling considerations'.[43]

Barristers

Barristers who specialise in medical negligence litigation were identified as suitable participants given their expertise and involvement in the phenomenon under study. Barristers for this research were sampled using a combination of random purposive sampling and snowball sampling techniques, both of which will now be discussed.

The use of purposive sampling has been criticised for its potential for bias.[44] Accordingly, random purposive sampling was employed to overcome this limitation. Random purposive sampling is a form of purposive sampling whereby the researcher identifies participants utilising a random generator tool from a list of those who meet the criterion, i.e. those that are deemed to be information rich and of interest to the study in question.[45] This sampling strategy is useful when there is no apparent reason to select one participant who meets the criteria over another.[46] The sampling framework in this research involved junior counsel and senior counsel who self-identified as specialists in medical negligence litigation on the Bar Council website.[47] From this sample (34), practitioners were chosen at random using a generator tool, as this represented one-third of the population under study. Qualifying participants were sent an introductory e-mail inviting them to participate and following a response, an interview was scheduled, the location of which was mutually agreed upon. A total of 12 barristers participated in this research, and sampling concluded at this number once the data had reached

[43] A Bryman, *Social Research Methods* (5th edn, OUP 2015).

[44] RS Barbour, 'Checklists for improving rigour in qualitative research: a case of the tail wagging the dog?' (2001) 322(7294) British Medical Journal 1115; K Malterud, 'Qualitative research: standards, challenges, and guidelines' (2001) 358(9280) The Lancet 483.

[45] MD Tongco, 'Purposive sampling as a tool for informant selection' (2007) 5 Journal of Plants, People and Applied Research 147.

[46] M Quinn Patton, *Qualitative Research and Evaluation Methods* (3rd edn, Sage 2002) 240.

[47] See generally, www.lawlibrary.ie.

the point of saturation (saturation is said to occur where no new information or themes arise).[48]

Whilst the majority of participants (nine) were recruited for this research via the purposive sampling strategy described above, three participants were also accessed through a process of snowball sampling whereby contact with an initial participant led to contact with and the involvement of another participant.[49] Patton describes this sampling method as:

> '... an approach for locating information-rich key informants or critical cases. The process begins by asking well-situated people "Who knows a lot about...? Who should I talk to?" By asking a number of people who else to talk with the snowball gets bigger and bigger.'[50]

Barristers who participated in this research as a result of snowball sampling were part of the population, detailed previously, from which participants were purposively sampled. However, snowball sampling was necessary as although participants were selected on the basis of their expertise in medical negligence, a core aim of this research was to explore experiences of medical negligence mediation and gain insights into the process in practice. Therefore, snowball sampling was particularly useful in this context as it allowed participants with experience, as well as expertise, of medical negligence mediation to be included in this research. Snowball sampling was achieved by developing a rapport with participants, building trust by communicating through e-mails, phone calls, and the face-to-face interview. It was also achieved by explaining the purpose of the study and why they were selected, and ensuring integrity throughout the process.[51]

Data collection took place over a four-month period, and a total of 12 interviews were conducted with legal practitioners. Interviews lasted between 40 and 60 minutes, depending on the willingness of the individual participant to elaborate beyond the standard interview questions.

---

48 G Guest, A Bunce and L Johnson, 'How many interviews are enough? An experiment with data saturation and variability' (2006) 18(1) Field Methods 59.

49 Margarete Sandelowski, 'Combining qualitative and quantitative sampling, data collection, and analysis techniques in mixed-method studies' (2000) 23(3) Research in Nursing and Health 246.

50 M Patton, *Qualitative evaluation and research methods* (Sage Publications 1990) 176.

51 J Hermanowicz, 'The great interview: 25 strategies for studying people in bed' (2002) 25(4) Qualitative Sociology 479; M Guillemin and K Heggen, 'Rapport and respect: negotiating ethical relations between researcher and participant' (2009) 12(3) Medicine, Health Care and Philosophy 291.

Data analysis

The analysis of the qualitative data was a continuous process that occurred over a number of stages including: transcription, coding, and thematic analysis. I transcribed each semi-structured interview myself. This was an arduous task, but it was also useful, as it allowed me to re-familiarize myself with the data. I endeavoured to have each interview transcribed before the next interview was conducted. The coding process commenced as soon as the first interview was conducted and transcribed. Thus, it was an iterative process in that data from the interviews was simultaneously collected, coded and analysed on an on-going basis with each stage informing the next. Consequently, the aide-memoir changed as new and unexpected themes emerged from the data.[52] The flexibility of this approach ensured that interesting opportunities for questioning were not missed. The process of transcribing the interviews also assisted with re-familiarisation with the data, and helped to identify emerging themes.

As aforementioned, once transcribed, interviews were coded and analysed thematically.[53] Vogt et al describe coding as attaching key words to passages of interview data.[54] As such, coding involved reading the interview transcripts and attributing a code to a sentence or group of sentences in the transcript.[55] Once the descriptive codes were established, the next stage of analysis involved grouping common patterns and themes and placing them into categories.[56] Thematic analysis is a process that involves identifying passages of text that are connected by a common theme which enables the organisation of text into categories. This then leads to the development of a thematic framework of ideas, informed by theory.[57] Codes were both generated inductively and drawn from the literature.

As the 12 interviews generated a large quantity of data, Nvivo (a qualitative computer software program) was used to aid the management and organisation of this information. As Bryman notes, computed assisted analysis of

[52] MB Miles, MA Huberman and J Saldana, *Qualitative Data Analysis* (3rd edn, Sage 2013); DR Thomas, 'A general inductive approach for analyzing qualitative evaluation data' (2006) 27(2) American Journal of Evaluation 237.

[53] Graham Gibbs, *Analysing Qualitative Data* (Sage 2008).

[54] PW Vogt and others, *Selecting the right analyses for your data: Quantitative, qualitative and mixed methods* (Guildford Press 2014) 40.

[55] J Creswell and V Plano Clark, *Designing and conducting mixed methods research* (2nd edn, Sage 2010).

[56] JW Creswell, *Qualitative Inquiry and Research Design: Choosing among five approaches* (3rd edn, Sage 2013).

[57] JW Creswell, *Qualitative Inquiry and Research Design: Choosing among five approaches* (3rd edn, Sage 2013); G Gibbs, *Analysing Qualitative Data* (Sage 2008).

qualitative data can improve the rigor and speed of the data analysis process.[58] Using the tools available in Nvivo it was possible to build a picture of the current dynamic of medical negligence litigation and its impact on those involved.

Finally, once the coding and thematic analysis of the data was complete, categories were analysed and connected to interrelating themes within the research, and a narrative was constructed.

V – Ethical Considerations

Ethical issues must be considered and should be at the forefront of the researchers' considerations from the start of the research project. Accordingly, and as required by the Faculty of Arts, Humanities and Social Sciences (AHSS) Research Ethics Committee in the University of Limerick, permission for this research was sought and obtained prior to engaging in any empirical research.[59] As part of this process, potential ethical issues which may have arisen throughout this research were considered. In addition, the ethics committee required the submission of a detailed application. This included an overview of the aims and objectives of the research, along with the proposed research methodology, and suitable procedures to be taken with regard to ensuring informed consent, confidentiality and volunteerism. The ethics process heightened my awareness of the ethical issues inherent in this research from an early stage, and ensured that this research complied with ethical standards at all times.

Ethical issues arose in the context of both the quantitative and qualitative elements of this research study. These included issues surrounding volunteerism, informed consent, and confidentiality.

Volunteerism

The first ethical issue which arose was in relation to the ethical principle of volunteerism. Volunteerism essentially means that research participants should not feel obliged to take part in the research. In addition, participants should be aware that they can withdraw from the study at any stage.[60] In order to ensure that volunteerism was achieved, participants were sent an information and consent letter prior to the interview which explained that they were not obligated to take part in the research, but should they decide to participate they could withdraw their consent entirely at any stage. This was

---

[58] A Bryman, *Social Research Methods* (OUP, 5th edn, 2015).

[59] For further information, see, <https://www.ul.ie/artsoc/ethics> accessed 5 December 2018.

[60] J Sieber and M Tolich, *Planning ethically responsible research* (Sage Publications 2012).

reiterated prior to commencing the interview. In addition, all participants were informed that they were entitled to a copy of the interview transcript to review and if they were dissatisfied with any aspect of the interview they could clarify elements or withdraw from the study.

Informed consent

It was necessary to obtain informed consent from all participants, prior to conducting this research. In order to achieve this, the information letter and consent form, approved by the AHSS Research Ethics Committee at the University of Limerick, was given to each participant at the outset of my communication with them. The information letter and consent form provided a detailed explanation of this research and what involvement in the study would entail. In addition, sufficient time to consider the consent form and to ask further questions about the research was afforded to all participants. At the beginning of each interview, informed consent was acquired from each participant, wherein if they were happy to proceed with the interview, they signed the consent form.

Anonymity and confidentiality

As individual case files from the MNU are not publically available, access may have been an issue in conducting this research. For instance, Scott notes the difficulty in obtaining access to such documents and suggests that these sources are often only available after 'behind-the-scenes' negotiations.[61] In the context of this research, access was sought from and granted by the Managing Director of the MNU to conduct an analysis of closed case files. Whilst individual case files were accessed to complete the analysis, identifying details of individual litigants were not recorded. Anonymity was guaranteed for any individual whose case file was included in the sample, however, the MNU chose to be identified in the research.

Anonymity was guaranteed to all legal practitioners, by assigning each participant an alpha-numeric code e.g. B1 = barrister 1 and by removing any identifying details from the interview transcripts. Due to the small nature of the jurisdiction, if barristers were to be categorised as 'male' or 'female', or 'senior' or 'junior' counsel, participants would be potentially identifiable. Similarly, the analysis did not differentiate between barristers acting for the plaintiff or defendant, as a number of barristers undertook work from both plaintiffs and defendants and therefore, would be easily identified. Thus, whilst these categorisations would have been an interesting mode of analysis,

---

[61] J Scott, *A Matter of record: Documentary sources in social research* (John Wiley and Sons 2014) 14.

in order to ensure anonymity, these distinctions were not made when reporting the research findings.

Finally, confidentiality surrounding all of the data collected was maintained. The data gathered throughout the course of this research was stored in accordance with the terms set out by the Research Ethics Committee. Furthermore, I was the only person with complete access to the data collected. Soft copies of the data, e.g. interview recordings, are stored on an encrypted external hard drive and secured in a locked cabinet in my home. Similarly, data collected in hard copy format, e.g. consent forms, are also stored securely in a locked cabinet in my office. These will be destroyed securely after a period of seven years, in accordance with the guidelines.

Protecting research participants

Ethical issues are frequently associated with qualitative research as the researcher seeks to access subjective life experiences and the meaning they hold for the interviewee. Consequently, issues arise as a result of 'researching private lives and placing accounts in the public arena',[62] which can be further compounded in situations where there is power imbalance between the researcher and interviewee.[63] However, as participants in this study comprised professionals – legal practitioners (barristers), it is argued that no power imbalance between the interviewee and participants existed, and therefore, ethical issues in this context were minimal.

VI – Reflections and Challenges

The employment of multiple research methods enabled significant empirical data to be gathered, which captured the nuances of delay as it pertains to medical negligence claims. However, throughout the course of conducting this research a number of challenges and limitations were encountered. In this section of the chapter, I hope to give a comprehensive overview of some of the obstacles I was faced with when conducting this research and how I dealt with same.

Challenges and limitations

Challenges arose in both the quantitative and qualitative studies. However, I found the quantitative study to be personally, more testing. This was in

[62] M Birch and J Jessop, 'Introduction' in M Mauthner, M Birch, J Jessop and T Miller (eds) *Ethics in Qualitative Research* (Sage 2002).

[63] S Brinkmann and S Kvale, 'Confronting the ethics of qualitative research' (2005) 18(2) Journal of Constructivist Psychology 157.

part, due to my discomfort with numbers, but more so, due to some unexpected issues that arose during the course of the research which I am now going to discuss.

As previously mentioned, NTMA annual reports were identified as a suitable source from which length of medical negligence litigation could be analysed. However, the research uncovered several issues with these reports, notably, inconsistencies in information presented annually, and discrepancies in figures presented. Thus, it was not possible to ascertain the length of medical negligence litigation to the State with certainty. I was also quite worried about how this research would progress when my FOI request was refused. However, the lack of information provided by the State in relation to this issue became a significant finding of the research. If we are to understand and problematise an issue, with a view to reform, reliable information is required. Thus, although I was initially worried about this finding, and viewed it as a limitation, the paucity of information available was in fact a significant finding in and of itself.

There were also several limitations to the quantitative analysis of closed case files at the MNU. First, whilst the study conducted at the MNU enabled me to gain insights into the duration of medical negligence litigation, a potential weakness of the design arose in connection with the sample size. Although the process of sampling is designed to identify individuals or data that can give us a picture of all such individuals,[64] only 14 cases at the Medical Negligence Unit (MNU) met the research criteria. I also found this to be a cause for concern, however, upon speaking with a colleague in the Department of Sociology, I realised that while a small sample may be viewed as a limitation, it can also be viewed as a strength as this was a complete sample of case files. Additionally, as the sample from the MNU is well-defined, it is illustrative of the experience of the population under study – those who have litigated a medical negligence claim.[65] Furthermore, the fact that relatively few cases reached the stage of litigation was a significant finding in itself, illustrating the difficulties in bringing a medical negligence case.

A final limitation of the MNU study arose in the context of the period under study. The claims analysed were from the date of issuance of proceedings to the date the claim was settled. Therefore, the analysis did not account for

[64] R Schutt, *Investigating the Social World: The Process and Practice of Research* (Sage Publications 2015).

[65] The sample need not be representative of the general population, but it must be representative of the population of interest.

other factors before proceedings are issued or after they are settled which may lengthen the litigation process and therefore, may not represent the total time involved in these claims. For example, before proceedings can be initiated in medical negligence litigation, the plaintiff's medical records must be reviewed and assessed, and, if deemed necessary, opinion from counsel and/or an expert medical report may be sought. These measures are necessary as evidence supporting the claim of negligence must be obtained before proceedings can be issued.[66] Therefore, it can frequently take up to a year to get a claim 'off the ground'.[67] Delays can also arise post-resolution of a claim. For example, McGarry has estimated that taxation of costs can take between 18 months to two years to reach conclusion.[68] He notes that this is problematic as 'a claim must wait until the costs issues are resolved before they [plaintiffs] can be reimbursed'.[69] Thus, the research findings may not reflect the total duration of a medical negligence claim from start to finish. However, the approach adopted was chosen to ensure consistency and accuracy,[70] as for instance, some claims analysed went to several solicitors before reaching the MNU,[71] and there would have been no way of documenting the date of first complaint. It was therefore decided that the most accurate and traceable dates should be taken into account, and these were identified as the date proceedings were issued to the date of claim resolution.

It is well documented that qualitative research is time-consuming and costly. This was the most significant challenge in the context of the qualitative study. Given the emphasis on people and environments in qualitative studies, conducting research employing qualitative methods is likely to involve more preparation than other approaches. Doherty notes that qualitative research techniques requires a number of important skills, including:

> '... the ability to manage relationships, to interact with others, to empathise, and to listen. They also require the researcher to be extremely well-organised and flexible, to have the ability to think on his/her feet and respond to challenges and setbacks, and to develop extremely good

[66] *Reidy v National Maternity Hospital* [1997] IEHC 143.

[67] M Boylan, 'Medical Negligence Litigation Challenges for the Plaintiff's Lawyers' in C Craven and W Binchy (eds), *Medical Negligence Litigation: Emerging Issues* (First Law 2008).

[68] P McGarry, 'Action needed now for system of legal costs' (2017) 22(3) Bar Review 85.

[69] P McGarry, 'Action needed now for system of legal costs' (2017) 22(3) Bar Review 85.

[70] Furthermore, dates were independently cross-referenced by conducting a High Court search on <www.courts.ie>.

[71] Cases frequently moved from private practitioners to the Unit because of the specialised nature of the claim and/or the client's financial status.

> negotiation skills. An appreciation of, and adherence to, high ethical standards is also crucial.'[72]

Recognising the limitations of my undergraduate training in the context of the methods I proposed to utilize, in consultation with my supervisors, I decided to engage in methods training. Thus, prior to commencing the research study, I completed modules in qualitative and quantitative research methods taught in the Department of Sociology. Thus, the length of the research project, the resources, and skills of the researcher should be key considerations when deciding upon methods and a methodological approach.

Strengths of the design

Although both the quantitative and qualitative elements of the research encountered limitations, the research design also had significant strengths.

Bryman, building on Greene et al's research, identified 16 reasons for conducting mixed methods research.[73] The main strengths of this approach include: 'completeness' which essentially means that through engagement with a variety of approaches a more comprehensive picture of the study phenomenon is provided; 'offsetting weaknesses' which provides that the weaknesses of a single approach can be minimalised, while strengths are built upon thereby providing more accurate data; 'complementarity' which elaborates or clarifies the results from one method to another; 'triangulation' which enables corroboration through the employment of a variety of methods; and 'explanation' whereby one method is used to help explain the findings which are generated by another.[74] Furthermore, qualitative research can build upon and assist in illustrating and illuminating the importance of the quantitative findings, which Bryman describes as being akin to putting 'meat on the bones' of 'dry' data.[75]

An example of putting 'meat on the bones' of 'dry' data in the present study related to the findings from the MNU. In order to surmount the limitation of the small dataset which emerged during the quantitative phase of the research, I decided to verify the findings from the MNU closed case files during the

---

[72] M Doherty, 'Getting Down and Dirty: The Case for Empirical Legal Research' in L Cahillane and J Schweppe (eds) *Legal Research Methods: Principles and Practicalities* (Clarus Press 2016) 132.

[73] A Bryman, *Mixed Methods* (Sage Publications 2006); J Greene, V Caracelli and W Graham, 'Toward a conceptual framework for mixed-method evaluation designs' (1989) 11(3) Education evaluation and policy analysis 255.

[74] A Bryman, 'Integrating quantitative and qualitative research: how is it done?' (2006) 6(1) Qualitative Research 97.

[75] A Bryman, *Mixed Methods* (Sage Publications 2006).

qualitative stage of the research. In order to achieve this, 12 legal practitioners were presented with the research findings from the MNU, and asked based on their own experience whether or not they found this to be representative. By adopting this approach, the research elicited insights into the causes of delay in medical negligence litigation, as well as supporting the quantitative research findings.

VII – Conclusion

Although mixed methods research often requires significant resources and time, the employment of mixed methods in this study helped answer questions that could not have been answered using a singular methodological approach.

Using a case study approach, this chapter has provided some discrete examples of how mixed methods research operates in practice. It is hoped that this discussion, along with the other contributions in this book, will be of use to students and legal researchers.

Chapter 13

Research at the Law Reform Commission

*Ciarán Burke and Raymond Byrne**

I – Introduction

Legal research may be directed to many ends. However, when asked to describe what those ends are likely to be, most scholars furnish one of two answers: either legal research is undertaken in order to provide background arguments, and precedents—and, if we are feeling Kelsenian,[1] the solution—to a particular case; or else, research is seen as the preserve of academics, which has been described in the past as having 'no other objective except an exploration in depth of the position on the particular topic of research.'[2] Although the second description may seem a little ungenerous to the sterling work of the academic community, particularly in modern times, it is nonetheless a common complaint that legal academic research is sometimes far removed from the real world, while research for practice often amounts to little more than unpicking the minutiae of the individual case.

Research for law reform purposes may be seen as situated somewhere between the two poles, a happy medium, as it were. Research is an essential prerequisite to high-quality law reform, undertaken with a definitive end, namely to propose improvements in the law on specific matters, and to formulate these proposals in as precise and concrete a manner as possible. Any research must take account of, amongst other things, the existing law in the jurisdiction in question; the reasons underpinning any need to reform the

* Professor Ciarán Burke, Director of Research, Law Reform Commission and Raymond Byrne, Commissioner, Law Reform Commission.

[1] Kelsen argued that behaviour is prescribed in a norm, and that therefore, the content of that norm means that one ought to behave in a certain way. Such a position is associated with the idea that there is a single correct solution to any legal question. H Kelsen, 'Der Begriff der Rechtsordnung' Logique et Analyse, vol 1 (1958), 150–67, reprinted in H Klecatsky, R Marcic, and H Schambeck (eds) *Die Wiener Rechtstheoretische Schule* (Vienna: Europa Verlag, 1968), vol 2, at 1395–1416.

[2] PM Bakshi, 'Legal Research and Law Reform' Journal of the Indian Law Institute 24, No 2/3 (1982): 391–415.

existing law; best practices from other jurisdictions and their potential for transposition; and policy considerations weighing in favour of particular courses of action as opposed to others. As such, law reform research cannot be cast as an abstract exercise. Nor should it fall prey to the practitioner's dictates of circumstance, which sometimes ensure that hard cases may make bad law.[3]

Located in this 'Goldilocks zone' of legal research, law reform lends itself to a distinct methodological approach that balances pragmatism and innovation. In Ireland, the Law Reform Commission is the only statutory body tasked exclusively with formulating proposals for law reform – although it is important to note that the Oireachtas, usually acting on Bills prepared by government departments and drafted by the Office of Parliamentary Counsel to the Government, has the exclusive power to enact legislation, that is, to actually put law reform in place. The Law Reform Commission Act 1975 provides that the Commission is tasked with keeping the law under review, and conducting research with a view to law reform. The 1975 Act defines law reform as including: the development of law; its codification (including its simplification and modernisation); and the revision and consolidation of statute law. This is a broad mandate, and one that is loosely sketched in the relevant legislation. The purpose and statutory basis of the Commission are modelled to a significant degree on the British Law Commissions Act 1965, which established the Law Commission of England and Wales and the Scottish Law Commission a decade earlier than its Irish counterpart. However, one might well argue that Ireland has a unique vocation for law reform. The first Attorney-General of the Irish Free State, and later Chief Justice, Hugh Kennedy, memorably described the common law as 'an alien structure imposed by statute, an exotic from which a cutting has been artificially fostered in Ireland but which has not taken root or become acclimatised in any real sense….'[4] Similar sentiments were expressed by the first President of the Executive Council,[5] WT Cosgrave.[6] On a similar note, early Irish legal scholarship lamented the lost tomes of the Brehon law,

[3] The phrase is derived from the English case *Winterbottom v Wright* (1842) 10 M & W 109.

[4] The National Archives/Public Record Office (United Kingdom) CAB 23/30, SFB 60.

[5] This office corresponded to that of the Taoiseach in present-day Ireland.

[6] See T Mohr, 'Law in a Gaelic Utopia: Perceptions of Brehon Law in Nineteenth and Early Twentieth Century Ireland' in O Brupbacher et al (eds), *Remembering and Forgetting: Yearbook of Legal History* (Martin Meidenbauer 2007), 247–276.

expressing a yearning for an autonomous *Volksgeist.*[7] The adoption of the common law of our Anglo-Saxon (or perhaps more accurately, Anglo-Norman) neighbours owed more to pragmatism than any attachment to its wisdom. Law reform in Ireland may thus be seen as a means of belatedly putting a uniquely Irish stamp on the common law.[8]

II – Methodological approaches

Reducing the methodology of law reform research performed in an Irish context to a typology is not an easy task. Due to the Commission's broad mandate, and the variety of projects it addresses, there are considerable divergences in the approaches employed. There is no typical Commission project. Some may involve a relatively narrow area,[9] whereas others may cover a large range of headings and sub-headings over a broad topic.[10] However, certain generalisations may be drawn from four decades of practice.

All law reform research is undertaken with a defined goal in mind. This goal may entail the compilation of a paper that explores the scope of the project when it is at a tentative stage, or a paper that sets out the issues related to the project in detail with the purpose of provoking submissions from the public on law reform, or a final report containing the reform proposals upon which

[7] ibid. Several authors have also made much of the destruction of many of the core Brehon law texts, contributing to a lack of understanding of the legal system that predated the common law. The piecemeal state of the original Brehon law corpus creates barriers to scientific study, as well as significant anomalies. As MJ Gorman has noted, our understanding of core concepts of Brehon criminal law and family law is incomplete, while we have access to a fairly complete code on the laws relating to beekeeping. See MJ Gorman, 'The Ancient Brehon Laws of Ireland', University of Pennsylvania Law Review and American Law Register, vol 61, No 4 (1913), 217–233 See also R Thurneysen, *Irisches Recht* (Verlag der Akademie der wissenschaften 1931), and N Higgins, 'The Lost Legal System: Pre-Common Law Ireland and Brehon Law' in Gerner-Beuerle and Frenkel (eds), *Legal Theory Practice and Education* (Atiner 2011), 193–205.

[8] This indeed occurred even prior to the Law Reform Commission's inception in 1975. In 1966, the English Lord Chancellor Lord Gardiner (one of the key architects of the British Law Commissions) had described Ireland as a country in which law reform was 'extremely active'. This was largely because the then Minister for Justice, Charles Haughey, had, in 1962, published a White Paper entitled *A Programme of Law Reform* and had followed that up with progressive reforming legislation that included the Guardianship of Infants Act 1964 and, in particular, the Succession Act 1965. The 1965 Act represented a broad transposition of several sections of civil codes to Ireland, a departure from the common law if ever there was one. See the Law Reform Commission's *Report on Prevention of Benefit from Homicide* (LRC 114—2015), para 1.13 (noting that s 120 of the 1965 Act drew on codified provisions on unworthiness to succeed in the French, German and Swiss civil codes) and the *Report on Section 117 of the Succession Act 1965: Aspects of Provision for Children* (LRC 118—2017), para 1.13 (noting that the provision for fixed shares in the 1965 Act also reflected a civil law influence, mediated through Scots succession law).

[9] For example, the *Report on Aspects of Domestic Violence* (LRC 111—2013).

[10] For example, the *Report on Regulatory Powers and Corporate Offences* (LRC 119—2018).

the Commission has convened. Any project will need to include an analysis, first of all, of the history and rationale underpinning the existing law as well as a detailed explanation of it, in order to introduce the non-expert reader to the matter at hand. This should include a full literature review, as well as any relevant input from outside the legal field, such as statistical analysis, if this is available. Following on from this, it is necessary to set out the (perceived) problem or problems with the law as it currently stands, and the reasons why it may be ripe for reform. The Commission also invariably engages in comparative research designed to inform the reader what other jurisdictions have done to engage with similar issues. Finally, a justification of the reasons underpinning any proposals for reform in Ireland should be set out.[11]

Broadly speaking, then, the following methodological approaches are employed in law reform research.

The doctrinal approach, supplemented by economic analysis

Firstly, a *doctrinal* approach is employed in identifying and examining the existing law. This may be supplemented by *historical* research,[12] explaining the evolution of the law, and why and how it has changed in the past. Then, *comparative* research is a necessary component, firstly in locating equivalent provisions in other jurisdictions, and then in discerning whether the approaches employed in those jurisdictions may lend themselves to transposition to the Irish context.[13]

The Commission's work on personal insolvency and debt[14] provides a clear example of how law reform needs to involve a significant stretch beyond

[11] The steps mentioned in this paragraph apply chiefly to Reports, Issues Papers (formerly known as Consultation Papers and Working Papers) will (aside from setting out final recommendations for reform, which along with draft legislation, are key components of Commission Reports) also engage in much of the same process, aiming to explain the issues to be addressed in relation to a particular area of law, and inviting submissions from interested stakeholders and the broader public.

[12] In this respect, it is germane to note that the Commission's historical research may be said to follow the six-stage test proposed by Garraghan, albeit with a strong focus on the sixth condition, namely the evidentiary value of the source consulted. G J Garraghan, *A Guide to Historical Method* (Fordham University Press 1946).

[13] This two-stage approach, containing comparability and transposability, represents a standard, albeit rudimentary approach to comparative law. See ML Izorche, 'Propositions méthodologiques pour la comparaison', Revue international de droit comparé (2001), 289–325 and N Jansen, 'Comparative Law and Comparative Knowledge', in: M Reimann and R Zimmermann (eds), *The Oxford Handbook of Comparative Law* (OUP 2006) 305–338.

[14] See *Report on Personal Debt Management and Debt Enforcement* (LRC 100—2010).

doctrinal legal research. The Commission's 2010 Report recommended that a primarily non-judicial process should be established for resolving personal insolvency and non-payment of debts (to supplement the existing judicial personal bankruptcy regime), and this was implemented in the Personal Insolvency Act 2012. The Report contained a detailed description of this new non-judicial architecture for resolving insolvency disputes. This derived from an extensive comparative review of relevant systems that had been in place in other jurisdictions for many years. However, arriving at its proposed solution required the Commission to ask quite fundamental questions about the then-existing law in Ireland on how personal insolvency was addressed: put simply, to ask whether the existing system of court-based bankruptcy was consistent with a modern society and, more narrowly perhaps, a modern economy.

The bankruptcy system, while located in a law enacted relatively recently, the Bankruptcy Act 1988, was in reality a modern consolidation without much significant reform of 19th century bankruptcy legislation. The 1988 Act, like its predecessors, appeared to be based on the concept that non-payment of debt was morally unacceptable. Indeed, it appeared to operate on the basis that a system in which personal debts might be forgiven ran the risk of what economists like to call 'moral hazard': the risk that forgiveness would lead to a perception that personal debt defaulters would see this as emanating from a 'soft system' and might decide to become serial debt defaulters.

The Commission, first of all, had to understand that, although 'moral hazard' was not mentioned in the 1988 Act, it represented a key part of the thinking behind it. The Commission then had to think beyond that status quo; and here, the more recent economic literature on debt default strongly indicated that the 19th century moralistic approach was just as outdated as other ideas from that era. The evidence from the literature indicated that the bankruptcy system was counter-productive. Apart from requiring an entry fee into the system (from a person who was already broke), the particular bankruptcy regime in place in the Irish Bankruptcy Act 1988 as enacted meant that a bankrupt person was likely to be effectively placed in suspended animation for over 20 years, prohibited from playing an active part in the economy because he or she was subject to strict bankruptcy control. The regime therefore had to be replaced by a system in which the law allowed a person a 'fresh start', so that he or she could initially pay back what he or she could, leave the past behind and return to participating in the economy, and thereby making a positive contribution to society. The Commission's approach rejected the concept of punishment for non-payment of debt (the Commission recommended that imprisonment for non-payment of debt should be abolished) and looked towards social and economic rehabilitation. So, in this instance, law reform required not just the painstaking task of detailed legal analysis, but also a completely fresh insight into the problem that focused on the importance of giving those who acted in good faith through the bankruptcy process to be allowed to have a fresh start and thus continue to contribute to society in a way that benefitted both the individual citizen and society as a whole.

Empirical research, workshops and focus groups

Where the nature of the project facilitates a statistical analysis, and where such data is available, *socio-legal research* which, for example, might employ a quantitative methodology consisting of a secondary analysis of statistical data may also be employed. Socio-legal research will also allow us to explore the justifications for adjudging the current law to be sub-par which might include drawing upon such diverse sources as: public opinion; previous law reform reports and papers or publications of other bodies; academic literature; judicial decisions; and the practical experience of legal professionals, consulted via focus groups or through written correspondence.

Also included in the socio-legal approach might be a requirement to engage in *empirical* research, though owing to resources, the Commission rarely carries out in-depth fieldwork. It has, however, on occasion, used structured workshops and focus groups to gather qualitative information, for example, in its analysis of harmful communications and digital safety.[15] In order to formulate its final recommendations, the Commission went through its usual consultative process, soliciting the views of interested parties, including legal professionals, social media companies and young people. The Commission had in-depth conversations with a group of young people called Future Voices, and these proved extremely helpful in ensuring that it garnered an insight into what young people thought about social media in particular.

However, the Commission does not have the experience to carry out structured consultations with any group. Thus, in addition to its usual consultative process described above, it turned to those who did, the Public Participation Unit in the Department of Children and Youth Affairs. That Unit facilitated, with Comhairle na nÓg, a two-day consultative event with 70 young people, from which the Commission gathered extremely important

[15] Appendix B to the *Report on Harmful Communications and Digital Safety* (LRC 116—2016) describes the two- day workshop consultation with young people discussed in the following paragraphs.

information concerning the attitudes of young people to harmful communications, and on the practical steps needed to address online harmful behaviour. This was an example of how evidence-based qualitative research assisted the Commission's recommendations for law reform that emerged from this project.

The cohort of 70 young people was asked for their views concerning the types of behaviour that should be unlawful, and those that should not. Their answers broadly reflected what was already captured by the existing criminal law, namely that hateful material intended to damage another person, as well as catfishing and other forms of cyber-harassment, should be illegal. They were also of the view that 'vulgar abuse' should not be illegal. The two-day consultation also emphasised the real need to have accessible systems in place for effective take-down of harmful online material as quickly as possible: this mirrored the Commission's view that a statutory Digital Safety Commissioner should be established, modelled in many ways on comparable bodies in Australia and New Zealand. Arguably, these workshops merely reinforced what the Commission's comparative review had already found, but in fact they added a vital additional dimension: an internal view, based on those personally affected, that some version of the solutions seen in other jurisdictions was needed in Ireland. In recommending that the Australian and New Zealand Digital Safety Commissioners were useful models on which to base a solution for Ireland, the Commission did not propose a straight transplantation. The Commission recommended that the proposed Digital Safety Commissioner in Ireland would not have criminal law enforcement powers, as is the case for the Australian and New Zealand comparators; but, rather, would have a civil law regulatory and supervisory role, in which the courts could enforce by declaratory orders the Commissioner's statutory online standards for takedown of harmful material. The Commission considered that this more modest role would represent a sufficient 'first step' on the regulatory ladder in the Irish legal setting. At the time of writing (March 2019), the Government is engaged in a public consultation process which appears to suggest that it may go beyond the Commission's recommendations in this Report and confer significant regulatory powers on what may be named the Online Safety Commissioner.

Multidisciplinary influences on law reform research

Legal research must move with the times, and the impact of other disciplines upon legal research methods cannot be ignored. As such, a move from a monodisciplinary approach toward a more *multidisciplinary* outlook is clearly required in some instances. The discussion above of the Commission's work on personal debt is an example of where modern economic analysis was brought to bear.

Another Commission project, on disclosure and discovery in criminal cases,[16] involved the need to address competing rights, between the long-established right of the accused to a criminal trial conducted with due process and the right of a recovering victim to receive effective counselling. This required the Commission to understand clearly, through direct discussion with relevant health care professionals, the processes involved in recovery and counselling and how they interacted with the criminal trial process. The Commission's project arguably involved a relatively straightforward analysis of how to translate a general principle into statutory form – the principle that the prosecution must disclose to the defence not only the material on which the prosecution will rely at trial but also any additional material that the prosecution and/or investigating authorities have collected and which may be of benefit to the defence. Most of this project involved collecting some of the detail of how this principle is applied in practice through consultations with those legal professionals involved in the criminal trial process, including setting out guiding criteria, and then examining the timing of when the disclosure ought to take place. However, the Commission was also aware of an especially problematic issue in sexual offence cases: how to deal with records of counselling sessions with a person who is recovering from a sexual assault.

This matter appeared at first sight to involve a clash between, on the one hand, the right to a fair trial in which the defence is entitled to receive all relevant information that may be helpful to the defence and, on the other hand, society's interest in seeing a person recover from a sexual assault and that person's right to receive effective health care to assist that recovery. The dilemma: if the recovering person is required to reveal the content of their counselling interviews to the defence, will they decide to drop out of the case and maintain their path to recovery, rather than giving the defence the opportunity to delve into this recovery process through cross-examination at trial? What appeared at first sight like a clash turned out to be, in fact, more like a false dilemma. This emerged from consulting with and meeting health care professionals involved in providing counselling to those recovering from sexual assaults – a type of volunteer sampling in that these professionals

[16] See *Report on Disclosure and Discovery in Criminal Cases* (LRC 112—2014).

had responded to the Commission's public consultation on this project.[17] As a result of the interdisciplinary nature of this consultative process, the Commission gained a clear insight into the precise form of the counselling process, and that those involved in counselling were fully aware of how counselling related to the criminal trial process. The counselling process could be divided into two fairly clear phases, the first of which, consistent with the aim of recovery, could (and does) incorporate a clear explanation to the complainant that certain forensic tests and associated statements would be needed for trial purposes. The second phase could then concentrate on counselling aimed at recovery, in which the person would talk through their feelings and thoughts about what had occurred with a view to their future path. This second phase required a high degree of confidentiality to facilitate recovery in a safe environment.

The legal process could facilitate this by ensuring that the counselling process was, to a large degree, separate from the forensic, evidence-related, process of the criminal trial. What had concerned counsellors in particular was that the prosecution might seek counselling records just before a trial started, without any kind of filtering process to separate out and protect the 'thoughts and feelings' elements from the forensic material that had to be disclosed to the defence.

The Commission, having obtained an insight into the counselling and recovery process, was able to formulate a process that fully met the disclosure principle while respecting the confidentiality of counselling and the recovery process. This involved recommending that where counselling records were at issue, there should be a pre trial filtering process in which an application would be made to a court to determine whether none, some or all of the counselling records passed the test of forensic and evidential relevance for disclosure purposes. This process meant that counselling records would not be handed over to the defence on a blanket basis, but instead would be subject to a judicial filter: the result would be that the defence would not have access to counselling records that were related to 'thoughts and feelings' and that had no forensic or evidential value.

[17] The Commission published a consultative *Issues Paper on Disclosure and Discovery in Criminal Cases* (LRC IP 5—2014), which was followed by a public seminar on the topic; and the Commission also received a number of written submissions from a wide range of persons, including health care professionals. See *Report on Disclosure and Discovery in Criminal Cases* (LRC 112—2014), at vii (Acknowledgements) and 6 (summary of consultation process).

While this process does not guarantee complete confidentiality to counselling records, it would appear that, arising from the Commission's consultations and discussions with counsellors, this recommendation for reform would provide sufficient protections to the relationship between the counsellor and the recovering person that recovery would not be inhibited; and would also provide clarity for the recovering person as to the scope of what is, or is not, relevant for the trial process. This proposed pre-trial filtering process was implemented in s 19A of the Criminal Evidence Act 1992, which was inserted by s 39 of the Criminal Law (Sexual Offences) Act 2017. Clearly, a 'black letter' approach to the issue might not have resulted in such a nuanced and survivor-appropriate reform.

Comparative legal research

While all of the above approaches present challenges, and while their employment in a law reform context may invite occasional criticism, comparative research, in particular, warrants further comment. Ireland is a small country, with limited resources, the legal system of which has, throughout its modern history, been strongly influenced from external forces, from the imposition of the English common law, to the modelling of parts of both the 1922 and 1937 Constitutions on that of Weimar Germany,[18] to the impact of directly applicable European Union norms on domestic law. Ireland's diminutive size (as well as that of the Law Reform Commission) means that true innovation based on original, blue sky thinking is rarely a feasible *modus operandi* for law reform projects, though there are notable exceptions in that regard.[19] The State's successful history

[18] In fact, the 1922 Constitution took inspiration from many sources, with the Weimar model providing a template for the human rights clauses; the US Constitution, the idea of judicial review of legislation (a radical idea, almost unknown in the Europe of its day); and Switzerland, the idea of direct democracy and recourse to referendums. The 1937 Constitution borrowed from the Weimar model in structural terms, in areas as diverse as the length of the term of the head of state, the power of the head of state to refer Bills to the Supreme Court/*Bundesgerichtshof*, and the rejection of noble titles. See G Hogan, *The Origins of the Irish Constitution, 1928-1941* (Royal Irish Academy 2012).

[19] In truth, the capacity for any law reform agency to be truly original is limited, due to resources as well as the need to ensure that any solution proposed is effective. However, the *Report on Personal Debt Management and Debt Enforcement* (LRC 100—2010), discussed above, demonstrates that, on occasion, significant paradigm shifts can occur through law reform, in this instance moving from conceiving of personal debt and bankruptcy as a shameful social ill (a relic of 19th century mores) to a model in which it was considered as part and parcel of a modern economy, and in respect of which it is necessary to allow a person to make a 'fresh start' and, subject to a 'good faith' test to avoid moral hazard risks, to facilitate the person to become an active economic participant in society. Another example of an *avant garde* approach is visible in the Commission's *Report on Child Sexual Abuse* (LRC 32—1990), which at the time recommended far-reaching reforms some of which, notably mandatory reporting of child abuse, were ultimately implemented after a quarter century of further debate: see the Children First Act 2015.

of absorbing diverse and repeated transplantations of law means that comparative research methods are particularly useful for law reform projects. The challenges faced by Ireland in relation to the law are likely to have been experienced elsewhere, and building upon the work of others may represent a good means of maximising the resources available to the Commission.

III – Challenges

A number of challenges arise in the context of conducting research for the purposes of law reform. Questions of project management and scaling, quality assurance, interdisciplinarity, and impact assessment are, for example, of considerable relevance in this context. However, for the purposes of the present section, and in the interests of brevity, one principal challenge is treated, namely the usage of legal research theories and methods that have primarily been refined and developed in the context of academic settings for law reform purposes.

When assessing the *métier* of academic lawyers, Becher's study from 1981 provided a lens as to how they were viewed by the non-academic community. Academics were variously described as 'not really academic ... arcane, distant and alien: an appendage to the academic world ... vociferous, untrustworthy, immoral, narrow and arrogant'.[20] Their research output was further dismissed as 'unexciting, uncreative, and comprising a series of intellectual puzzles scattered among large areas of description'.[21] Such perceptions mean that academic output is sometimes viewed with a degree of scepticism in the practical world. Despite these reservations, it is undoubtedly the case that law reform agencies must lean heavily upon the tools developed by the legal academic community in conducting research. Law reform agencies are a comparatively new invention, dispose of limited resources, and have not been in a position to develop a truly *sui generis* branch of legal science. In addition, progress in the academic field in recent decades away from purely doctrinal legal research is nothing short of remarkable, and some of the fruits of this transition have proven exceedingly useful in the context of law reform. The Commission has taken note of both socio-legal research and academic works proposing law reform in the past.[22] However, as noted above, the law reform scholar must proceed with an awareness of the

[20] T Becher, 'Towards a definition of disciplinary cultures' (1981) 6 Studies in Higher Education 109.

[21] ibid.

[22] For example, Schweppe, Haynes and Carr, *A Life Free From Fear: Legislating for Hate Crime in Ireland, An NGO Perspective* (2014) was referred to repeatedly in the Commission's *Report on Harmful Communications and Digital Safety* (LRC 116—2016).

limitations of drawing on either practice or academia. In his seminal 1983 work, Arthurs set out a taxonomy of legal research styles.[23] While his study used Canada as a case study, it carries significant lessons, to which any legal researcher would do well to pay attention. The vertical axis of Arthurs' matrix represents the distinction between, on the one hand, 'pure' research, generally seen to be the preserve of academia, and, on the other hand, applied project-focussed work, generally seen as representing the output of practitioners. On the horizontal axis, a distinction is drawn between doctrinal and interdisciplinary research. The logic of this analysis is reproduced below.

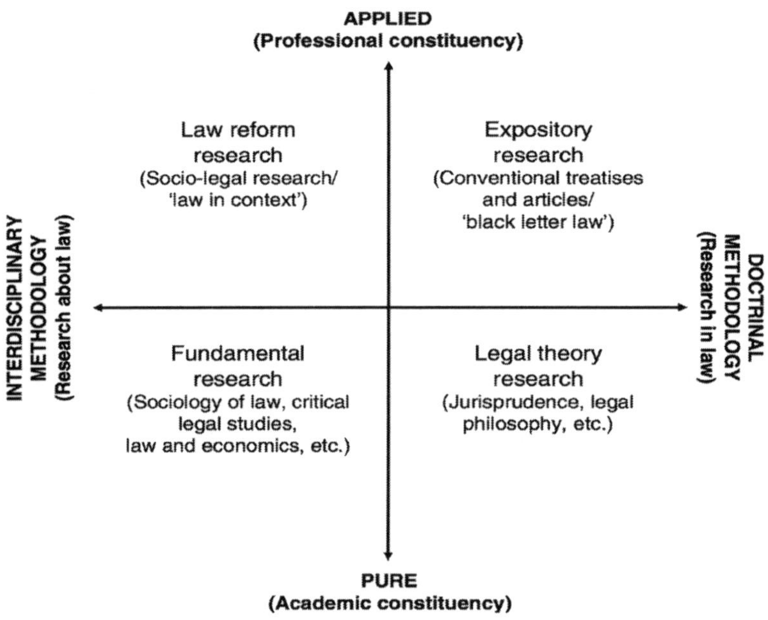

Arthurs' model places law reform research at the applied end of the vertical axis, and at the interdisciplinary end of the horizontal one. This would seem logical, as law reform is not merely an academic pursuit; rather, it is intended to engender real change, thus implying a practical element.[24] Nor is law reform a purely doctrinal discipline, envisaging, as it does, societal change

[23] HW Arthurs, *Law and Learning: Report to the Social Sciences and Humanities Research Council of Canada by the Consultative Group on Research and Education in Law* (Information Division, Social Sciences and Humanities Research Council of Canada 1983).

[24] This statement is without prejudice to the fact that much academic research includes proposals pertaining to improvement and reform of the law, and that other bodies, such as the Irish Human Rights and Equality Commission, may also publish documents containing ideas for law reform.

on foot of legal regulation, though even proposals for new regulatory solutions to relatively recent phenomena, such as the impact of smart phone usage on social media platforms (neither of which existed until the first decade of the 21st century), could be described as reactive, reflecting societal change in the law reform proposed.[25] Clearly, Arthurs' model has limitations, and is not fully representative of the activities of academics or practitioners today, providing general postulates rather than absolute truths. However, it is clear that it contains some elements of wisdom, given that the goals of law reform research are, in no small part, distinguishable from either academia or legal practice. Such a conclusion may be seen as problematic, because those who conduct law reform research are likely to be drawn from either the academic community or from the corps of practitioners, since most legal professionals work in one or other of these branches. Neither *milieu* appears, at first sight, to furnish adequate and readily transposable skills to prepare an individual for law reform research, with law schools at undergraduate level focusing mainly on doctrinal research. Equally, if law reform is an exercise in legal practice, then it is one far removed from the everyday life of courtroom lawyers and judges.[26] Neither practitioners, nor indeed academics, function chiefly through the medium of interdisciplinary research. Rather, legal research, traditionally understood, is a highly doctrinal discipline, while even modern academic legal research, while embracing interdisciplinarity, is often overly self-referential and is undertaken in the context of the 'safe space' of the academy.[27] It may be, of course, that those lawyers who are attracted to research with a law reform focus have already developed a capacity to consider that the law as they have found it may not be suitable or

---

[25] The relative novelty of these phenomena may render controversial some reform proposals that affect them. Thus, the Commission's *Report on Harmful Communications and Digital Safety* (LRC 116—2016) proposed: (a) reform of the existing criminal law concerning harmful communications to reflect some new forms of digital communications, which was not deemed controversial; and (b) the establishment of a supervisory statutory Digital Safety Commissioner, deemed more controversial but which, at the time of writing (March 2019), appears to have been accepted in principle by Government, having been the subject of ongoing debate within Ireland's National Parliament where this proposal had been supported by a number of parliamentary committees between 2016 and 2018.

[26] Of course, court decisions occasionally go beyond viewing law as a closed system. See B van Klink and U deVries, *Academic Learning in Law: Theoretical Positions, Teaching Experiments and Learning Experiences* (Edward Elgar Publishing, 2016) 153, citing: *Cattanach v Melchior* (2003) 215 CLR 1 (wrongful birth); *Woods v Multi-Sport Holdings* (2002) 208 CLR 460 (extra record social scientific material); *St Helen's Borough Council v Derbyshire and Ors* [2007] 3 All ER 81 (working lives of women); and *Stack v Dowden* [2007] 2 All ER 929 (cohabitation).

[27] The perspective of at least some lawyers may be seen as that of a group of insiders, examining a system without being able to step out of it. See C McCrudden, 'Legal Research and the Social Sciences' (2006) 122 Law Quarterly Review 632.

meet contemporary needs, a capacity that may even have been inspired by some inspiring law teachers at undergraduate or post-graduate level.

Doctrinal research, occupying the right end of Arthurs' horizontal axis, essentially consists of analysing legal rules to reveal patterns, meta-rules generally dubbed 'doctrines'.[28] Bringing such doctrines to light is generally accomplished by examining legal texts, thus coming to be known as 'black-letter law'. As research, the interpretive nature of this process is readily distinguished from the natural sciences, where causal relationships between variables are often used to explain natural phenomena. The doctrinal tradition is certainly closer to the *verstehen* model long employed by the social sciences.[29] However, core distinctions between the two remain, insofar as social science generally relies on empirical data, either in order to base theories (inductive reasoning) or to test them (deductive reasoning). Whichever method is employed, research outcomes may be tested through a method involving empirical tests. Social science research methodology has developed as a means of refining the way in which such methods are employed, demanding robustness in terms of sample sizes, coding and the use and choice of variables.[30]

Doctrinal research, by contrast, is not typically associated with a rigorous usage of empirical methods.[31] This is particularly true of the commentary model prevalent in civil law jurisdictions, where the opinions of leading scholars serve as an authoritative subsidiary canon, effectively glossing black-letter law in the manner of ecclesiastical scholars in the Brehon tradition.

Common law scholars, by contrast, employ a doctrinal method that depends heavily on the study of case law. This approach, on the surface, has much to recommend it to social scientists. After all, what is case law if not empirical practice? However, the superficial attractiveness of the practice preference of common lawyers in terms of facilitating robust research methods is undermined by the manner in which case law is understood by lawyers.

[28] G Holborn, *Butterworths Legal Research Guide* (2nd edn, Butterworths 2001).

[29] TA Schwandt, 'Three epistemological stances for qualitative inquiry: Interpretivism, hermeneutics and social constructionism', in NK Denzin, and YS Lincoln (eds), *Handbook of Qualitative Research* (2nd edn, Sage Publications 2000).

[30] D Proverbs and R Gameson, 'Case Study Research' in A Knight and L Ruddock (eds), *Advanced Research Methods in the Built Environment* (Blackwell 2008) 99–110.

[31] See Kilcommins, 'Doctrinal Legal Method (Black-Letterism): Assumptions, Commitments and Shortcomings' in Cahillane and Schweppe (eds), *Legal Research Methods: Principles and Practicalities* (Clarus Press 2016).

Firstly, the cases that influence common law doctrine are not typical cases, but are, rather, difficult, atypical cases in which a complex point is at issue. As Holmes himself noted, 'great cases are called great, not by reason of their importance ... but because of some accident of immediate overwhelming interest which appeals to the feelings and distorts the judgment.'[32] It is such 'great' cases that pepper our textbooks, thus distorting our understanding of the law. While it is true that generally it is only those cases in which 'law' is made that appear in the law reports, this furnishes us with a limited picture, since such cases are generally far from typical, and do not reflect how law is usually practiced, or indeed its societal impact, an issue to which law reform scholars do well to pay heed. Secondly, when efforts are made to avoid such cherry-picking, and to furnish a more representative doctrinal analysis of how law works in general, they are usually relegated to the fringes of academic circles, a curiosity rather than an advance in the discipline.[33] The aversion of lawyers to social science research methods immediately becomes apparent in such circumstances. The average social scientist would view the wisdom of the selective 'important cases' approach of many legal textbooks as anecdotal at best.

Understanding and engaging with such shortcomings must be at the forefront of our thoughts when we conduct research for law reform purposes. As Kelsen has noted, legal rules are *normative* insofar as they prescribe how individuals *should* comport themselves.[34] They are simply not designed to engage with, predict, account for, or indeed, help us to understand the behaviour of the common man or woman in the street. Thus viewed, doctrinal research may be viewed as research *in* law, rather than research about the law, taking an internal, participant-oriented approach to law, and thus revealing severe limitations in offering input on how society could—or should —be regulated.[35] It cannot, of itself, provide the wisdom upon which law reform proposals are grounded.

[32] *Northern Securities Co v United States*, 193 US 197 (1904).

[33] By way of example, see IH Scheltema, the application of public international law by the European Court of Human Rights: a legal empirical analysis, (thesis) Florence, European University Institute (2014). Scheltema's methods involve a Large-N analysis of all cases in which the European Court of Human Rights has employed extraneous norms of public international law in order to place the European Convention on Human Rights in context. His thesis examines the text of the judgments, using a statistical model, to test the hypothesis that such extraneous norms are usually employed in a manner that supports, rather than diminishes, any rights that the claimant might be due, and are interpreted in a manner that is not altogether congruent with their normal usage. Such a Large-N analysis allows Scheltema to rigorously assess his research question, whereas typical doctrinal analysis, centred on individual cases, would not permit this.

[34] See H Kelsen, *Reine Rechtslehre*, 1 (Aufl 1934).

[35] See HLA Hart, *The Concept of Law* (OUP 1961).

Despite these reservations, doctrinal research continues to occupy a dominant position in legal scholarship (though there are signs in academia that this may slowly be changing somewhat and academic research is rarely solely doctrinal today),[36] and represents the vernacular of the legal community – a key stakeholder with which any law reformer must engage. As such, doctrinal research must nonetheless form a core component of any research conducted with a view to law reform. However, the danger of applying these tools crafted for a different end in the context of law reform is great indeed. As Chynoweth has noted:

> the actual process of analysis by which doctrines are formulated owes more to the subjective, argument-based methodologies of the humanities than to the more detached data-based analysis of the natural and social sciences. The normative character of the law also means that the validity of doctrinal research must inevitably rest upon developing a consensus within the scholastic community, rather than on an appeal to any external reality.[37]

Overcoming these shortcomings involves having recourse to methodologies beyond the black letter. This is not, in fact, entirely unusual. In practice, all but the most rigidly inclined positivists are inclined to occasionally include some reference to the historical and social context in which legal judgments have been made. As one begins to give credence to such external factors, research begins to gravitate left along Arthurs' horizontal axis toward *interdisciplinary* research.

Moving beyond a purely doctrinal paradigm in terms of law reform research also involves the use of tools that were crafted for a different purpose, in this instance, tools belonging to a different discipline entirely. Such endeavours typically bring lawyers far from their comfort zone. It is unlikely that many legal researchers will have garnered a great deal of experience in economic theory or sociological modelling. However, for the purposes of law reform research, embracing such methods is indispensable. Avoiding the pitfalls associated with research in other disciplines that fails to reach the highest standards of rigour is far from an easy task, but may be addressed by recourse to specific professional training, through engagement with universities, or by confirming one's results against a methodology from another discipline. Law

[36] For broader discussion on this point, see R van Gestel, HW Micklitz and EL Rubin, *Rethinking Legal Scholarship: A Transatlantic Dialogue* (Cambridge University Press 2017).

[37] P Chynoweth, 'Legal Research' in A Knight and L Ruddock (eds), *Advanced Research Methods in the Built Environment* (Blackwell 2008) 30.

reform researchers must be unafraid to seek help in such circumstances, and may need to solicit outside aid to ensure high quality outputs.

Nonetheless, a cautious and critical perspective must always inform the law reform researcher in his or her work. Social science is not an exact science. Seemingly robust statistical methods often reveal bias in terms of sample group and coding. Further, even if the extraneous methods employed reflect best practice *inter se*, the very choice of such methods may lay the law reform researcher open to charges of methodological bias, with law and economics approaches typically favoured by right-wing policy makers, while their left-wing counterparts often prefer sociological methods, for example.[38] As law reform agencies are intended to be neutral, technocratic, and non-partisan, such pitfalls are potentially very serious indeed.[39]

As already noted, another essential element of the law reform researcher's toolkit is that of comparative law. The best law reform research involves sensible application of the principle 'think global, act local'. This entails scouring the world for analysis of models that might work better than what is currently in place at home, but also ensuring that any suggested solution is apt for transposition to the Irish context. Typically, such an analysis involves moving from the local to the global and back again. Approaching each issue, it will usually be germane to examine: (1) the existing law in Ireland, in order to appraise the current legislation and case law, as well as to identify any areas in need of reform; (2) the various jurisdictions of the United Kingdom, given the many communalities, both historical and legal-cultural between the countries, and the likelihood that many problems may arise in the UK and

[38] This point was originally made by F Böhm. F Böhm, 'Left-wing and right-wing approaches to the market economy,' Zeitschrift für die gesamte Staatswissenschaft (1979) 442–448.

[39] It should perhaps be conceded that a standard such as 'neutral, technocratic and non-partisan' disavows the human element of any law reform body, represented both in its workforce and its executive. However, there are compelling reasons why such a standard should at least represent a *desideratum*, and one that is taken seriously, by law reform agencies. Such a posture allows the latter to detach themselves from the political life of the state, proposing reform measures that solve problems that have not been deemed by the legislature to warrant its direct consideration. This is particularly useful in terms of projects that pertain to the *Rechtstaat*, allowing the Commission to propose measures such as consolidation and improving the accessibility of legislation without fear that such moves will be interpreted as pursuing an agenda to the benefit of one particular group and to the detriment of others. Equally, when the Commission's proposals have policy implications, employing a work ethic that keeps this *desideratum* to the fore lessens the potential for arguments that rob the Commission's work of its legitimacy and reformative potential on the basis that the research has been conducted in a partisan manner. That the Commission has been successful in this regard is borne out by its standing in the state and the high implementation rate, over 70 percent, that its reports have achieved.

Ireland contemporaneously, as well as the often easy transposition of solutions devised for one jurisdiction to the other[40]; (3) other common law jurisdictions, especially Australia (both at federal and state level), Canada (both at federal and provincial level), New Zealand, and the United States (federal and state level), for similar reasons to those associated with the UK; (4) civil law countries (paying particular attention to our fellow EU member states, especially in areas of shared EU/member state competence)[41]; and (5) international legal materials (emanating, for example, from the European Union, the Council of Europe, the Hague Conference on Private International Law, or the United Nations).[42]

However, while the above represents a fairly sensible ordering of *which* comparative research should serve law reform in Ireland, *how* it should be accomplished is somewhat more complicated. One may be reminded of Gutteridge's observation:

> A busy practicing lawyer cannot, as a rule, be expected to pay much heed to other systems of law. His main concern is to make himself master of the rules of law which are the subject matter of his vocation; he will, for the most part, have neither the leisure nor the inclination to embark on a course of study which is more than usually exacting, and unlikely to prove profitable in the professional sense.[43]

While one may take issue with Gutteridge's generalisation if one's vocation is private international law, for example, the truth is that it holds much wisdom.

The challenge in employing comparative methodology, then, is similar to that of using both black-letter law and interdisciplinarity. The tools have been crafted for theoretical, rather than practical, purposes. While they may

[40] It bears noting that since devolution of the late 1990s, we need to be increasingly aware that this involves four separate legislative entities: Northern Ireland, Scotland, England, Wales, as well as a Westminster parliament that legislates for between one and four of these jurisdictions, depending on the area.

[41] It perhaps be noted at this juncture that, clearly, not all EU Member State jurisdictions will warrant consideration on each project, and that for practical reasons, a selection will have to be examined for exemplary purposes.

[42] While this final category does not pertain directly to a domestic jurisdiction, and therefore may not be classed as comparative law *stricto sensu*, it is nonetheless germane to note that many international standards agreed by the bodies mentioned may have direct repercussions, or may serve as inspiration or guidelines for legislative reform in Ireland. They are therefore typically considered at this stage of the process.

[43] H Gutteridge, *Comparative Law* (1949) 23.

push leftward on Arthurs' horizontal axis, on the vertical axis, they remain firmly toward the lower end. As such, fundamental questions, such as whether policy can ever truly be informed through a comparative exposition of common law using common law methods (case-law analysis) versus civil law using civil law methods (commentaries), are not satisfactorily answered. Equally, and on the contrary, whether using common law methods to analyse civil law jurisdictions is likely to yield better results, is difficult to divine from the words of leading comparativists.[44] In time, it is to be hoped that law reformers might themselves contribute to curing legal science of some of these *lacunae*. In Ireland, the Law Reform Commission makes extensive use of comparative analysis while at the same time recognising that what it proposes in terms of reform must fit within and work in practice in the Irish setting.[45]

Another particular challenge may be identified in the context of law reform research, for which many scholars are often unprepared, namely that posed by the usage of plain English. *Ignorantiam iuris neminem excusat* remains one of the most poignantly ironic dicta of legal wisdom. The principle that ignorance of the law is no defence is an excellent reflection of the *desideratum* of the order that law is supposed to confer. Since not knowing a law cannot excuse one from the consequences of breaking it, there is no premium on ignorance, and citizens are expected to be aware of what the law expects of them. Yet, the fact that the phrase is most commonly rendered in Latin (or occasionally in French – *nul n'est censé ignorer la loi*) illustrates the logical fallacy at the heart of the principle. How can the common citizen, the 'man on the Clapham Omnibus' of English common law,[46] or the person on the

[44] The divergent methodologies of examining the common law and civil law are occasionally touched upon by comparative law scholars, but given that few have truly immersed themselves in foreign legal systems, such attempts are often acknowledged by the authors as superficial. This discussion has typically taken place amongst continental scholars. See R David, C Jauffret-Spinosi, and M Goré, *Les grands systèmes de droit contemporains* (Dalloz 2016), A Flessner, *Wegfall der Bereicherung: Rechtsvergleichung und Kritik* (Vol 37. Walter de Gruyter GmbH and Co KG 2017).

[45] By way of example, see the discussion of the *Report on Harmful Communications and Digital Safety* (LRC 116—2016) in Part II, Methodological Approaches, above.

[46] The phrase was first used in a reported judgment by Collins MR in *McQuire v Western Morning News* [1903] 2 KB 100 at 109. However, he attributed it to Lord Bowen, said to have coined it as junior counsel in a notorious *cause célèbre* of the 1870s usually referred to as the 'Tichborne Claimant' case, in which a man commonly referred to as Thomas Castro or Arthur Orton claimed to be the long-lost heir to the Tichborne baronetcy. He lost his civil claim, was later convicted of perjury and served a lengthy prison term. The fact that the moniker itself is somewhat arcane is mildly ironic in the context of the present discussion.

Cabra bus or Dart of Irish common law,[47] be expected to remain compliant with a system steeped in arcane maxims and dicta in foreign languages? The fact is that the language of the law—as well as its undoubted substantive complexity—has an exclusionary effect. This observation applies to law as it is practiced in courts (*sub judice* contempt?), as it is studied in law schools (feoffment of seisin?), and as it is written about in academic essays, including, no doubt, the present contribution.

However, the law reformer is explicitly charged with *improving* the law, and while this task is usually seen as principally confined to substantive improvement, linguistic improvement is also relevant. Employing a simpler vocabulary automatically increases accessibility of law, thereby rendering the system fairer and more ethically defensible. This can usually be achieved without unduly simplifying the substantive content of the law itself, and law reformers can rely on the already-established science of plain language to aid them in their work.

It has been noted that lawyers[48]:

> … do not write plain English. We use eight words to say what could be said in two. We use arcane phrases to express commonplace ideas. Seeking to be precise, we become redundant. Seeking to be cautious, we become verbose. Our sentences twist on, phrase within clause within clause, glazing the eyes and numbing the minds of our readers. The result is a writing style that has, according to one critic, four outstanding characteristics. It is '(1) wordy, (2) unclear, (3) pompous, and (4) dull.'

Most lawyers now agree that this situation could be improved. Wydick cites the idea that '[g]ood legal writing does not sound as though it had been written by a lawyer.'[49] However, achieving such a sea change in the legal profession in general is likely to represent a major challenge, even though most lawyers are acutely aware of the connection between comprehensible language and access to the law. Lawyers seem to be almost universally attracted to purple prose, while there is also an awareness that linguistic complexity represents another reason for which individuals might need to consult—and pay—a legal specialist.

---

[47] Mr Justice Niall McCarthy, Foreword to *Byrne and McCutcheon on the Irish Legal System* (6th edn, Bloombury Professional 2014).

[48] R Wydick *Plain English for Lawyers* (4th edn, Carolina Academic Press 1998) 3.

[49] ibid 5.

However, the motivations for law reform researchers are somewhat different. Improving accessibility of law is amongst the core objectives to be pursued. Such a position may be seen as part of Ireland's belated introduction to the concept of the *Rechtstaat*, with the benefits to the state, its economy, its citizens and general welfare from improvements in the quality of laws and legislation—including the quality and accessibility of language used—gradually becoming an accepted truth.[50] This is borne out by the Law Reform Commission's practice. In its *Report on Statutory Drafting and Interpretation: Plain Language and the Law*,[51] the Commission strongly supported the use of plain language. Chapter 6 of the Report contains recommendations on the use of plain language in legislation. It recommended that familiar vocabulary should be used where possible. The Report stated that the use of Latin and French terminology or other archaic language obscures the law's meaning and should be avoided.

The Commission's Report also recommended that we should not use anachronistic words, such as 'herein', 'heretofore', 'aforesaid' and 'aforementioned'. It also recommended that we should avoid the unnecessary use of excessively formal words, for example 'furnish' instead of 'give', or 'save' instead of 'except', and of superfluous phrases such 'that is to say' and 'as the case may be'. The Report also provided numerous examples of unnecessary use of synonyms and words with similar meanings, such as 'last will and testament', 'give and bequeath', 'null and void' or 'rest, residue and remainder'. Gradually removing these vestiges of yesteryear from the *lex lata* remains an ever-present tenet of the law reformer's *métier*. Or, to put it another way, making legal language simpler is part of the job.[52]

[50] See R von Mohl, *Die deutsche Polizeiwissenschaft nach den Grundsätzen des Rechtsstaats*. Tübingen (1833); and K Sobota, *Das Prinzip Rechtsstaat. Verfassungs- und verwaltungsrechtliche Aspekte* (Jus publicum; Bd 22), Mohr Siebeck, Tübingen (1997).

[51] LRC 61-2000.

[52] The tide may be turning in the direction indicated by the Commission in its 2000 Report. In 2017 the Irish National Adult Literacy Agency (NALA) published a booklet called *Plain English and the law: the legal consequences of clear and unclear communication.* The booklet provides examples from three Irish court decisions of the consequences of unclear communication in contractual and statutory language. The three cases were: *Ickendel Ltd v Bewleys Café Grafton Street Ltd* [2013] IEHC 293, [2014] IESC 41 (on the interpretation of a rent review clause); *Corbally v Medical Council* [2013] IEHC 500, [2015] IESC 9 (on the interpretation of "poor professional performance" in the Medical Practitioners Act 2007); and *ACC Bank plc v Kelly* [2011] IEHC 7 (on the interpretation of a bank loan contract).

IV – Reflections

The main focus of this contribution has been to identify to what extent law reform legal research mirrors, or differs from, other forms of legal research, and indeed research in other related disciplines such as the social sciences. The general answer is that much law reform research reflects the approach of academic lawyers, because it principally involves a reflective analysis of current law, a kind of detailed literature review. However, because, increasingly, legal research nowadays also goes further and includes at least some reflection on wider policy and even sociological contexts, with socio-legal research sometimes incorporating speculative proposals for change, this permits law reform researchers to adopt a broad perspective, which may incorporate approaches that are also seen in the academic milieu.

Of course, for a law reform agency, this is not a matter of choice, because it is clearly a mandatory part of its mandate; this means not just making general suggestions for reform, but providing detail of how such reform might appear in legislative form (as well, as, on occasion, including supporting soft law codes of practice).[53] Some law reform agencies may at one time have opted out of preparing draft legislation to accompany their final Reports, but most eventually reassessed the need to include draft legislation alongside detailed recommendations for reform. The reason is fairly straightforward: draft Bills provide a clear linguistic testing ground for recommendations. Even what may appear a sensible enough recommendation for reform will be tested to the limits in the white heat of translation into legislative form. To that extent, law reform research must of necessity always involve answering the question: how would that proposed reform work in practice? Increasingly, academic research includes that approach: for law reformers it is simply an inescapable element of the work.

[53] A good example of this is the recommendation, in the *Report on Harmful Communications and Digital Safety* (LRC 116—2016), discussed in Part II, above, for a code of practice for takedown procedures for harmful communications to be prepared by the Digital Safety Commissioner.

Index

A

D

E

F

G

H

J

K

L

M

N

T

U